Army under the command of Lt. General Burgoyne, took poſt on the 20th Sep. 1777
azer's Funeral.)
m Lane, Leadenhall Street, London.

GENTLEMAN JOHNNY BURGOYNE

*Courtesy of Macmillan & Co., Ltd.*

John Burgoyne, Rome, 1750

From a painting by Ramsey, in possession of Miss Burgoyne, at Hampton Court Palace. Taken from De Fonblanque's "Life of Burgoyne"

# Gentleman Johnny Burgoyne

*Misadventures of an*
ENGLISH GENERAL
*in the Revolution*

*By*

F. J. HUDLESTON
*Librarian of the British War Office*
*Author of* Warriors in Undress

*ILLUSTRATED*

THE BOBBS-MERRILL COMPANY
INDIANAPOLIS PUBLISHERS

*Printed in the United States of America*

PRINTED AND BOUND
BY BRAUNWORTH & CO., INC.
BROOKLYN, NEW YORK

TO

THOSE WHO WON

AND

THOSE WHO LOST

THE BATTLE OF SARATOGA

# PREFACE

I must first express my thanks to Messrs. Macmillan and Company for their kindness in allowing me to quote from the letters included in E. B. De Fonblanque's *Political and Military Episodes in the Latter Half of the Eighteenth Century Derived from the Life and Correspondence of the Right Honorable John Burgoyne, General, Statesman, Dramatist,* a work published by them in 1876. De Fonblanque, who was a son of John Fonblanque, editor of the *Examiner* and perhaps the most brilliant journalist of the early nineteenth century, was, like myself (and Mr. John Pownall! See page 45), employed in the War Office, so I feel that, if he had been born later, or I earlier, we should have been colleagues. His book is a mine of information, not only for the life of John Burgoyne, but also for the political history of the days in which he was one of the best known men in town, whether at the gaming house, the theater, or, that less entertaining establishment, the House of Commons.

Secondly I must thank most cordially Mr. David Chambers Mearns of the Library of Congress who has furnished me with most valuable material for the North American period, that is to say the most important and most interesting period, of John Burgoyne's career. Mr. Mearns has, to put it briefly, ransacked the American records for me. Happy indeed the Englishman who, writing in England on any period in the history of the United States, can find a friend in that country so keen upon his subject and with so wide a knowledge of it, as I have found, thanks to my publishers, in Mr. Mearns. I think that he is, like myself, so interested in the career of Gentleman Johnny that this was to him a labor of love. The shade of John Burgoyne, who perhaps now and again in the Elysian Fields fights his battles over again with Arnold and Schuyler and Gates (with Charles Lee, accompanied by his phantom hounds, looking sardonically on), should be as grateful to Mr. Mearns as I am.

And finally I must thank my friend and colleague, Mr. A. S. White of the War Office Library. One of the most amiable of men, his indignation when he discovers a mistake in a military record is, like the tameness of the fauna who wanted to play games with Alexander Selkirk on his desert island, "shocking" to see. He has, very kindly, read every page of this book, and I am glad to remember that he has not often exploded.

F. J. H.

# CONTENTS



## APPENDICES

# LIST OF ILLUSTRATIONS

# GENTLEMAN JOHNNY BURGOYNE

# GENTLEMAN JOHNNY BURGOYNE

## CHAPTER I

### EARLY DAYS

ON THE morning of March 10, 1760, at the Horse Guards, that building which is familiar to every Londoner and to every visitor to London, and which had then been standing just ten years, there began the "Fourth Day's Sitting on the Tryal of Lord George Sackville, being charged with Disobedience of Orders while he commanded the British Horse in Germany."

Colonel Sloper in his red uniform and with his jolly red face—which one may assume in view of his rank, the age in which he lived, and the Treaty* with Portugal—was sworn and gave evidence. And, for an Englishman, it is very painful evidence to read. He told the Court how on August 1, 1759, early in the morning in the open country near Minden, on a heath, a "blasted heath" so far as the honor of the British Army was concerned, thanks to a white-livered scoundrel, Captain Winschingrode, aide-de-camp to Duke Ferdinand, rode up to Lord George Sackville and told him in French that "it was the Duke's orders he should advance to the left with the right wing of the cavalry." "The Duke" was

*The Methuen Treaty of 1703. The Portuguese got British woolen goods and in exchange we got a far, far better thing—port. As a nation we began drinking it then and have never stopped doing so. I have a bottle by my side as I am writing this.

Prince Ferdinand of Brunswick. He sent his orders for the advance of the Horse with the words: *"Voici le beau moment pour la cavalerie: courez y."*

Colonel Sloper went on: "My Lord said, *'Mais comment, mais comment?'* Captain Winschingrode, like Captain Nolan at Balaklava, pointed with outstretched sword the direction for the advance. "I heard my Lord say," continued Colonel Sloper, " 'I do not comprehend how the movement is to be made.' " The movement was not made, *le beau moment* passed and was lost, and the French army escaped annihilation. Later Captain Ligonier galloped up and, to continue the Colonel's evidence:

> "I spoke to Captain Ligonier. As to what I said the Court must tell me whether I am to go on.
>
> *"Judge Advocate.* Yes, proceed.
>
> *"Colonel Sloper.* I said to Captain Ligonier, 'For God's sake repeat your orders to *that man,* that he may not pretend not to understand them, for it is near half-an-hour ago that he has received orders to advance, and yet we are still here.'
>
> *"Question.* Who did you mean by the words 'that man'?
>
> *"Answer.* My Lord George Sackville. My oath obliges me to say all I said. I said to Captain Ligonier, 'You see the condition he is in.' "

Further questioned, Colonel Sloper said, "My Lord was alarmed to a very great degree: he seemed in the utmost confusion."

There was a very patient hearing of evidence on both sides, and the accused was allowed a free hand in cross-examination, but after Colonel Sloper's evidence it is not surprising to learn that the judgment of the court-martial ends with the words, "It is the Opinion of this Court that the said Lord George Sackville is, and he is hereby adjudged, unfit to serve His Majesty in any Military Capacity whatever." What *is* surprising is that he was not shot on the Horse Guards Parade. Still, one must remember that he was "My Lord."

The court filed out of the Horse Guards into Whitehall and made its way to the coffee-houses, the gaming-houses, the pleasure-gardens and (perhaps) the bagnios, and honest old Colonel Sloper must have felt like a terrier that has just killed a rat. But it is a pity that the court in its sentence could not have left out the word "Military." For in 1775 "that man" emerges from "the trap-door of history," if one may use a favorite phrase of a brilliant, not to say coruscating and glittering writer, as Secretary of State for the American Colonies and also for the American War.

The War of American Independence was won by Washington and his troops in spite of Congress: the loss of the American Colonies was due, not so much to the incapacity of the British generals in the field, as to the stupid bungling of affairs in London by "that man," by this time Lord George Germain. He changed his name to Germain on inheriting some property.

Of the British commanders who fought and lost in North America none had a more variegated and romantic career than John Burgoyne. There is a legend, which still persists, that he was the illegitimate son of Lord Bingley, who had been ambassador in Spain and who was certainly Burgoyne's godfather. This legend has been repeated in a book which was published so recently as 1926. It was started by Lady Bingley, who was not on the best of terms with her husband, and that gossiping old woman, Horace Walpole, repeated it. There is no Lord Bingley now. Any eighteenth-century peer with so slap-dash, reckless and devil-may-care a name as Bingley must have had many love-affairs. And I say this in spite of that gentlemanly Mr. Bingley who was "a single man of large fortune, four or five thousand a year. What a fine thing for our girls." (If you do not know who he was, you are not a Janeite.) As a matter of fact, it *is* recorded of Lord Bingley that he "left annuities to two or three widows." They can not, of course, all have been his—unless he was a trigamist.

John Burgoyne was born in London in 1722. The family was of good old stock and acquired their estates in 1387 from "time-honoured Lancaster," who granted them to Roger Burgoyne by the following quaint deed:

> I John of Gaunt
> Do give and do graunt
> Unto Roger Burgoyne
> And the heirs of his loyne
> All Sutton and Potton
> Until the world's rotten.

His father was the younger son of the third baronet, Sir John Burgoyne. His mother, Anna Maria, was the daughter of a London citizen, called Burnestone, and "worth a plum,"* as they used to say in those days. She was also a great beauty, and her son inherited her looks. The third Sir John married a daughter of Richard Lucy of Charlecote in Warwickshire, of that Lucy family which in the person of that member of it who served as a

---

*That is to say, had a handsome fortune.

model for Mr. Justice Shallow, objected to young William Shakespeare killing deer which did not belong to him. John Burgoyne had in this way a roundabout connection with the theater and the drama of which he was in his time both a devotee and an ornament. His father was a man about town who, like so many men about town of his day, finished a glorious, gambling career in the King's Bench. Nowadays men of fashion who have come to grief go beyond the King's Bench, into the City, where, if they are sufficiently distinguished, they become Directors of Companies. But they do not as a rule direct, fortunately perhaps for the Companies.

John Burgoyne, like another famous soldier who was not exactly a success in the field, Lord Raglan, went to school at Westminster, where, unhappily, for it had rather a sad effect upon his style, he became well acquainted with the classics and, also, happily, formed a great friendship with Lord Strange, heir to the eleventh Earl of Derby.

Burgoyne was in later life much addicted to tags of Latin, and probably many of his brother officers did not understand them. Latin and Greek are not really much use to a soldier. It is all very well to know every move in the Siege of Troy, but, as a matter of cold hard fact, this siege was, even in the eighteenth century, from a practical point of view, as much out of date as the Siege of Jericho, where Joshua initiated a system of Siege Warfare which has never since been surpassed, although there certainly have been in military history commanders who could blow their own trumpets to some purpose. Burgoyne himself was not guiltless in this respect. His friendship with Lord Strange led to an acquaintance with the latter's family and also to an elopement with

Lady Charlotte Stanley,* when he was a young officer in the 1st Dragoons. He had had a "priory tachment," as Sam Weller puts it, to Miss Frances Poole, who ultimately married the Lord Palmerston of the day. Burgoyne dedicated to the bridegroom a poem on the charms of Fanny to which he had nearly succumbed:

'Twas mine to see each opening charm,
New beauties rise—new graces charm;†
'Twas mine to feel their power;
Nature and morals just and pure,
For that has made the fruit mature
Since I adored the flower.

After hard conflict passion cool'd;
Discretion, honour, reason ruled
O'er the subsiding flame;
Till Charlotte to my vacant breast,
With kindred charms and virtues blest,
A sweet successor came.

"Subsiding flame" for the cooling-off of a flirtation is excellent. But one can not help wondering what Charlotte thought of Fanny, and vice versa.

Burgoyne, as we shall see, was not indifferent to female charms, but he loved his Charlotte dearly and was a good, kind and most considerate husband to her. Her family, except Lord Strange, at first frowned upon the match, but ultimately, won over by the dashing young cavalryman's charm of manner, accepted him with great kindness and ever did what they could for him. And in the eighteenth century a peer could do a great deal.

He joined the army in 1744, but, chiefly owing to cards, sold out in 1747. He went with his wife to France

---

*Sixth daughter of the eleventh Earl of Derby.

†Rather a poetic license, this repetition.

where they settled down near Canteloup, and where he acquired that knowledge, or rather, smattering of the French language which in those days was indispensable to any man of fashion. And yet most of them mangled it; not more, however, than they did English,—witness that creation of Burgoyne's friend, Sheridan, Lord Foppington with his "As Gad shall jedge me," "Stap my vitals," "Rat me," and so forth. But one loves Lord Foppington, if only for his remark that he was "passionately fond of music—on Tuesdays and Saturdays, for then there is always the best company at the Opera."

It was at this date that Burgoyne with his wife paid a visit to Italy, where in Rome his portrait was painted by Ramsay,* and a remarkably handsome fellow the artist depicts him as being, with large and lustrous eyes. No wonder Lady Charlotte fell in love with him. In 1756 he rejoined the army and, thanks to the interest of the house of Stanley, was gazetted Captain in the 11th Dragoons. It was not long before he saw service in the field. The Seven Years' War had for its main theater Germany, but at this date England was constantly fitting out expeditions to the coast of France. These were called "diversions," and to read about them is certainly diverting, for as a rule the admiral who took the troops over and the general who commanded them were not on the best of terms. The "general idea," as soldiers say, was that by landing men somewhere on the coast of France, the French troops serving in Flanders, or High Germany, or wherever Bellona may have been belloning about, would be "diverted" thence to deal with the invasion of Normandy or Brittany. These expeditions might have been called Tip-and-Run Expeditions: they

*Official portrait painter at George III's Court.

were not cricket, for they usually ended in a draw. Fox compared them to "breaking windows with guineas," and it is an apt simile. What a wit said of the Rochefort Expedition of 1757 might be said of most of them:

> We went, we saw, were seen, like Valiant Men
> Sailed up the Bay, and then—sailed back again.

Young Burgoyne took part in three of them, the attack upon Cherbourg in 1758, the expedition against St. Malo in the same year, and the Belle Isle adventure in 1761. The St. Malo enterprise, known in its day, but now quite forgotten, as "The misfortune at St. Cas"—St. Cas being the bay from which the troops reembarked—had some interesting features. It was commanded by General Bligh, whom Horace Walpole describes as "an old General routed out of some horse armoury in Ireland." In other words, he was what we now call a "dug-out." One can not blame this poor old boy, for his instructions were of the vaguest: they were to the effect that he should "carry a warm alarm along the coast of France." An indignant and ungrammatical pamphleteer of the day demanded, "Who could the descent alarm but a few peasants and a few old women for fear they should not be ravished?" (A very cynical *"not"* this, I think.) But the "Misfortune" deserves to be remembered, if only for one incident. When the troops were driven on to the beach of St. Cas, the Quartermaster-General, a certain Colonel Clerk, instead of worrying about such trifling details as arrangements for the reembarkation, sat on the shingle, "Spending his time in the trivial amusement of reading a Gazette which accidentally fell into his hands." This is the right British phlegm which helped us to win an empire and also, incidentally, later on in the eighteenth century, to lose a large part of it. Burgoyne learned in this expedition to assume responsibility. He writes, "C. and myself who were upon the right perceived a very large body of the enemy pushing with great expedition upon the hill on the right in the intention to flank us. Of this we immediately informed the Generals, but received no order how to act and were obliged to determine upon our own authority to wheel the divisions we commanded so as to front the enemy." And it is most probable that the generals were anxiously waiting each his turn, all queued up, to borrow the Quartermaster-General's *London Gazette* to see who had been promoted. Our troops had to swim for it to the boats and many were killed in the water. It is not to be wondered at that the first of the dug-outs, General Bligh, when he got back to England found himself in disgrace. But the odd thing is that the Duc d'Aiguillon, the French commander, was also heavily censured. So this particular show was emphatically a draw. The subsequent history of Colonel Clerk is not known. But one might wager that the coffee-houses buzzed with stories of his calmness.

In 1759 it was decided to raise two regiments of Light Horse, and George II gave Burgoyne the command of one of them, the 16th Dragoons. (The other was given to Eliott, afterward Lord Heathfield, the hero of the Siege of Gibraltar: you can see his portrait in the National Portrait Gallery, and a fine red-faced, hook-nosed old gentlemen he is, a typical British general of the period.) The ranks of Burgoyne's regiment soon filled up, and no wonder, for the recruiting advertisement said, "You will be mounted on the finest horses in the world, with superb clothing and the richest accoutrements; your pay and privileges are equal to two guineas a week; you are everywhere respected; your society is courted; you are admired by the Fair, which, together with the chance of getting switched to a buxom widow, or of brushing with a rich heiress, renders the situation truly enviable and desirable. Young men out of employment or uncomfortable, 'There is a tide in the affairs of men, which, taken at the flood, leads on to fortune': nick in instantly and enlist." I think we may be pretty sure that it was Burgoyne who suggested the Shakespearian quotation. He soon licked his regiment into shape.

George III after his accession took a special pride in, and never wearied of inspecting, "Burgoyne's Light Horse," so smart a regiment had it become. Later on, when it returned from Portugal, the King gave it the title of The Queen's Light Dragoons, and used to review it regularly every year on Hounslow Heath or Wimbledon Common. Burgoyne drew up a Code of Instructions for the guidance of his officers, which is of peculiar interest. He was in advance of his time. He actually, anticipating Sir Joseph Porter, K. C. B., told them not to swear. An occasional joke, in talking to the men, is also recommended as "an encouragement to the well-disposed and at the same time a tacit reproof to others"—though surely such a joke must have been rather like Lord Burleigh's nod. To the private, soldiering was no joke in the mid-eighteenth century. Army punishments were horribly severe. They included flogging,* tying neck and heels (akin to the Scavenger's Daughter,† a form of torture used in the Tower of London), riding the

*The Bostonian taunt of 1770, "Bloodybacks," referred to the floggings then almost of daily occurrence in the British Army.

†Said to derive its odd name from Sir William Skevington, Lieutenant of the Tower, who invented it in the time of Henry VIII.

wooden horse, picketing and running the gauntlet, or "gantlope," as it used to be called. Minor punishments were clubbing, bottling, booting, and, perhaps most terrible of all, "Removal to the Navy." One need not go farther than Smollett to learn that a Life on the Ocean Wave, And a Home on the Roaring Deep, was not exactly a home from home in those days. But Burgoyne was no bullying martinet. We shall see later on, in North America, that if ever there was a general popular with the rank and file, it was Gentleman Johnny, chiefly indeed because he was a gentleman.

It is but poor consolation to reflect that the men in other armies were even more savagely treated. In that crack corps, the Prussian Guards, between 1740 and 1800 there were over one thousand six hundred desertions and one hundred and thirty suicides. The Prussian method is what Burgoyne calls in his code "Training men like spaniels by the stick,"* and he contrasts it with the French system of "substituting the point of honour in the place of severity." These are significant words: the "point of honour" was (after women) the lodestar of John Burgoyne's life. He goes on to say, "An Englishman will not bear beating so well as the foreigners," and he even urges that soldiers should be treated as thinking beings! Here he is enormously in advance of his age.

Regimental officers of his day regarded their men not as thinking, but as drinking, beings. "You have no business, Sir, to think," was a common army phrase of the period. And, as a matter of fact, the private who thinks

---

*"A spaniel, a woman, a walnut tree,
The more you flog them the better they be."

Of the three it would seem wiser to deal with the *Juglans Regia.* It can not bite, kick, scratch, or call you unpleasant names.

has always in the past been rather an anomaly. Trooper Silas Tomkyn Comberback (otherwise known as Samuel Taylor Coleridge) thought a good deal when he was in the 15th Dragoons. But his thinking led to his writing Greek inscriptions—not unpleasant ones, one trusts—upon walls while he was on sentry-go. And probably a famous writer of the present day could not refrain from thinking when the Sergeant-Major at Caterham told him that he "looked like a plateful of warmed-up Death." Burgoyne gives his officers excellent advice, though it must have given rise to many an oath of astonishment.

The ignorance of the British officer of this day was, in the biting words of Colonel J. F. C. Fuller, "of a Stygian density." Burgoyne actually urges them to read books and to learn foreign languages, though he admits that they should first learn English, and to "write it with swiftness and accuracy." When he comes down to brass tacks he is extraordinarily sensible. A dragoon officer should acquire "the knowledge of every article that concerns the horse," in other words he puts his officers through it, they had to "accoutre and bridle a horse themselves till they were thoroughly acquainted with the use of each strap and buckle." This is as sensible as the Duke of Wellington, who, anxious to know the exact weight carried by a private, instead of calling for a return on paper, made out by a clerk, sent for an infantryman, fully accoutered, put him into a pair of scales, weighed him and noted the weight. He then made him strip stark naked, weighed him again and noted the difference. Burgoyne also animadverts upon "the small allowance given by the Government for corn." This stinginess persisted for centuries, certainly up to 1880, or thereabouts, when there was a very popular ditty:

Captain Jinks of the Horse Marines*
Fed his horse on corn and beans,
Which surely far exceeds the means
Of a Captain in the Army.

In 1761 Burgoyne took part as a volunteer in another "diversion," the attack on Belle Isle. His Charlotte, quite naturally, did not want him to go. He tried to console her with a poem which begins:

Still does my Obstinate repine
And reason's voice reprove;
Still think him cold who would combine
Philosophy with Love.

Perhaps "my Obstinate" was right. Philosophy and Love go ill together. Though of course there is the classic case of Lord Lytton, who, on one occasion, told his wife that he was going into the country "to study philosophy." Lady Lytton, who appears to have smelled a rat, followed him and, as she put it, "found Philosophy in pink muslin upon my Lord's knee." "How charming is divine Philosophy," especially when you can dandle it and address it as "Honey."

The expedition to Belle Isle is remarkable for one very curious episode. The governor, Sainte Croix, did his best by stratagems to deceive the British as to his strength. In this the ladies of the garrison—was there ever a French lady who was not at once both strategist and tactician?—gave him valuable aid. Clad in red uniforms, they rode on horseback along the coast where they could be seen by the English fleet then lying in that

*No such regiment, of course, ever existed. Which seems a pity, as the British Army is so frequently engaged in what is called Amphibious Warfare.

vague—to landsmen—quarter generally known as "the offing." Such was the patriotism of these daughters of France that "those who had no horses rode on cows." Which must have soured, if not the milk, at all events the cows. This is very like the Welsh women who, in their red cloaks and steeple-crowned hats, completely took in the French soldiers* when they landed at Fishguard in 1797. There was no battle at Fishguard and there is no mention of the Pembrokeshire Yeomanry in Lord Cawdor's despatch dealing with this very trivial affair. Which is, no doubt, the reason why the corps in question was in 1853 given by the Home Secretary, Lord Palmerston,† "Fishguard" as a battle honor—a most Palmerstonian proceeding. And yet many regular regiments had to wait until 1882 before they got battle honors which they had won in Flanders under the great Duke of Marlborough. Probably in 1853 there was some Welsh M. P. whose vote was valuable.

Belle Isle was very futile. A verdict of the day on it was, "There was not wanting some in England who did not sufficiently estimate the value of this conquest, yet all the parties agree in applauding the valour of the officers by whom it was obtained." This may be said of every diversion, or side-show, as we call them now, in military history. The latest, the Dardanelles, has given a word, Anzac, to history which will certainly never be forgotten. In a contemporary account of Belle Isle there is a quaint passage. "The French began to fire from behind a breastwork: the English returned it every

---

*They had just been recruited from the French jails and were hardly real soldiers.

†At this date the Militia and Yeomanry were administered by the Home Office, not the War Office.

time, squatting themselves on their backsides every time to unload, which saved them from the shot of the enemy." The word of command "Backsides!" is not to be found in the old drill-books, though these contain some very odd directions. Those interested in such should read *The Sergeant-Major,* by Colonel F. J. Davies,* published in 1886. This highly entertaining work ends with an extract from an old drill-book which I should love to quote. But I dare not, lest I be denounced by some censor as a turp., and lest this my book be Ellis-Islanded upon some *Index Librorum Prohibitorum.* John Burgoyne got taken prisoner once, and I do not want this to happen to him again.

Burgoyne was now to see more serious campaigning than these "Tag you're it" kind of expeditions to the coast of Normandy and Brittany. France and Spain had made up their minds to bully Portugal, and England, mindful of her favorite wine and ever the champion (when convenient) of small countries, fired up on behalf of her old ally, declared war on Spain and in 1762 sent a contingent of seven thousand troops to the Peninsula. These troops were placed under the command of Wilhelm, Count of Lippe Buckeburg (some add Schaumburg, but this makes it painfully long), a field-marshal in the army of Prince Ferdinand of Brunswick. He had held a commission in the British Foot Guards and had fought at Dettingen. After the Seven Years' War he set up a kind of Woolwich for the training of young Brunswick sapper and gunner officers at which he himself instructed them in mathematics. The Portuguese army filled this old martinet with dismay and horror. The officers were

*Now General Sir F. J. Davies, K. C. B., Lieutenant of the Tower of London.

ill-paid,* so much so that many of the captains did a little job-tailoring in their spare time and their wives took in washing. There is a British regiment pleasantly known as The Slashers,†—perhaps Portugal then had one called The Cutters. The Generals could not afford to pay their servants wages, so instead gave them commissions, and the guards on duty outside the King's palace in Lisbon would beg alms from those who passed by. Probably if any one had thrown a copper on the parade-ground while they were being drilled—if they ever were—there would have been an unseemly scuffle, or, in the odd phrase of the newspaper reporters, "an ugly rush." That distinguished Spanish officer, that "unaffected, undetected, well-connected nobleman," the Duke of Plaza Toro, would probably not have seen anything odd or unseemly in this, but La Lippe was horrified. To show his lack of appreciation of Portuguese gunnery he gave a dinner to the Portuguese generals in a large marquee and offered a prize to any gunner who should hit the flag flying on the top of it. One can only hope that the Portuguese generals took the cannonade as a salute in their honor; Burgoyne, always a fire-eater, must have thoroughly enjoyed it—I can hear him asking with a pleasant smile on his handsome face, "Where did that one go?"

The Count de la Lippe was given to grim practical jokes of this kind. Once, in Germany, after maneuvers,

*It was painful to read in the French press in December, 1926, that in the French Army there were cases of officers whose pay was so inadequate that they were reduced to supplement it by cleaning motor-cars and collecting railway-tickets in their spare time.

†The 28th Foot, now 1st Battalion The Gloucestershire Regiment, won this nickname in North America at the battle of White Plains in November, 1776.

he gave a dinner in his tent to a number of distinguished visitors, and toward the end of it was observed to be perpetually looking at his watch. He had, like Mr. Winkle, just said, "Let's have another bottle," when he was asked why he was so anxious about the time. "Why," he replied, "I have ordered this tent to be mined by a new method: it is to be blown up at a certain moment, and I want to go out in time to see the explosion." His guests did not wait to empty that bottle.

Burgoyne had come over in command of his Light Dragoons and was given the local rank of brigadier-general, with a brigade of three thousand troops, two thousand of which were Portuguese and not very enthusiastic soldiers, for a large proportion of the inhabitants of Portugal took no interest whatever in the operations that had been undertaken in the defense of their country; they appear to have regarded the whole matter as a lot of unnecessary fuss. Burgoyne and his regiment greatly distinguished themselves in the surprise and capture of Valentia d'Alcantara. He started at midnight, forded the Tagus and, though misled by his guides, arrived at dawn in front of Valentia and, without waiting for the infantry to come up, rode, sword in hand, at the head of his Dragoons into the place and captured it. And the first thing he did was to "raise a contribution for sparing the convent and the town to be divided among his troops." Otherwise the town would have been pillaged and the convent—well, the less said about the fate of its inmates the better. And yet, though it is no excuse for pillage and rape, there is a story in a novel by Paul de Kock* dealing with 1814, when certain old maiden ladies

*He was the favorite reading of Pio Nono, in spite of the fact that in London you generally see him in rather furtive shop-windows, in the

in a town on the road from the Western Front to Paris, instead of flying from it with the rest of the inhabitants, are, rather unkindly, represented as eagerly demanding, *"Les Cosaques! Où sont les Cosaques?"*

It is pleasant to read in Burgoyne's despatch: "I am conscious that the chief merit of the success was due to the admirable though not uncommon valour and activity of the troops I had the honour to command." This is in the right Gentleman Johnny vein. La Lippe was greatly pleased and issued a General Order in which he extolled *"la glorieuse conduite de Monsieur le Brigadier Burgoyne qui après avoir marché quinze lieues sans relâche à emporté Valentia d' Alcantara, l'épée à la main; fait prisonnier le général qui devoit envahir l'Alentejo; détruit le régiment Espagnol de Seville, pris trois drapeaux, un colonel, plusieurs officiers de distinction et beaucoup de soldats."* And he further urged his officers and men to strive to imitate *"un aussi bel exemple."* King Joseph, too, was delighted, and told Burgoyne that the colors he had captured were at his disposal to send back to England, if he so thought fit, and presented him with a diamond ring.* "My Obstinate," who accompanied him to the Peninsula, must have been very proud of her *beau sabreur.*

In the Public Record Office (W. O. 1.-165) there is an interesting letter concerning his regiment written by

---

company of Cora Pearl, Maria Martin and—*que diable allait-il faire dans cette galère!*—Aristotle! When the Pope heard that this lively, if somewhat free, story-teller was dead, he is said to have exclaimed in sorrow, *"Mio povero Paolo di Kocko!"*

*The King's reward to La Lippe took the form of "six pieces of golden cannon and carriages of such a weight that a strong man could not sustain one of them at arm's-length horizontally without being over-poized." The King left legacies to all the foreign officers down to the rank of colonel, with the solitary exception of Charles Lee, of whom more hereafter, whose manners were never ingratiating.

Burgoyne, Lisbon, June 26, 1762, to Charles Townshend, Secretary at War. In this he recommends Captain Walpole for promotion to major: "His behaviour since his arrival in Portugal, where he has been trusted with a separate command, allows me the satisfaction of mentioning his name to you in a very different manner from what his habit of dissipation authorised me to do when I had the honour to talk to you upon his preferment in England. I never doubted his talents for the service; I am now convinced he is capable of steadiness to employ them and think I can make myself answerable that in the rank of major he will do his part to support the credit of the English cavalry." Alas! the "habit of dissipation" was too strong to be thrown off, as we shall see later. Burgoyne was very proud of, and keen about, his regiment. In this same letter he recommends that Cornet Duperron should be placed in a regiment of foot, because though "a diligent, good officer," he is "very unfit for the Dragoons as an incorrigible bad horseman and unacquainted with every part of horse service." The Colonel kindly adds, his circumstances "make him a subject of compassion," and "could he be transferred to a regiment of foot, it would make him and his family happy." The letter ends, "Lady Charlotte begs you to accept her compliments."

In October Burgoyne brought off another surprise, that of Villa Velha. This was largely due to the dash and enterprise of his subordinate, a certain Colonel Lee, who got into the enemy's encampment without being perceived, and, when the Spanish troops had rallied, "pursued them upon a brisk run" and chased them out of the camp. We shall meet Colonel Lee again, later on, in North America. It is one of the Romances of

War that Colonel Charles Lee, who led Burgoyne's fine regiment into action in the Peninsula* in October, 1762, should have been captured by these his old comrades in North America, in December, 1776, at Basking Ridge near Trenton. The Regimental Record contains an illustration showing Lee handing over his sword to Colonel Harcourt on this occasion. There appears to be a whimsical smile of recognition upon both faces.

Peace was concluded early in 1763, and Burgoyne and his regiment returned with their laurels to England. While in Spain he had defeated not only the Don but, a far more formidable antagonist, the War Office in London. His friends, Lieutenant-Colonel Brudenell, Lieutenant-Colonel Clinton and Lieutenant-Colonel Fitzroy, had all been promoted colonel. This was an age of nepotism; there was no such damned nonsense as merit leading to promotion. Burgoyne wrote to Charles Townshend, Secretary at War, a pretty warm letter. He says plainly, with pardonable indignation, that he had "family support" and adds, "upon any other ground I should blush to ask preferment, and I doubt not that the gentlemen who have succeeded likewise waived the claim of service." And yet we won a good many victories in the eighteenth century. He goes on, should he not be promoted he would take it, not as a disappointment to himself, but as a slight to his patron and connection, Lord Strange. The Secretary at War was quite hurt; he had "a personal regard for Burgoyne as a man as well as an officer." And he adds the noble words, "I am not

*Lee was every inch a cavalryman. When, after Portugal, he was in the Russian service, he wrote to a friend: "I am to have a command of Cossacks and Wollacks, a kind of people I have a good opinion of. I am determined not to serve in the line: *one might as well be a churchwarden.*"

The American General Lee

Taken prisoner by Lieutenant Colonel Harcourt of the English Army, in Morris County, New Jersey, 1776

Engraved for Barnard's "New Complete & Authentic History of England"

cold in any interest or to any person Lord Strange recommends and loves, my life and conduct will be a full answer to that charge." The upshot was that Lord Bute* wrote personally a very flattering letter to Burgoyne saying that he had procured him the rank he desired. For great people these were great days: plain Captain John Smith had to wait much longer before he got promotion—if he ever did.

It is a good thing that this correspondence never came the way of Charles Dickens; he was so prejudiced. He would have written something unpardonably bitter about it, for he did not like the army. Even "the flower of ours," that fine old rough and tough soldier and strategist (yes, strategist, for your true strategist is always "devilish sly"), Major J. Bagstock, is represented by Dickens as having a few venial faults, such as gluttony, curiosity, snobbishness and selfishness.

*Then Prime Minister.

# CHAPTER II

## PARLIAMENT

BURGOYNE had been elected Member of Parliament for Midhurst in 1761, but did not take his seat until he returned from Portugal in 1763. And I almost wish he had not, for parliamentary proceedings and debates are, as a rule, terribly tedious to read, though possibly the *Congressional Record* is not much more lively than the British Hansard. I have waded through many pages of the *Annals of Parliament* in mid-eighteenth century and have only once or twice found the reporter's (or rather the compiler's) interpolation (Here a great laugh). How often the scribe might have put in (Here a great yawn), even in modern times, for it is reported of the Marquis of Hartington of the Victorian era that he once yawned terrifically in the middle of—one of his own speeches. I wish some statistician would compute the total amount in sovereigns of the emoluments (a dignified word) received by Speakers of the House of Commons since the appointment first came into existence. The amount would probably be colossal. But, however great, it must have been well-earned, as would be very evident if the same statistician could also reckon the number of yawns that have been yawned in the House during the same period.

In 1765 Burgoyne, like the keen soldier he was, did a sort of grand tour on the Continent to see what foreign armies were like. His reports are, from a military point of view, of considerable interest. Lord Chatham gave him a letter of introduction to Prince Ferdinand of Brunswick, and Burgoyne's letter thanking him ends in such a grand eighteenth-century style that it is worth quoting for the benefit of those interested in the Art of Polite Writing:

> "I have the honour to be
> "With the most profound respect, attachment and sense of obligation
> "Your Lordship's most obedient, humble servant
> "JOHN BURGOYNE."

These were leisurely days indeed.

Just as young officers from the Staff College make, and have for many years past made, in time of peace, tours of continental battle-fields, so did John Burgoyne, Charlotteless, of course, "wander with enthusiasm over what is to a soldier classic ground." He may even have seen a certain Old Peterkin still engaged in the melancholy and monotonous task of digging up skulls on his farm near Blenheim, or rather Blindheim. Unless, of course, old Kaspar cut off his grandson, then Young Peterkin, with a rixthaler for being such a dreadful little bore with his constant and reiterated parrot-cry as to "what they fought each other for." For this offensive imp, as you will remember, would not take his grandfather's "Nay, that I do not know" as a satisfactory answer.

Burgoyne managed, with some difficulty, to be present incognito at the maneuvers of the army of the Emperor of Austria. He thought the infantry the best he had ever seen, the cavalry not quite so good, and the general officers "very knowing," devilish sly, in fact. But he points out that there were no less than three hundred and thirty-eight of them. When one remembers what a general—of those days—cost, directly and indirectly, it seems excessive. Indeed it reminds one rather of the realms of King Goodheart, of whom the Grandest of Grand Inquisitors used to sing:

> On every side Field Marshals gleamed,
> Small beer were Lords-Lieutenant deemed,
> With Admirals the ocean teemed
> Throughout his wide dominions.

And though they were knowing, some of them seem to have been past mark of mouth. Burgoyne writes, "Some are superannuated; others owe their preferment (and have no other pretensions to it) to family rank* and court intrigue; many have risen by gradual seniority, without faults, and without merits, whom it would be unjust to put by, yet whom the state can never employ for great purposes." He pays a high compliment to the Irish.† "In the Austrian service many of the most distinguished characters will be found among men of Irish extraction; and in the lower ranks the army swarms with the offspring of the best Roman Catholic families of that country," and he regrets that the Roman Catholic Irish were not allowed to serve as officers in the British Army. In this he was far in advance of his time, for though it was

*A Daniel come to judgment! (See page 20.)

†In the old days the Irish scrapped all over the continent. The Irish Brigade which fought for Louis XIV against William III made the odd stipulation that they should wear the English uniform and fight under the English flag. Which is very Irish, and therefore very difficult to understand.

winked at later on in the eighteenth century, it was not until about 1800 that Roman Catholics were admitted to the army with the cognizance of the Crown. In the old Half-Pay Lists at the Public Record Office there is an entry against many an officer's name: "Suspected Papist." Which means that a proved Papist could have drawn no half-pay.

Burgoyne also noted the horse-breeding studs for which Hungary has always been famous. And, practical soldier that he was, he gives details about "the caps made so as to let down and cover the ears and neck in inclement weather, and the Hungarian trousers and half-boots without stockings," the general object of the uniform being to "unite as much as possible lightness, warmth and ease." And yet, in later years, in spite of these notes, Burgoyne was destined to command in North America Brunswick troops who were, as regards uniform and equipment, about as fit for fighting in the thickly-wooded country there as the White Knight. He gives details about the Prussian infantry drill and shows great admiration for its simplicity. Later on this was introduced into the British Army by Dundas, who, from his attachment to it, was affectionately known as "Old Pivot." Burgoyne finds the Prussian cavalry indifferent, and he is very critical about the rank and file in general, many of whom are "strangers, deserters, prisoners and enemies of various countries, languages and religions."* As the King of Prussia had a royal weakness for kidnaping any one who looked a likely soldier, this is not astonishing. The result was, as Burgoyne points out, "Their army is more harassed with precautionary guards against their

*Which might be said of much of the German riffraff which let him down on the Hudson in 1777.

own soldiers deserting than against the enemy, and, after an unsuccessful action, the number missing usually trebles the number to be accounted for by death or capture." Not lost, in fact, but gone behind. He gives the King of Prussia full credit for his secrecy. "He is jealous of prying eyes in all his employments. If he means to manœuvre ten thousand men in private, he shuts up a country as effectually as his palace." Poor Burgoyne! When he came down from Canada, not so much like "a wolf on the fold" as an invader whose march had been widely heralded as though by advance agents, he was to find how difficult it is to keep anything secret in the field, especially if there is a lady (or ladies) in the case.

His report on the French Army is mixed. He greatly admires their cavalry, though he notes that their horses are much inferior to British horses, and he also very shrewdly observes, "The Prussian severity of command together with the free use of the stick is very ill-suited to a nation where even in the lowest classes a blow is regarded as an irreparable disgrace." And no doubt this, in a minor way, helped toward the French Revolution. "Monsieur the Marquis," Charles Darnay's uncle, had, we may be pretty sure, been an officer in this army.

Lord Chatham, to whom Burgoyne's *Reflections and Observations* were sent, thanked him for them in very flattering terms. They are, in effect, the comments of a very keen if slightly pedantic soldier, always noting, as is natural, his own arm, cavalry, and whatever pertains to it, with a peculiar interest. They are what military attachés, or military observers as they used to be called, have covered reams and reams of paper with: sometimes these have been noted and acted on, more often pigeon-holed and forgotten. The classic instance, in the latter class, is furnished by Colonel Stoffel, the Cassandra of the Second Empire. As French Military Attaché in Berlin from 1866 to 1870 he narrowly observed the Prussian Army and sent in to Paris detailed reports showing what a fine fighting machine was being put together across the Rhine. These were pigeonholed. Had any one dared to bring them to the notice of, and explain their significance to, the Emperor, Napoleon III could not but have realized that his army, though "ready to the last gaiter-button," as the French Field-Marshal rather vaingloriously put it, had as much chance of marching *à Berlin* as it had of marching to Timbuctoo. The moral is, Destroy all pigeonholes: they have ever been the curse of Ministries of War, as we shall see later in the case of "that man."

There is, by the way, a remarkable instance in the history of the United States Army. General Emory Upton, who died in 1881, wrote *The Military Policy of the United States,* which is now a military classic. "Yet his voice was as the voice of one crying in the Wilderness: the Government did not even print his Report, it was filed in Manuscript and forgotten among the millions of documents in the archives of the War Department." It was ultimately discovered and, thanks to the wisdom of Mr. Secretary Root, printed in 1903.

Horace Walpole never lost an opportunity of saying something unpleasant about Burgoyne, and now we come to the reason for the Horatian bitterness and backbiting. A nephew of his, Major Walpole, serving in Burgoyne's regiment—we have already made his acquaintance—had applied to Lord Townshend, then Lord-Lieutenant of Ireland, for the appointment of aide-de-camp. The matter was naturally referred to Burgoyne. He wrote to

Lord Townshend a very honest letter. The Major was a slacker who had been on leave for a year. Burgoyne said "he could not help complaining aloud of the impropriety of his solicitations." He added, "If after this representation Major Walpole thinks proper to persevere in his application, I have only to hope that he may speedily find from your lordship's patronage a rank more worthy of his attention, and that an opening may be made in my regiment for a Major whose views of future preferment will rest upon a diligent discharge of a present trust." And Major Walpole probably said "Od rot him," for Burgoyne's testimonial to him was pretty plain speaking, and unusual in an age when family influence was all-powerful.

In 1768, King George made Burgoyne governor of Fort William, North Britain, which added considerably to his income. He was now quite a figure in London, smiled on at Court, and a friend of Johnson's* friend, the great Sir Joshua Reynolds, who is said to have painted Burgoyne's portrait. Tom Taylor, Sir Joshua's biographer, says, "They must have been in the constant habit of meeting in the Green Room of Drury Lane, at the dinners of the Thursday Night Club,† at the Star and Garter, at every place of amusement where the gay, the witty, and the well-bred of London gathered together." There have been two famous Star and Garters near London, one at Greenwich and one, more famous, on Richmond Hill. Sir Joshua had a villa almost next door to the latter. About 1890 this "villa," which means a

*Oddly enough there is no mention of Burgoyne in Boswell's *Johnson,* except a curious remark of Johnson's about the Convention of Saratoga, which I will quote when we get to Saratoga.

†Not Night-Club—probably much more cheerful than those dreary, if dissipated, haunts.

good-sized house, was to let, and I remember being vastly pleased by the notice-board which described it as "Once the Property of the *late* Sir Joshua Reynolds."

But the Royal Borough of Richmond is full of strange bits of bygone history; you may, for example, see there The Original Maid of Honor Shop. Perhaps it should be explained that maids of honor are a kind of cheese-cake and excessively good, even to those whose livers resent pastry. Visitors to Richmond who take any turning to the right from the crowded street which leads up to the picturesque old bridge will find themselves in a real Kate Greenaway Green which has, with its red-brick Queen Anne houses, so old-world an air that one would never be astonished to see there a Sir Plume, clouded cane and all, coquetting with some Lady Gay Spanker, all be-patched and be-powdered, and vastly obleeged and coquettish, bless her. Undoubtedly many ghosts must saunter there—if only one could meet them! And on the other side of Richmond Green, toward the river, there is still a bit left of Richmond Palace where Queen Elizabeth died.*

At the General Election of 1768 Colonel Burgoyne and Sir Henry Hoghton, Lord Derby's nominees, stood in the Whig interest for Preston, in opposition to Sir Peter Leicester and Sir Frank Standish—two delightful names which might have come straight out of some Sheridan comedy. It was a spirited election, Eatanswill had nothing on it. As Mr. Shaw so pleasantly says, Burgoyne literally fought it, a loaded pistol in each hand.

*She was born at Greenwich Palace, which fact impelled Doctor Johnson to write the lines:

> Pleased with the spot which gave Eliza birth,
> We kneel, and kiss the consecrated earth.

There was much rioting, and an inhabitant of the town writing in March, 1768, said, "The contest here is attended with imminent danger, I have just escaped with many friends."

There are some interesting notes about this election in Lord Kenyon's Manuscripts, where it is noted, November 10, 1768, "This day was presented by Lord Strange the petition of Sir Henry Hoghton and Col. Burgoyne, complaining of a false return and partiality in the late election for Preston. There is another petition from the inhabitants setting forth that they were rejected by the Mayor. . . . Col. Burgoyne gives out that he hath engaged Government on his side and is sure of success." On March twenty-fourth of the following year we read, "Yesterday the information against Burgoyne came on at six o'clock in the morning and lasted thirteen hours, when Burgoyne and several others of the defendants were found guilty. . . . An indictment was tried at Lancaster against one of Burgoyne's mobbers for plundering Jackson, the linen-draper's house, and forcing him to deliver up his money on his knees." And finally on May ninth of the same year we are told, "This morning Sir Joseph Yates, after a very pathetic and proper speech, wherein he laid it on very hard upon the Colonel, pronounced the judgment of the Court, viz., fined Burgoyne £1,000, but no imprisonment, and the fine was paid in Court." Others were fined one hundred pounds and given three months' imprisonment and "the three sergeants and drummers six months imprisonment, but no fine, being poor." The writer adds, "I do think they should have sent the Colonel to keep Mr. Wilkes* company as well as the rest, and then everybody would have been satisfied; most people

*Jack Wilkes, the demagogue. We shall meet him again later.

think that part was wanting to make the sentence complete."

The mystery man of the age, the Man in the Literary Mask, Junius, got hold of this and made great play with it. He attacked the Duke of Grafton* and charged him with having given Burgoyne three thousand five hundred pounds "to re-imburse him for that fine of £1,000," and went on to charge "the noble Colonel with unfair play in the gaming-houses and with watching with the soberest attention for a fair opportunity of engaging a drunken young nobleman at piquet." Even Horace Walpole remonstrated against this—not that a young nobleman should have got drunk, for in this age that was their nightly custom, but that Burgoyne should have been accused of foul play. Horry says, "Junius was thought unjust, as Burgoyne was never supposed to do more than play very well." Burgoyne himself, when some one brought this charge up against him in the House of Commons, said, "If the wretch Junius is now lurking here in any corner of the House, I would tell him to his face that he was an assassin, a liar and a coward." In his day, of course, Junius "intrigued," to use a modern cant-word, his contemporaries as much as Fiona Macleod did the last generation, and the authoress of *The Young Visiters* did the present. And, of the three, one would very much rather read *The Young Visiters.* Procurio will, it is to be hoped, live forever, while Junius will be of no interest to any one save to the Dryasdusts who

---

*Grafton rather laid himself open to attack. He had the amiable but indiscreet weakness of taking his *chère amie* (Fanny Parsons) to the Opera when it was known that the Queen would be present. And when there was a race-meeting at Newmarket, despatch-boxes could wait, he had better business to despatch. "He thought the World should be postponed to a Whore and a Horse-race." Very flattering for *cette dame.*

arise in every age and write enormous tomes proving that Shakespeare could have spelled his name in thirty-six different ways—what a trial he would have been nowadays to his banker—and that the *Iliad* was not written by Homer but by "somebody else of the same name." You can see them at work doing this any day in the Reading Room at the British Museum.

In the House of Commons Burgoyne appears to have been a bit of a free-lance. He voted according to his conscience, which, on occasion, King George thought "so extraordinary" that I almost imagine it was a mistake. We heard of the Falkland Islands in 1916. Their previous, and only important, mention in the history books was in 1770. A Spanish admiral had descended on them, driven out the English garrison and "taken the rudder off the only English vessel in the harbour."* It was some months before the Spanish Government made a very grudging, half-hearted apology. This made Burgoyne's blood boil and he said in the House, "Spain gave fifteen minutes to an officer to evacuate a garrison; Great Britain slept four months after the insult. It has been the fashion to maintain (I have seen it in print and I have heard it in conversation) that military men were prejudiced judges in questions of this nature. Sir, I disdain the idea, and denounce it in the name of my profession. The man who would wantonly promote bloodshed, who upon private views of advantage or ambition would involve Europe in war, would be a promoter of ferocity—a disgrace to his profession, to his country, and to human nature. But there are motives for which

*A Captain Walsingham said in the debate that "if the Spanish admiral had attempted to remove the rudder from a ship of his, he would have thought it his duty to knock his head off."

a soldier may wish for war; these are a sense of satisfaction due for an injury inflicted; a desire to make a return to our country for the honours and rewards we receive at her hands; a zeal to be the forward instrument to battle for the honour of the Crown, and the rights of the people of Great Britain." This is very eloquent, of course, but I think I prefer the breeziness of the sailor, Captain Walsingham; the Navy has a habit of putting things in a nutshell.

In 1771 Burgoyne voted for the Royal Marriage Act,* which later on, was to prove poor Mrs. Fitzherbert's undoing on her marriage with that punch-drinking rascal Prinny, better known as the Prince Regent and the "First Gentleman in Europe." It is odd to read that George III wrote to Lord North, "Had Burgoyne failed to do so, I should have felt myself obliged to name a new Governor for Fort William."

We next find him as an authority on that dreary subject Economics, or Political Economy, as this "dismal science" used to be called. The East India Company had been getting into debt. Burgoyne, who had often had a similar experience, wrote in the most sensible and Micawberish manner upon this: "It is impossible to produce anything out of nothing: the Company have no money, and therefore it is impossible that they should pay any of their creditors." One can not help thinking that this is an echo of some letter which, in earlier days, he may have sent on his own behalf to some Mr. Moses Shentpershent of the period. He is very modern in his

*George III himself was said at the time, by gossips, to have secretly married a pretty little Quakeress, Hannah Lightfoot. He also had a great admiration for Lady Sarah Lennox, later mother of the Napier soldiers. He wanted to get married, since, as he told Lord Bute, "his passions were similar to those of other young men."

phraseology. He says of one scheme which had been put forward to assist the company: "What a noble harvest would such a scheme produce for the Bulls and the Bears, and what a crop of ruin for those who were not perfectly in the secret." And he goes on with a warning to North. "A Minister who would be concerned in a business of this sort would deserve to be hanged, and I am confident that if Lord North thinks of it at all, it is from his not being at all acquainted with the ways of 'Change Alley.' "

These were the days of shaking the pagoda tree and returning from Hindoostan with lacs and lacs of rupees, and ivory, apes and peacocks and all the rest of it. Burgoyne does not spare John Company and alludes caustically to "the rapacity of their servants abroad and the knavery of the Directors at home." "Knaves" and "Directors" coupled together! We have indeed advanced far in the last hundred and fifty years: such a concatenation is, of course, impossible nowadays. In April, 1772, Burgoyne moved for a Select Committee to Inquire into the Affairs of the East India Company. He made a spirited speech: the "honour of the nation"—honor ever came first in Burgoyne's eyes—asked for it; the servants of the company had misconducted themselves; its affairs were "huddled together in one promiscuous tumult and confusion" and his peroration, in spite of its eighteenth-century pomposity, has really a fine appeal to humanity: "The fate of a great portion of the globe, the fate of great States in which your own is involved, the distresses of fifteen millions of people are involved in this question. Good God! What a call! The native of Hindoostan, born a slave—his neck bent from the very cradle to the yoke—by birth, by education, by climate, by religion, a patient, submissive, willing subject to Eastern despotism, first begins to feel, first shakes his chains, for the first time complains under the preeminence of British tyranny!" This ended in 1773 with the impeachment of Clive. As Macaulay puts it: "Burgoyne, a man of wit, fashion and honour, an agreeable dramatic writer, an officer whose courage was never questioned and whose skill at that time was highly esteemed, appeared as the accuser." Clive made a spirited and humorous defense. He complained that he had been "examined by the Select Committee more like a sheep-stealer than a Member of this House." He added: "I am sure, Sir, if I had any sore places about me, they would have been found: they have probed to the bottom: no lenient plasters have been applied to heal: no, Sir, they were all of the blister kind, prepared with Spanish flies and other provocatives." He ended by suggesting that "as the heads upon Temple Bar had tumbled down, Jacobitism having apparently come to an end,* his head should be put upon the middle pole and should have as 'supporters' on either side those of the late Chairman and Deputy Chairman of the India Company."

*Temple Luttrell jocularly said in the House that Bute, "that mighty Northern Thane," had had them taken down and kept as honored relics "in an interior cabinet." These heads, which included that of the old villain Simon Lovat, gave rise to Goldsmith's famous witticism. He and Johnson had been in Westminster Abbey and when they were in Poets' Corner, Johnson, pointing to the great names all round them, quoted the lines:

*Forsitan et nostrum nomen miscebitur istis.*

From the Abbey they "took a stroll down Fleet Street." (Which words, by the way, Johnson never used: they were put in his mouth by the late George Augustus Sala.) When they reached Temple Bar, "Goldy," pointing to the heads there, slyly repeated the quotation:

*Forsitan et nostrum nomen miscebitur* ISTIS.

"The House," says the Parliamentary History, "burst out into applause and remained in a fit of laughter for nearly ten minutes."

But not long afterward Clive committed suicide.* And Burgoyne was soon to set out upon that Great Adventure which ended in the death of his military reputation, and which was to cause him more bitterness than Clive ever felt.

---

*Had he lived he would in all probability have been sent to North America. He might perhaps have been as successful a general there as he was in Hindoostan.

# CHAPTER III

## BUNKER HILL

VOLUMES and volumes have been written on the causes of the American War of Independence, though really it ought to be called the First Civil War in America. They deal at enormous length with Taxation without Representation, Taxation No Tyranny, the Stamp Act, clergy dues paid in tobacco, the Molasses Act, Tea (Hysons and Congoes), Olive Branches unacknowledged and left to wither in a Whitehall pigeonhole, blundering Ministers, Sons (and Daughters) of Liberty, Writs of Assistance, the Bunch of Grapes, drawbacks on china earthenware, clandestine running of goods, the stupidity of Lord North,* the general cussedness of the British Government and the pig-headedness of Farmer George.† It is pleasant to see that a more lenient view of this sovereign is now being taken in the United States. I read not long ago in an American

*That easy-going nobleman. In February, 1775, Lord Hillsborough said that North, who had called on him, "talked about Almack's and the Pantheon, but not one word of America," though Hillsborough had begged him even with tears to resign.

†Farmer, because when he "opened the Session" on January 19, 1770, he began with: "It is with much concern that I find myself obliged to open the session of Parliament with acquainting you that the distemper among the horned cattle has lately broken out in this kingdom." America was kept for a casual mention in the last paragraph. George III and North were very like each other in face and figure. Contemporary scandal said there was an obvious reason for this.

weekly paper that he was now regarded "not so much as a tyrant as a snuffy old German who liked train-oil in his salad." There is one point in this question which, though of great interest, is not much stressed in, at all events, the English history books, and that is England's lack of appreciation of American courage. This is very well brought out in a speech made in the House of Commons, March 27, 1775, by David Hartley.* It is as follows:

> "Everything is asserted about America to serve the present turn without the least regard for truth. I would have these matters fairly sifted out. To begin with the late war: the Americans turned the success of the war, at both ends of the line. General Monkton took Beausejour in Nova Scotia with 1,500 provincial troops and about 200 regulars. Sir William Johnson in the other part of America changed the face of the war to success, with a provincial army which took Baron Dieskau prisoner. . . . Nor did they stint their services to North America: they followed the British arms out of their continent to the Havannah and Martinique, after the complete conquest of America. And so had they done in the preceding war. They were not grudging of their exertions—they were at the Siege of Carthagena†—yet what was Carthagena to them, but as members of the common cause, of the glory of this country! In that way too, Sir, they took

*Son of the philosopher, David Hartley, whom Coleridge admired so much that he named his son Hartley after him. He helped Benjamin Franklin with the negotiations which led to the Treaty of Peace of September 3, 1783.

†Washington's half-brother Lawrence served there and became a friend of the Admiral, Vernon. Hence Mount Vernon. Massachusetts sent five hundred men on this expedition. Barely fifty returned.

Lord George Germain

Painted by Sir Joshua Reynolds. From a print in possession of Messrs. T. H. Parker, 12a, Berkeley Street, London, W. 1

Louisburg* from the French, singlehanded, without any European assistance; as mettled an enterprise as any in our history! an everlasting memorial of the zeal, courage and perseverance of the troops of New England. The men themselves dragged the cannon over a morass which had always been thought impassable, and they carried the shot upon their backs. . . . Whenever Great Britain has declared war they have taken their part. They were engaged in King William's wars and Queen Anne's, even in their infancy. They conquered Nova Scotia, which, from that time, has always belonged to Great Britain. They have been engaged in more than one expedition to Canada, ever foremost to partake of honour and danger with the mother country. Well, Sir, what have we done for them? Have we conquered the country for them from the Indians? Have we cleared it? Have we drained it? Have we made it habitable? What have we done for them? I believe precisely nothing at all, but just keeping watch and ward over their trade, that they should receive nothing but from ourselves, and at our own price. . . . In all the wars which have been common to us and them, they have taken their full share. But in all their own dangers, in all the difficulties belonging separately to their situation, in all the Indian wars which did not immediately concern us, we left them to themselves to struggle their way through."

---

*In 1745. The expedition was engineered by Governor Shirley, of Massachusetts. It sailed from Boston, consisting of four thousand men, more than three-quarters of whom were provided by Massachusetts alone. The news of this brilliant exploit was a tonic to England, and England wanted a tonic. For it arrived just after Prince Charlie landed in Scotland, and not long after Fontenoy. Sir Charles Lucas calls this Capture of Louisburg "perhaps the most brilliant feat of arms ever achieved by British Colonists." (*The Empire at War*. Vol. I.)

My apology for quoting this long speech is that it is a heavy indictment of the stupidity of those who like Lord Sandwich* (who gave his name to the arid curse of Railway Refreshment Saloons), thought that the Americans would not fight, or if they did, would run away. Burgoyne himself is not guiltless in this respect. But probably in his days, at Westminster, they did not teach modern history any more than they do nowadays in most English schools.

To revert to the causes of the war, in that uncanny way in which a woman will go straight to the point, brushing aside all the clouds of prejudice and passion, Miss Kate Hotblack in her *Chatham's Colonial Policy* has put the case in a nutshell. After the peace of 1763 the colonies were exhausted; "all they wanted," says she, "was a little wholesome neglect." Beckford, now forgotten save for the fact that he was the father of the author of that queer romance *Vathek,* said much the same in the House of Commons in 1767. "Do like the best of

*Better known as Jemmy Twitcher. He had been a boon companion of John Wilkes, and when Wilkes got into trouble over the "Essay on Woman" denounced him in the House of Lords. When, just after this, Macheath in a performance of *The Beggar's Opera* came to the line "That Jemmy Twitcher should peach, I own, surprises me," there was a roar of laughter, and Sandwich never lost this nickname. An epigram of the day said that he was

Too infamous to have a friend,
Too bad for bad men to commend.

The best thing that can be said for him is that he had a trenchant style. Mr. Eden, later Lord Auckland, ratted and joined William Pitt. He sent Sandwich a letter, trying to justify himself. Sandwich wrote back: "Sir, your letter is before me, and it will presently be behind me. I remain, Sir, your most humble servant, Sandwich." He is chiefly remembered now from the fact that his mistress, Miss Ray (whom he kept in his official residence), was murdered as she left the theater by a clergyman who was in love with her, and who took this singular method of showing his affection.

physicians and heal the disease by doing nothing." The Dean of Gloucester went further. He wanted to give up the Colonies for the singular reason that "the Swiss Cantons have no colonies, but are a most flourishing state." Deans will be deans.

But, instead of being left alone, the Colonies were worried and badgered and bullied like naughty children. Briefly, Farmer George thought that they wanted chastisement, and North knew that he would lose his job if he did not agree with George. It is to be feared that in these days England was a bully. Though the nation was crippled with debt (£148,000,000), too many people were prosperous. There were too many nabobs.* We drank too much, even of the innocuous cup of tea.† We had too many *nouveaux riches,* we gambled heavily at Almack's, White's (blameless name!), and even at the still more innocuous-sounding Cocoa Tree Club. An observer of the day said, "If gallantry was the characteristic of Charles the Second's reign and religion of his father's, politics of Queen Anne's and chivalry in times of yore, gaming is undoubtedly the predominant feature of the present." (Earl of Carlisle's Manuscripts.) We would bet (John Burgoyne in particular) on anything: whether old Lord Methusalem, just married to young Miss Susan Simper, would have issue within a year (twenty guineas to one against, eagerly snatched at by those who knew

*An indignant American said of George III: "He carried an offensive war into the East Indies and deprived many thousands of those innocent people of their lives and properties, that he might snuff the spices of the East and repose his sluggard limbs on the sofa of a nabob." *(Brusher's Journal.)*

†In 1664 the East India Company gave the King, as a curiosity, two pounds of tea. In 1762 the Company sold four million pounds of it. What we drank of Jamaica Rum and Mother Geneva (gin) it would be too tantalizing to estimate.

Miss Susan), and one thousand guineas a side as to who was likely to be victorious in the first engagement in North America.

Where the Colonies were concerned the nation as a whole was guilty of more than what James Russell Lowell was to call later "a certain condescension." Franklin said, "Every man in England seems to consider himself as a piece of a Sovereign over America; seems to jostle himself into the throne with the King and talks of *our subjects in the colonies.*" There were, of course, many who sympathized with the Colonies. Admiral Keppel said in so many words that "he would not draw his sword against them." Howe told his Nottingham constituents, the year before he went out, that he would not hesitate to refuse if invited to lead English troops against the Colonies and, when appointed to a command, asked if it was a proposal or an order. The Earl of Effingham threw up his commission, with the words, "I cannot without reproach from my own conscience consent to bear arms against my fellow-subjects in America in what, to my discernment, is not a clear cause," and that very keen young soldier Ralph Abercromby, destined to fall at the head of his troops fighting against the French in Egypt, thanked his stars that his regiment was not sent to fight against the Americans. The famous Jeffrey Amherst refused to serve, though George III had personally tried to persuade him to go out with the chief command. But Amherst's refusal was probably due, not so much to sympathy with the Americans as to his wife's arguments and a feeling that he would not be allowed sufficient troops for what he realized was a very difficult task. Lord Pitt, Chatham's heir, aide-de-camp to Carleton, Governor of the Canadas, was ordered by his father to resign his commission. It is unusual to send in your papers when hostilities are imminent, so Carleton, very kindly, sent him home with despatches and thus Lord Pitt "saved his face," as the Chinese say. Lastly, to come to less important people, a Member of Parliament, James Wilson, who was also a Captain of Marines, sent in 1776 to Lord George Germain a memorial to lay before His Majesty, "requesting leave to lay down his commission, as he cannot, he says, consistently with his own conscience, serve in the present dispute against the Americans." For this he has been called a conscientious objector. Which is unfair, for most conscientious objectors have a conscientious objection not so much to fighting as to being killed.

There was practical sympathy also. The Constitutional Society, Cornhill, raised one hundred pounds "for the relief of the widows and orphans MURDERED by the KING'S troops at or near Lexington and Concord in the Province of Massachusetts."*

Burgoyne took the part of the stern parent; he reminds one rather of Mr. Barlow, regarding Massachusetts and Virginia as though they were young Masters Sandford and Merton. In April, 1774, when voting against the repeal of the tea-duty, he said, "I look upon America as our child, which we have already spoilt by too much indulgence." The Parliamentary Annalist adds in brackets in the middle of the General's speech: "(The House here seemed very noisy, and did not attend,

---

*Horne Tooke, then plain John Horne, whose work this was, got into trouble over it, was fined two hundred pounds and sentenced to twelve months' imprisonment. Tooke wrote a curious work called *The Diversions of Purley,* dealing with etymology. The present-day diversions of Purley—that charming suburb—are, I believe, Golf and Beer. And then more Beer.

being tired with the debate, thinking that the general belonged rather to the heavy than the light horse.)" I wish Mr. Hansard would interpolate remarks like this. Lord Chesterfield was wiser than Burgoyne. "For my part, I never saw a forward child mended by whipping; and I would not have the Mother Country become a step-mother." I think really Burgoyne was too keen a soldier to lose a chance of a fight. Ministers seem to have been dubious if he would accept an appointment for Boston. Mr. Jenkinson (later Lord Liverpool), leaving the House of Commons in his company, "wished I was in that country (America) with a look and emphasis that conveyed more than accidental conversation." It was all very mysterious and furtive, and even when Lord Barrington finally told him of the King's commands he began with "common chit-chat observations upon the late American debate."

For one reason only, Burgoyne was most reluctant to leave England, and that was on account of his wife. About her he wrote in a manner which, though tinged with pomposity, is affecting.

> "To separate for a length of time, perhaps for ever, from the tenderest, the faithfullest, the most amiable companion and friend that ever man was blessed with—a wife in whom during four-and-twenty years I never could find a momentary act of blame! The narrow circumstances, perhaps the distressed state in which she might find herself at my death, added severely to my anxieties. To supply the requisites of her rank, to reward the virtues of her character, I could only bequeath her a legacy of my imprudence. Men of the world in general are too callously com-

posed to conceive what I endured. My intimates, even those of most sensibility, acquainted with the levities, the inattentions, and dissipations of my common course of life, might have wanted faith in my sincerity; I therefore concealed my heart from all; and I even suffered my dearest Charlotte herself—not, I hope, to doubt that I felt—but rather to be ignorant how much I felt, than expatiate on a subject that could be so afflicting to her in the tender and delicate state of her mind and health."

The rest of this document, is, in places, significant. He had an interview with Lord North, who "listened to me attentively and answered me with politeness," but was "very cautious of committing himself in any engagement further than to lay all I had said before the King." As a matter of fact, Burgoyne was obviously burning to go to North America, and was pulling strings and canvassing everybody who, he thought, could help. He saw Lord George Germain and found him "communicative and friendly."

He also saw a humbler individual, Mr. John Pownall, who really deserves a little space as a typical civil servant of 1775. He was a brother of "Governor Pownall," or "that fribble," as a stern New England Puritan called him. The Governor was one of the many who were supposed to be Junius.* John was not a "fribble": he was

*It seems pretty certain that Sir Philip Francis was the real Simon Pure. He was a clerk in the War Office and, in the character of Junius, pleasantly alluded to his official chief as "Bloody Barrington." Barrington got Francis nominated to the India Council at six thousand pounds a year—and Junius stopped fulminating. How times change! If a clerk in the War Office were, nowadays, to allude to his chief as "bloody," he would not, however Junius-like, get six thousand pounds a year but (and rightly) the Order of the Boot, the proud motto of which is "You're Fired."

Secretary in Lord Dartmouth's office, which looked after the Colonies and also the American War, and he was serious and a trifle pompous. There is a good deal about him in the *Diary and Letters of Thomas Hutchinson,* "Captain-General and Governor-in-Chief of His Late Majesty's Province of Masachusetts Bay in North America," the predecessor of Gage. Hutchinson was not popular in North America during the war, and in more modern times Bancroft, the historian, talked of his "fawning treachery." Still, his *Diary* is full of queer things: thus he notes on August 11, 1760, "Mr. Otis stopped at my house and after salutations desired to see me in private; tho' in the morning about 8 or 9 he smelt strong of rum." He also has a note "in Boston the dried French white haricot beans are much in demand, stewed soft with meat and eaten as a Sunday dish between the services."* He was also courageous: when he returned to England and had the famous interview with George III, the King said, "I see they threatened to pitch and feather you." Hutchinson interrupted with "Tarr and feather, may it please your majesty," and Dartmouth, who was present, corroborated him, casually alluding to the Boston "Committee for Tarring and Feathering." In 1774-75 Hutchinson was constantly going to Pownall's office in Whitehall, which was once the Duke of Monmouth's bedchamber, to get the latest news from Boston. At various times he finds "Mr. P." thunderstruck with American news, exceedingly anxious, "unsteddy" (not early rum I hope) ; one day all fire and another depressed and in despair. "Mr. P. tho't some extraordinary measures should be taken." And occasionally Mr. P., very unlike modern War Office clerks, would be seen, like Brer

***When was Boston first called the Baked Bean Town?**

Tarrypin, "lowngin' " about in office hours* and also, no doubt, "sufferin'," for his health was indifferent. One entry about him is typical. He and Lord Pitt (fresh back from Canada with despatches from Carleton) were attacked by a highwayman on Blackheath. Being armed they got out of the coach and "Mr. Pownall burnt priming, but the pistol did not go off." I do not suppose that anything he ever undertook "went off" with any success and I am sure that he himself never "got off." He is constantly cropping up in the Dartmouth Manuscripts. We find him "indisposed," "laid up with a fever," "awakened by an express from Liverpoole" and going to Margate to recuperate. Anon he is "oppressed with infirmity" and tries Bath for a change. And on another occasion, writing to a fellow clerk on leave, he says *(horresco referens!)*, "I have done nothing but play truant since you left." But he was very polite and must have had ingratiating if slightly pompous manners. "He conversed with Hey about the Quebec Act: Hey preferred his (Pownall's) plan to his own, but he (Pownall) thinks Hey's is best." And he uses two delightful phrases: on one occasion, writing to his chief, Lord Dartmouth, he actually alludes to the Office as "Our Shop," and when he retired he called the pension given him "a Cup of Comfort."

Burgoyne, first and foremost a man of the world, obviously had the greatest contempt for poor Mr. Pownall. He writes of him: "He entered into a long, formal, and sometimes unintelligible discussion of American affairs. He talked to me as I imagined he might be accustomed to do with men really inferior to him in in-

*Lord Shelburne, afterward first Marquis of Lansdowne, who knew it well, called it "a very idle Office."

formation, or whom he supposed to be so. Gentlemen in trade and other situations in life, which set them at a distance from great men in office, or even from the subalterns and apes of official greatness, diffident of their own judgment, and believing men in power to be better informed because they ought to be so, are generally patient hearers, and hence a secretary is very apt to contract an air of supercilious or ministerial importance. He was guarded—mysterious—obscure—— I acquired by the conversation (as I thought) some lights into his character, but none into American affairs."

Burgoyne also saw Pownall's chief, Lord Dartmouth, who was extremely affable but showed "a great deal of caution in committing an opinion upon nice subjects." He also mentions, which is interesting, that Howe was very reluctant to go to Boston, partly because of the "obligations his family owed to the Bostonians, who had raised a monument to the late Lord Howe,"* and partly because of the low opinion he held of the Commander-in-Chief (Gage) as a soldier. In which low opinion he was entirely justified.

Burgoyne again approached Lord George Germain, who "expressed his wonder that the major-generals were not called before the Cabinet, or by some other method consulted upon a plan of measures." He also thought that something might be done by Cabinet dinners, for "he had often observed that the surest means of collecting matter from professional men, especially if they were

*Brigadier-General Lord Howe, who was killed at Ticonderoga. The monument in question is in Westminster Abbey. Pitt (Chatham) called him "a character of ancient times; a complete model of military virtue," and Wolfe said of him, "He is the noblest Englishman that has appeared in my time, and the best soldier in the army." This, as we shall see, can not be said of William Howe.

modest men (here Burgoyne must have bowed), were to employ convivial hours for that purpose."* So a "convivial hour" was appointed; a dinner took place at Lord Dartmouth's, at which all the Cabinet were present and in addition General Harvey, our friend Governor Hutchinson and (of course) Mr. Secretary Pownall. "We talked," writes Burgoyne, "of every subject but America." Probably, as was always the case at Sir Robert Walpole's table, they "talked bawdy, for in that all men can join": on this occasion, all, I think, except Mr. Pownall. Even at bawdy talk I am sure he would have been most cryptic. I can fancy him gallantly starting a verse,

"I spied a maiden bathing in a pool,"

and then, when everybody's attention was arrested and their eyes bulging out with anticipation of something "warm," adding in his best official manner,

"She said she found the water wet and cool."

(Snorts of derision from the soldiers present.)

Burgoyne in his blunt way said that "he and his colleagues were totally in the dark upon all the plans of Government upon the campaign" and that he supposed that he had been selected for some other purpose than "to see that the soldiers boiled their kettles regularly." Even this did not move Lord North: like Mr. Pownall, he remained "mysterious and obscure."

*In 1758, when it was decided to send Wolfe on the expedition which resulted in the capture of Quebec, a "convivial hour," that is to say a private dinner at White's, was chosen to tell him of his appointment.

(The Government was equally vague and shadowy when preparing for a possible peace as when preparing for war. The Earl of Carlisle was one of the Commissioners sent to America early in 1778, with "conciliatory bills." Before sailing they met at Lord North's, Germain, the Attorney-General and the Solicitor-General and others being present. Lord Carlisle writes, "Little passed of any real importance, and I confess I came away by no means satisfied with the conversation, and not a little shocked at the slovenly manner with which an affair so serious in its nature had been dismissed." He adds that some were sulky, others childish, and all in a hurry. (Earl of Carlisle's Manuscripts.) Some of the "bills" were burned under a gallows in Rhode Island.)

Burgoyne's love for Charlotte—which was sneered at by Horace Walpole, who had no great affection for anybody except the gentleman who later became Lord Orford—is very evident from a letter which he wrote and left with a friend to be delivered to the King in case of his death in North America. This was written at Portsmouth, April 18, 1775, just before he sailed. It begins very like Mr. Tupman's historical letter to Mr. Pickwick, after Jingle had bolted with Rachel:

"Sire,

"Whenever this letter shall be delivered to your Majesty, the writer of it will be no more. It may therefore be esteemed an address from beyond the grave, and under that idea I am persuaded your Majesty will consider with indulgence both the matter and the expression.

"My purpose, Sire, is to recommend to your royal protection Lady Charlotte Burgoyne, who at my death will have to combat the severest calamities of life,—a weak frame of body, very narrow circumstances, and a heart replete with those agonies which follow the loss of an object it has long held most dear. What will be her consolation? Wretched state, when poverty is disregarded only because it is the least poignant of our sensations, and the pains of distemper are alleviated by the hopes that they send to our dissolution.

"The first comfort upon which my mind rests in regard to that dear woman, in a crisis so trying, is a knowledge of her piety; the next, a confidence in your Majesty's compassion and generosity. . . .

"Your Majesty, acquainted with the value of female excellence, will hear without impatience a husband's praises. I protest, with the sincerity of a man who meditates death while he writes, and calls God to witness to his testimony, that in the great duties of life, I do not know that Lady Charlotte ever committed a fault, except that, if a fault it can be called, of love and generosity which directed her choice to me without consulting her family—even that is now cancelled in their eyes—upon a review of our happiness during a course of twenty-four years, no moment of which has been embittered, except by sickness or separation.

"My heart tells me, Sire, that I am not presumptuous in this application. I received your Majesty's commands for America with regret, the first sensation of that nature I ever experienced in a call for service, but I have not less a sense of duty; I have scorned to propose terms to my obedience, or to take advantage of the crisis of receiving your royal orders to prefer a petition for the provision of my family.

"I rely on your Majesty's heart to accept with indulgence this humble mark of my respect, and I take confidence to assure your Majesty that, whatever may be my fate in my ensuing trials, I shall be found to my last moment

"Your Majesty's
"Zealous soldier
"And most faithful subject
"J. BURGOYNE."

The occasion for the delivery of this somewhat highfalutin letter did not arise; Lady Charlotte predeceased Burgoyne, dying in 1776. Hutchinson in his *Diary* for July 22, 1775, writes, "Before dinner walked in Kensington Gardens, where we met General Burgoyne's lady in great anxiety for news from America." Since that day I think many a soldier's lady must, from time to time, have paced Kensington Gardens in great anxiety for news from—well, pretty well every quarter of the globe, except, happily, save during that most unnecessary War of 1812, the United States.

Hutchinson also has a note about Burgoyne himself before he left for Boston. "He seems more anxious how to conduct affairs in case Martial Law should be declared in force, than how to withstand all the force the Americans can bring against him. He spoke freely of the present state of Administration; the want of one vigorous direction; the indecision in all the Councils; the aptness to procrastination; and though he expected to sail in eight days, doubted whether any Instructions had been prepared and rather feared he should go without any." Burgoyne seems to have suggested to Hutchinson that he was the Big Noise of the party about to sail on the

*Cerberus,* but in the House of Commons he spoke rather plaintively of his "inferior station," adding, "The utmost merit I shall be able to claim in this expedition will probably be that of an attentive, an assiduous, circumscribed obedience." It is painful to read that he also mentions casually that "the licentious prints of the times had alluded to Lord North as a 'sanguinary minister.'" What language!

The three generals who sailed in the *Cerberus** left with the town laughing over a witticism. "Our Generals may terrify the enemy, they certainly terrify me," and were greeted in Boston with another:

> Behold the *Cerberus* the Atlantic plough.
> Her precious cargo, Burgoyne, Clinton, Howe.
> Bow, wow, wow!

All three of them were taken off, later on, in a delightful American drama published early in 1776. This was *The Fall of British Tyranny:* the chief characters were Lord Hypocrite (Dartmouth), Lord Poltroon (Sandwich), Judas (Hutchinson), Lord Boston (Gage), Elbow Room,† (Howe), Mr. Caper (Burgoyne), and Admiral Tombstone (Graves). Admiral Tombstone talks of Bunker Hill with a sailorlike freedom: "Many powdered beaux, *petits maîtres,* fops, fribbles, skip-jackets, macaronis, jackpuddings, noblemen's bastards and whores' sons fell that day."

"Mr. Caper's" reputation as a man of pleasure had

---

*There was a young naval lieutenant on board, "Jem" Burney, brother of the celebrated Fanny, and, later, a friend of Charles Lamb.

†A name which recalls that delightful book by Max Adeler, a book which I read with joy as a schoolboy and can still read with the greatest of pleasure.

preceded him: the *Pennsylvania Packet* said severely, "Should the boasting General Burgoyne ridicule the simplicity of our American Cincinnatus (Putnam) and be asked at the same time where his master's orders found *him* when he was commanded to repair to Boston, the answer would most probably be 'in a gambling-house or brothel.' "

The first thing Burgoyne did—he ought to have had a fountain-pen, for he could not refrain from writing—was to draw up for Gage, who hated doing anything, a proclamation, a terribly pompous proclamation,* to the Bostonians.

With the possible exception of that tearful peer, Mr. Belloc's Lord Lundy, who was told by an indignant relative to "go out and govern New South Wales," there can have been few public men sent in a high position to a colony less competent than General Gage. Charles Lee, writing to Burke in December, 1774, said: "It is somewhat strange, but it is true, that this gentleman should reside so many years in America, and yet be as ignorant of the dispositions of the people of America as he is of those in the moon; indeed, he took all possible means of shutting up the avenues of truth. At New York he never conversed, as I can find, with any but place and contract hunters, the staff officers and his own family; and when he was sent to Boston with express orders to inform himself of the cause of the disturbances, he applied to the very men, and those only, from whom these disturbances were said to flow. He shut himself up immediately in Castle William with Bernard, Hutchinson and Sewell; under their inspection, and according to

*People say there is more attention paid to style than to policy." Brigadier-General J. Robertson. (Dartmouth MSS.)

their dictates, after three days' labour, he put the finishing hand to a narrative of the state of a province, by which the Ministry were to regulate their conduct. . . . Had he condescended to listen to the representations of the town at large, these pernicious measures had, perhaps, never been adopted." Gage reported that the "phrenzy," as he called it, was dying down, and Dartmouth complained that he allowed the Boston town guards and militia to drill in Faneuil Hall.

To be perfectly fair to Gage, he had one great admirer, and that was a Major Donkin, author of *Military Collections and Remarks,* published at New York in 1777. He says that the General was "endued with every talent that constitutes a great captain, excels in the art of thinking, reasoning and writing well;*—See his letters to Trumbull, Randolph and Washington. They are as capital pieces as any of antiquity. He has also the art of commanding to please all! for if he could not dispense favours to everyone, his refusal was accompanied with the language of the graces." Donkin's book is, bibliographically, of great interest. Page 190 deals with "bows." And I believe there are very few, if any, copies in existence in which a passage of this page has not been cut out. And no wonder. For this Major, who ought to have been ashamed of himself, actually proposed that arrows should be infected with smallpox and used against the Americans. Washington in a letter of December 10, 1775, wrote, "The information I received that the enemy intended spreading the smallpox amongst us, I could not suppose them capable of. I must now give some credit to it, as it has made its appearance on several

*Burgoyne was his pen. It should also be mentioned that Donkin served under Gage, so may have been prejudiced in his favor.

of those who last came out of Boston." Surely the explanation is that as Boston was full of smallpox, anybody who left the town, or stayed in it, was likely to develop it.

Burgoyne wrote a long letter to Lord North (June 14, 1775). He is in too humble a station to do anything good in "the military line." He therefore suggests that he should be given a kind of roving commission, not as a soldier but as an M. P., to try to bring the "rebels" to a better frame of mind. "Not charged with any direct proposal from Government, nor authorised to treat with them in a publick character, I have not less zeal in my capacity as a member of Parliament, a friend of human nature, and a sincere well-wisher to the united interests of the two countries, to forward as far as in me lies, the great work of reconciliation upon enlarged, solid, honourable grounds. This sort of language would not commit Government in anything." The real truth was that he did not like playing a minor rôle at Boston, but wanted to get into the limelight and return home with—perhaps—large laurels as a diplomatist.

Lord North rejected this proposal, but in a very flattering way. Writing from Bushy Park on July thirty-first,* he said:

> "His Majesty fears that your plan cannot be carried into execution. If taken, you would be a valuable hostage. We cannot send you† much above 2,000 men more in the course of this campaign, but in the spring you will have 20,000 regulars or more in the two armies. We are all perfectly sensible of the importance and difficulty of the contest, and mean to

*Marquis of Abergavenny's MSS.

†This "you" is flattering.

General Burgoyne

Engraved in 1786. From John Andrews' "History of the War with America"

exert every nerve to put a safe and honourable end to it. Our wish is not to impose upon our fellow-subjects in America any terms inconsistent with the most perfect liberty. I cannot help thinking that many of the principal persons in North America will, with the calmness of the winter, be disposed to bring forward a reconciliation. Now they are too angry, too suspicious and too much under the guidance of factious leaders."

Had Burgoyne got into trouble at home over his letter of July ninth* to Charles Lee, this letter of North's, though of a subsequent date, would have been rather useful to him.

At the same time that he wrote to North, Burgoyne wrote to General Harvey,† Adjutant-General at the Horse Guards, a soldier's letter, in which he severely criticized the Higher Command in Boston, particularly the Quartermaster-General and the Adjutant-General, and not sparing Gage himself, whom he described as "unequal to his present station." He also censures the authorities at home. Gage had been promised forty thousand pounds, and had only received ten thousand pounds. "Where," asks Burgoyne with shrewd common sense, "does the money lie and who receives the interest?" The furtive Pownall also gets a smack. The three Generals had been promised five hundred pounds apiece "equipage money," and Pownall said that orders had been trans-

---

*See page 79.

†A rough and tough old soldier, given to profanation and becoming "much heated"; he once reproached two officers who had served in North America, "How often have I heard you American Colonels boast that with four battalions you would march through America; and now you think Gage with 3,000 men and 40 pieces of cannon mayn't venture out of Boston!"

mitted to General Gage to that effect. No such orders had reached Boston, and the indignant Burgoyne says, "I acquit North and Dartmouth of the dirtiness of office but is it not fit that at a proper time and in a proper place the subalterns of office should hear of this treatment?"

I am sure Mr. Pownall was much too honest—and too stupid—to have regarded this "equipage money" as a rake-off. But it is rather a coincidence that John Wilkes brought the quaint and unpleasant charge against his brother, "Governor" Pownall, "of passing inferior oats" and falsifying his military accounts when Comptroller of the Commissariat in 1763. But it is only fair to add that the Governor was honorably acquitted. Besides, Wilkes was always stirring up dirty water, washing dirty linen and bringing dirty accusations. He actually, in his *Essay on Woman,* brings most unpleasant charges against what was called in those days The Fair Sex, or sometimes simply The Sex. There is little doubt this "equipage money" found its way into the capacious pockets of that champion place-seeker, Richard Rigby, Paymaster General to the Forces at the time. When he died it was said of him that he left "near half a million of public money." Had he not been such a terrific boozer—he drank brandy as if it were small beer—he would probably have left more. When present in the House of Commons he always wore a purple suit, but it was not so purple as his face. He was always, says the Parliamentary historian, "extremely violent against America."

We now come to that historic battle, Bunker Hill, or Breed's Hill (originally known as Breed's Pasture), fought on a hot summer's day, June 17, 1775. According to Howe's letter of June 12, 1775, to Lord Howe

(Dartmouth Manuscripts), the original British plan was to occupy and fortify Dorchester Neck and then, if found practicable, to attack the post of Roxbury and so secure Boston from attack on that side. Then to march to "Charles Town height and either attack the Rebels at Cambridge or perhaps, if the Country admits of it, endeavour to turn that post." The Americans got wind of this. Some say that Warren went over "in a small boat with muffled oars" and got and brought back information of the British designs. How did they become known? Well, Gage's wife had been, before her marriage, Miss Margaret Kemble (or Kembal) of New Jersey, and was related to the Van Cortlands of New York. Her sympathies were, not unnaturally, with her kindred. General Harvey had told Hutchinson that she had said "she hoped her husband would never be the instrument of sacrificing the lives of her countrymen," but the cautious General added that "he did not chuse to be quoted for it." It is significant that on the evening of April eighteenth General Gage told Lord Percy that he intended to send that night a detachment to seize the stores at Concord, that he had appointed an officer to command it, but had not yet told him his destination. "He meant it to be a secret expedition, and begged of Lord Percy to keep it a profound secret." Percy was told, shortly afterward, as a piece of news by some idlers on Boston Common, where the troops were going. He at once acquainted Gage with this. "The General said that his confidence had been betrayed, for that he had communicated his designs to *one person only* besides his lordship." I think General Gage—it is difficult not to allude to him as General Greengage—probably began this confidence with "Between you and me and the bed-post, my dear Peggy." (But for full details of this, see that most interesting book by Mr. Allen French called *The Day of Concord and Lexington.)* Mrs. Gage went to England in August, 1775, in a transport pleasantly called *The Charming Nancy.*

In any case, Boston was full of American agents and sympathizers, of whom Paul Revere, famous for his ride, is best remembered, and Gage was anticipated. On the night of June sixteenth, the Americans under Prescott passed over Bunker Hill and fortified Breed's Hill, and by daybreak were well dug in. As they worked during the night at the trenches they could hear the marine sentinels on the British men-of-war crying "All's Well," which from a British point of view it most emphatically was not. At daybreak Gage realized to his astonishment that Putnam and Prescott commanded Boston. Gage, looking at the hill through his spy-glass, said to Counselor Willard, "Who is that officer commanding?" The Counselor recognized his brother-in-law, Colonel Prescott. "Will he fight?" continued Gage. "Yes, Sir, depend upon it, to the last drop of blood in him, but I cannot answer for his men."

At Colenso, in the Boer War, where the British made a frontal attack, which did not succeed, the United States Military Attaché* asked, with horse sense, "if there was not a way round." There certainly was a way round for Gage. He could have landed his troops near the Charlestown Neck causeway, in Prescott's rear, and, aided by the guns of the fleet, have completely cut off the American force.† But a way round was undignified, neither British, nor frank, nor manly. Circumlocutions are all very well

*Captain S. L. H. Slocum of the Eighth Cavalry.

†General Ward thought that Gage would do this.

in a despatch, but "fetching a compass" in the field was (unfortunately) not the British way. So Gage decided on a frontal attack. As a keen young officer there present, Charles Stuart, son of Lord Bute (the Jack Boot of anecdotal history) put it in writing to his father: "In fact, you will see by the survey that the attack was made in the strongest place, the enemy, taking advantage of an imprudence, fought the ground inch by inch in a spot well calculated for defence by nature and assisted by all the artifice of a shrewd, artful, cunning people. The Rebels fought with a resolution that dependence on their breastworks and palings almost heightened to a frenzy." Both sides were spoiling for a fight, and they had it. The English troops, though it was a blazing summer's day, were "encumbered with blankets and knapsacks and three days' provisions,* although they were near home." They made three frontal attacks, climbing through "grass reaching to their knees," led by Howe, who, when the first and second had failed, said to his officers, "To be forced to give up Boston would, gentlemen, be very disagreeable to us all." To his men he said, "I shall not desire one of you to go a step further than where I go myself at your head." Until the Civil War it was by far the hottest fight in America: in Stark's picturesque phrase, "the dead lay as thick as sheep in a fold." Pitcairn, who led the marines, was, it is said, shot, his son close by him, by a negro, Peter Salem, once a slave, who fought throughout the war. The casualties among the British officers were very great: they were

*A contemporary writer, Stedman, says that each British soldier carried at least one hundred and twenty-five pounds. The blankets and provisions rather suggest that an easy victory with a triumphant march to Cambridge, was anticipated.

picked off and the American troops obeyed to the letter the orders, "Aim at the handsome waistcoats"; "Pick off the Commanders"; "Wait until you can see the whites of their eyes."* One marksman, or sniper, to use the modern word, as soon as he had fired one musket was handed another, and is stated to have killed or wounded at least twenty British officers.

There is a very curious note in the Round Manuscripts bearing on this point. Thomas Falconer, the scholar, writing to Charles Gray, M. P. for Colchester, after saying, "The best account I have seen of Bunker Hill was written by a lady in Boston to another lady at this place (Chester)"—is this account, I wonder, in the United States?—goes on: "How far the Bostonians can justify taking aim at Officers with rifled muskets I am not a military jurisprudent enough to determine. It seems to be contrary to justice and will not intimidate us I hope." Whenever any new weapon of war, from gunpowder to gas, has been invented the same complaint has gone up, all very much to the same effect as:

> It was great pity, so it was
> That villainous saltpetre should be digg'd
> Out of the bowels of the harmless earth
> Which many a good tall fellow had destroyed
> So cowardly.

But good Mr. Falconer knew more about Strabo and the geography of the ancient world than he did about military matters. He continues: "The Bostonians have all the barbarity which false zeal can inspire, mixed with the low cunning of a poor, commercial people." He is more

*This last order is attributed to Putnam, or "Old Put," as he was affectionately called.

sensible when he mentions "that heterogeneous substance General Lee, who has been fomenting disturbances on the other side: this man would be dangerous could he agree with any party, but he cannot submit long to any superior and consequently is at present rejected."

On the American side, three names stand out: Prescott, Putnam* and Warren. Prescott had a narrow escape. He said later, "The first man who fell† in the Battle of Bunker Hill was killed by a cannon-ball which struck his head. He was so near to me that my clothes were besmeared with his blood and brains which I wiped off in some degree with a handful of fresh earth." Warren, who earlier had expressed a wish: "I hope to die up to my knees in blood" was shot through the head. Nor must one forget Gridley, the Chief Engineer, who had made a name many years before at the Siege of Louisburg; Stark, that fine fighter with a fighter's name, and the gallant Pomeroy, a name which to an Englishman suggests cider, cockles and cream, and other delicacies dear to Bill Brewer, Jan Steuer, Peter Gurney, Peter Davy and the rest of them. Seth Pomeroy, seventy years old, had declined a commission as brigadier-general and found his way to the redoubt to fight in the ranks. He was well known, and "a loud huzza welcomed him to the post of danger." I should also like to mention Colonel Garrish, because, like many an officer in most armies of that day, he was "very corpulent." But on both sides at Bunker Hill almost all the officers were "stout fellows," and I need not explain that the word stout means, firstly, "brave, doughty, resolute." My old friend

*His family came from Aston Abbots, that pleasant place near Aylesbury in Bucks, one of the most British of British counties.

†Stated to be "a young man of Billerica called Pollard."

General Heath,* said, "Perhaps there never was a better fought battle than this," and, substituting harder for better, I think we will all, on both sides of the Atlantic, agree that he is not far from right. It made Putnam, like the British Army in Flanders, swear terribly. In later years he is said to have, metaphorically, worn a white sheet for this before the congregation of the church of which he was a member. The Americans ultimately retired because their powder was exhausted. A spy in their lines reported later to Gage, "If you will believe me, Mr. Pidgeon, the Commissary-General then, now declares that we had not one half-lb of powder left that night the bunker hill was taken and had you pursued the Camp must have been broken up—this they confess." He ends, rather like Miss Squeers, "Excuse my incorrect manner of writing, for I am in a tremor."

Bunker Hill was a curious battle in some respects. Both sides were put to odd shifts. On the American side the men had guns of every possible caliber and had to hammer the balls served out to them into shape. On the British side "most of the cannon-balls were found to be too large for the pieces." Such mishaps are not infrequent in war. In the Dardanelles, where the maps were few and indifferent, a British Yeomanry Regiment received a large case of maps. This was opened with great joy, but it proved to contain a number of beautifully-executed, large scale maps of—the country round Cromer, where the yeomen had been undergoing training, just a year before. I doubt if there was ever such astonishment at the opening of anything since an amazed

---

*I devoted a few pages to this very engaging old gentleman in my previous book, *Warriors in Undress.* We shall hear more about him later.

monarch was confronted with, not what he expected, pigeon-pie, but four-and-twenty melodious blackbirds.

Gage did not receive bouquets for Bunker Hill. He does not appear to have foreseen anything. It did not occur to him that you can not make an omelet without breaking eggs and that a battle is necessarily attended by casualties. An eye-witness wrote: "It is impossible to describe the horror that on every side presented itself—wounded and dead officers in every street; the town (Boston), which is larger than New York, almost uninhabited to appearance, bells tolling, wounded soldiers lying in their tents and crying for assistance to remove some men who had just expired. So little precaution did General Gage take to provide for the wounded by making hospitals, that they remained in this deplorable situation for three days; the wounded officers obliged to pay the most exorbitant price for lodgings, when near 30,000 houses belonging to proclaimed Rebels were uninhabited." Both sides claimed a victory, but a London wit put it extremely well when he said, "We certainly are victorious, but if we have eight more such victories there will be nobody left to bring the news of them." John Wilkes, too, put it well in the House of Commons: "What have we conquered? Bunker's Hill with the loss of 1,200 men. Are we to pay as dearly for the rest of America?" And Barré said that it "smacked more of defeat than victory." The loss on both sides was very heavy. We admitted that it was a more bloody battle than either Minden or Fontenoy. Ninety-two British officers were killed and wounded, "a melancholy disproportion," Burgoyne calls it, "to the numbers killed and wounded of the private soldiers." It ruined Howe's nerve, he never displayed any great energy thereafter.

Most of his energy had always been devoted to pleasure. A German officer who served under him in America said, "Sir William liked enjoying himself, so much so that he sometimes forgot his duties as a commander. He always had in his *entourage* an excellent *chef,* and often also a mistress." He liked to have a good time, and he liked his friends to share it. A Major Wemyss, a contemporary, bears him out: "He had a dislike to business, a propensity to pleasure, and was also addicted to private conviviality." But, whatever his faults, and we shall see more of them later, one must never forget his gallantry at Bunker Hill. An Englishman, Nicholas Cresswell, in North America at the time, went so far as to call Howe "the great Chucclehead." Cresswell, by the way, wrote a journal which is full of curious information. For example, when in New York he jots down: "Sunday May 18th 1777. In the forenoon went to St. Paul's Church and heard a Military Sermon by the Reverend Mr. O'Brien. This is a very neat Church and some of the handsomest and best-dressed ladies* I have ever seen in America. I believe most of them are Whores." I wonder if this very neat Church still stands.

The Duke of Wellington once said: "A battle is very like a ball." Those whom he met in the field, if they were honest might often have agreed with him, substituting for "ball" the old-fashioned word "rout." What the Duke meant was that nobody could possibly see the

---

*But in this respect Boston then ran New York close, as I daresay it still does. An English officer writing from the former town in 1774, paid it rather a left-handed compliment: "The women are very handsome, but, like old Mother Eve, very frail; the camp has been as well supplied in that way since we have been on Boston Common, as if our tents were pitched on Blackheath." But I must be careful, for did not a grand jury find a true bill against Gage "for slandering the town of Boston"?

whole battle-field, but only his own particular little bit of it. This was not Burgoyne's case at Bunker Hill; although he played only a very minor part in it he had, as it were, a seat in the stalls and the whole scene was unfurled before him. He wrote two very interesting letters about it, one to Lord Rochefort and one to Lord Stanley. But this is a long chapter, the bottle of port is now empty, so I think I will now begin a fresh bottle and a fresh chapter.

(Here followeth the sound as of a cork being drawn.)

## CHAPTER IV

### THE COMPLETE LETTER-WRITER

BURGOYNE'S letter to Lord Rochefort was a general review of the situation and of his impressions since his arrival. Though written after Bunker Hill, he was too John Bullish not to allude to the American forces as a "rabble in arms." "Never despise your enemy" should be one of the first items in the soldier's Book of Do's and Don't's. Despising your enemy generally leads to being surprised by them. In the Royal Military Tournaments in the eighties of the last century the opening scene was almost invariably a camp of British soldiers, and then "Surprise of the British Army," generally by whooping savages, really British rank-and-file blackened and disguised. In those days they whooped as if they enjoyed it. A year or so ago, when a fight between Normans and Saxons was being rehearsed at Aldershot, it was noted that the Saxons fought mum-chance. They were urged to assume Anglo-Saxon attitudes and to shout forth cries of defiance. The rehearsal was renewed, and as the Norman knights advanced, a stentorian shout was heard from the defenders of the White Cliffs of Old England: *Are we down-hearted?* And the rehearsal had to be stopped again.

Down-hearted, or perhaps disgusted, is rather a good word for Burgoyne's letter. It is one long grouse. Gage ought to have seized Adams, Hancock and the other leaders, ought to have trained the troops, got secret intelligence, and raided the surrounding country for supplies. Although he alludes to "the affair of April 19th" (Lexington) as a "paltry skirmish," he adds that had the enemy opened batteries upon Boston it would have induced "circumstances as rapid and as decisive as the Battle of Pharsalia; and the colours of a fleet and army of Great Britain, not wrested from us, but without a conflict kicked out of America." He grumbles about his rank, "the inferiority of my station as youngest Major-General upon the staff left me almost a useless spectator, for my whole business lay in presiding during part of the action over a command to assist the left." And he adds, "In the general regular course of business in this army, Major-Generals are absolute cyphers." Major-Generals cyphers! One can only comment: O! O! O! "My rank only serves to place me in a motionless, drowsy, irksome medium, or rather vacuum, too low for the honour of command, too high for that of execution." "The defence [at Bunker Hill] was well conceived and obstinately maintained; the retreat was no flight; it was even covered with bravery and military skill, and proceeded no further than to the west hill, where a new post was taken and new intrenchments instantly begun."

He then, commenting on the very heavy casualties among the British officers, pens a sentence which I think he must subsequently have regretted. "Though my letter passes in security I tremble while I write it; and let it not pass even in a whisper from your Lordship to more than *one* person;* the zeal and intrepidity of the

*Presumably the King.

officers, which was without exception exemplary, was ill seconded by the private men. Discipline, not to say courage, was wanting. In the critical moment of carrying the redoubt, the officers of some corps were almost alone." It is difficult to explain this, but it was probably due to the fact that Burgoyne had lost many personal friends among the officers' casualties on Bunker Hill and the bitterness of his heart found expression in his pen. In any case, he changed his mind. When, the following year, Colonel Barré said in the House of Commons that "the troops from an aversion to the service misbehaved at Bunker's Hill," Burgoyne, home on leave, "rose with warmth and contradicted him in the flattest manner." He allowed that the troops "gave way a little at one time, because they were flanked by the fire out of the houses, at Charlestown, but they were soon rallied and advanced and no men on earth behaved with more spirit,* firmness and perseverance till they forced the enemy out of their entrenchments." To this one may add the testimony of Sir John Fortescue, the historian of the British Army. "The return of the British infantry to the third attack after two such bloody repulses is one of the very greatest feats ever recorded of them." King George was fully satisfied. Lord Barrington, Secretary at War, sent Gage a despatch from the War Office, July 28, 1775, expressing His Majesty's approbation of "the firmness of spirit which distinguished the troops in the late action." In a thoughtful postscript, which, however, reads

*They were perhaps, on occasion, rather too spirited. In Howe's Orderly Book there are a good many instances of "lashes" being ordered to be laid on; and it is curious to read that in September, 1775, "Winifried" McCowen actually "stole the Town Bull and caused him to be Killed." For this poor Win, who probably had wearied of salt pork and wanted some roast beef, was, though a woman, ordered to receive "100 lashes on her bare back in the most public parts of the town."

rather oddly he "recommended to his consideration whether he should not be provided with more shoes, shirts, stockings, etc., which the troops might wish to purchase," and suggested that a Mr. Coffin (ominous name!) should be made use of in the matter.

North was more human. He wrote to Burgoyne, "The gallantry and ability of General Howe, and the bravery of the men whom he commanded on the 17th of June, are the admiration of their countrymen, but the number of wounded and killed makes my heart bleed. I would abandon the contest were I not most intimately convinced in my own conscience that our cause is just and important." (Marquis of Abergavenny's Manuscripts.)

Burgoyne, to return to his letter, is very sound on the general situation; the country near Boston is all fortification, the army could only proceed "by the slow step of a siege" and was sadly lacking in wagons, hospital carriages and horses. And above all Gage is not equal to his task, he might make an amiable governor but was incapable of rising to the opportunity; but this is qualified by the statement that even Cæsar would find the matter a difficult job. But Cæsar would have seen that he was properly supplied with the sinews of war, which is more than Gage had done. There was little money, and consequently no cattle, no forage and, above all, no intelligence: "we are ignorant not only of what passes in congresses, but want spies for the hill half a mile off." Howe, writing to General Harvey, June 12, 1775, (Dartmouth Manuscripts), entirely bears Burgoyne out in this:

"In our present state all warlike Preparations are wanting. No Survey of the adjacent country, no proper boats for landing troops—not a sufficient number of Horses for the Artillery, nor for Regimental baggage. No Forage, either Hay or Corn of any Consequence. No Waggons or Harness for Horses, except some prepared by Colonel Cleveland for the Artillery. No Fascines, or Pickets. The Military Chest at the Lowest Ebb, about three or four thousand only Remaining, which Goes fast for the subsistence of the troops. . . . Our Intelligence is So Scanty, that what we get from the Inland Country for the most part is sent to the General by the Rebels. Very few or no Spies. We are therefore Entirely Ignorant of what they are about in the Neighbourhood."

Wedderburn at home wrote to North: "In all undertakings carried on by the arms of this country the beginning has been unprosperous.* This country is never sufficiently prepared. The misconduct of the General and Admiral is the most obvious cause of the present bad posture of affairs in America." He then enlarges on the modern text, "Sack the lot."

To return to Burgoyne, he adds the rather astonishing statement, "There is hardly a leading man among the rebels, in council or in the field, but at a proper time, and by proper management, might have been bought." This is a hard saying, and I think it is the politician not the soldier who is speaking here.

Captain John Montresor, indeed, went further than Burgoyne.

"Even Israel Putnam, of Connecticut, might have been bought, to my certain knowledge, for one dollar

*Which is extraordinarily true.

per day, or 8 shillings New York Currency. The following Rebel Generals might have been obtained at a still 'melieur marchais' *(sic)*, viz:

Lasher, the Shoemaker of New York
Heard, the Tavern-keeper of Woodbridge
Pomeroy, the Gunsmith
Pribble, the Tavern-keeper of Canterbury, Old England."

(See that work full of curious information, *The Evelyns in America*, edited by G. D. Scull. Printed for private circulation, Oxford, 1881.)

No doubt people were bought during the war, Benedict Arnold for one. Is there not an empty niche in the Saratoga Monument? But it was wounded pride that helped his treachery. There was another individual bought, and in England, no less a personage than the famous Mr. Gibbon. He had been a bitter critic of the Ministry, remarking pleasantly at Brook's that "there was no salvation for England unless six of the heads of the cabinet council were cut off and [like Parliamentary Papers] laid upon the tables of the Houses of Parliament as examples."* But when the great historian was made a Commissioner of Trade his sympathy for North America and contempt for ministers declined and fell with a dull thud.†

*The nearest approach to this was when the desiccated ear of Master Mariner Jenkins was shown (Exhibit A) to an astonished House of Commons. England went to war with Spain over this.

†This inspired some wit to a pleasant epigram:

King George, in a fright
Lest Gibbon should write
The history of England's disgrace,
Thought no way so sure
His pen to secure
As to give the historian a place.

Burgoyne's criticism was not merely destructive. He puts forward for Lord Rochfort's consideration a plan of campaign. When the reinforcements, daily expected, arrive, he suggests that Dorchester Neck should be occupied, three thousand men left in Boston, and two thousand embarked for an unknown—to the Americans—destination. In short, he proposes "diversions." He would "chastise" Rhode Island, occupy Connecticut River, and "encourage" Long Island. And he also hints that if he had been sent with a force to New York, why, the war would have been practically over. (These things are so easy on paper.) He says he has interviewed many of the prisoners, most of them "men of good understandings, but of much prejudice and still more credulity," and that he has urged Gage to send them unconditionally back to their homes with the words, "You have been deluded; return to your homes in peace; it is your duty to God and your country to undeceive your neighbours."

This counsel of perfection was not acted on, but his next suggestions were, later on, and enormous controversy this caused. He proposes that a large army of foreign troops* should be hired, also a large levy of Indians,† and as many Canadians employed as possible. Poor Burgoyne! He was to know later the value of the Indians and the Canadians, and to discover how ill-suited heavy German troops were for fighting in the forests and swamps of North America. The general idea one gets

*Efforts were first made to hire Russian troops, but the Empress Catherine, or "Sister Kitty" as Horace Walpole calls her, would not hear of it.

†This question had come up before. On September 4, 1774, Gage wrote from Boston to Carleton: I am to ask your opinion whether a body of Canadians and Indians might be collected and confided in for the service of this country should matters come to extremities."

from this letter is that although poor old Grandmother Gage had better go home and knit stockings, a certain John Burgoyne might work wonders. In short, we find in this letter Burgoyne the politician and, I fear it must be admitted, the intriguer. But in his letter to his nephew by marriage, Lord Stanley, we have Burgoyne the dramatist, to whom the Bloody Battle of Bunker Hill appealed as a scene in a play, beginning with the old stage direction, "Alarms and Excursions Without."

> "As to the action of the 17th [Bunker Hill], you will see the general detail of it in public print. To consider it as a statesman, it is truly important, because it establishes the ascendency of the King's troops, though opposed by more than treble numbers, assisted by every circumstance that nature and art could supply to make a situation strong. Were an accommodation, by any strange turn of events, to take place without any other action, this would remain a most useful testimony and record in America.
>
> "To consider this action as a soldier, it comprised, though in a small compass, almost every branch of military duty and curiosity. Troops landed in the face of an enemy; a fine disposition; a march sustained by a powerful cannonade from moving field artillery, fixed batteries, floating batteries, and broadsides of ships at anchor, all operating separately and well disposed [*i. e.,* placed]; a deployment from the march to form for the attack of the entrenchments and redoubt; a vigorous defence; a storm with bayonets; a large and fine town set on fire by shells. Whole streets of houses, ships upon the stock, a number of churches, all sending up volumes of smoke and flame, or falling together in

ruin, were capital objects. A prospect of the neighboring hills, the steeples of Boston, and the masts of such ships as were unemployed in the harbour, all crowded with spectators, friends and foes, alike in anxious suspense, made a background to the piece; and the whole together composed a representation of war that I think the imagination of Le Brun* never reached. It was great, it was high-spirited, and while the animated impression remains, let us quit it. I will not engage your sensibility and my own in contemplation of humanity upon the subject, but will close *en militaire,* by lamenting that your brother Thomas was not arrived, because in a long life of service he may not, perhaps, have an opportunity of seeing any professional tragedy like it."

What a fine war correspondent he would have made! Burgoyne had some correspondence with his old friend and subordinate Charles Lee, who wrote to him from Philadelphia soon after his arrival in Boston. Lee was an odd and prickly character. In England he was called the arch-rebel; of his treachery to America we will read later. He had a violent temper, which resulted in 1778 in his court-martial for insubordination at the Battle of Monmouth. He was always nursing some fancied grievance. As Burgoyne was the handsomest man in the British Army so Lee must have been the ugliest in the American. He was tall and extremely thin, with an aquiline nose of enormous proportions. He was fond of

*Charles Lebrun whom Louis XIV took a-campaigning into Flanders in 1667 to tell the world, by his brush, what a fine General was Le Roi Soleil.

Charles Lee, Esqr.

Major-General of the American Forces

Caricature of Charles Lee

From "The Pageant of America," published by Yale University Press, after a portrait in Thomas Girdlestone's "Facts Tending To Prove That General Lee Was The Author Of Junius," London, 1813

dogs, and in a delightful caricature* of him he is shown as accompanied by one of these pets which, however, the artist has depicted more as an ant-eater than a dog. Born in 1731 (he was related to the Bunbury family), he received a commission at the age of eleven, and served in North America 1755-60, where he made friends with the Mohawks, who nicknamed him "Boiling Water." After being in Portugal with Burgoyne he served in several continental armies and was made a major-general by the King of Poland. He lost two fingers in a duel in Italy in 1770 and, like so many others, was supposed to be Junius. A caustic wit, a man of the world and a cosmopolitan soldier, he was not of a generous nature. When captured by the British he attributed it to the fortune of war, the activity of Colonel Harcourt, and the rascality of his own troops. When he was taken prisoner he was poorly clad and sent for a tailor to mend his clothes, but "Not a man in the regiment" (which he had once, in Portugal, led into action†) "would work for so great a rascal." George III was immensely pleased by Lee's capture and said, "I shall take care of Colonel Harcourt: leave his future to me." He did take care of him. Harcourt ended as a field-marshal. The little village of Tring (in Hertfordshire), which was interested in Colonel Harcourt, had a poster put up in the market-place:

"Feb. 13, 1777.

"This is to give Notis that Thursday next will be held as a day of regoicin in commemoration of the takin of General Lee, when their wil be a sermint preached, and other public demonstrascions of joye, after which

---

*By Barham Rushbrooke. The uniform Lee is shown as wearing is that as aide-de-camp to Stanislaus, King of Poland.

†See page 19.

will bee an nox roosted whole & everery mark of festivity & bell ringing imaginable, whith a ball & cock fiting at night in the Hassembly room at the black Lyone."*

Lee's letter (June seventh) to Burgoyne is very artful. He is chiefly concerned for Burgoyne's reputation. "I sincerely lament the infatuation of the times, when men of such a stamp as Mr. Burgoyne and Mr. Howe can be seduced into so impious and nefarious a service by the artifice of a wicked and insidious court and cabinet." Burgoyne must know what abandoned men the cabinet are, a man of such sense and integrity should not keep such company. Then comes some artful flattery. Burgoyne is a man of capacity, but Gage! Why, he has had his understanding so completely blinded by the society of fools and knaves that "he is no longer capable of discerning facts as manifest as the noonday sun: I assert, Sir, that he is ignorant, that he has from the beginning been consummately ignorant of the principles, temper, disposition, and force of the colonies." He misstates facts and derives "tortured inferences from them." This must have been "jam" to Burgoyne. We have seen what he thought of Gage, and human nature is such that we all simply love to hear that those placed in authority over us are a pack of ignorant fools.

Lee then proceeds to give his old friend what is really most sensible advice. "You cannot possibly succeed. No man is better acquainted with the state of this continent than myself. I have run through almost the whole colonies, from the north to the south, and from the south to the north. I have conversed with all orders of men, from the first estated gentlemen to the lowest planters

---

******The Evelyns in America.*** Tring is much nearer London than Frome. See page 220.**

and farmers, and can assure you that the same spirit animates the whole. Not less than a hundred and fifty thousand gentlemen, yeomen, and farmers, are now in arms, determined to preserve their liberties or perish. As to the idea that the Americans are deficient in courage, it is too ridiculous and glaringly false to deserve a serious refutation. I never could conceive upon what this reputation was founded. I served several campaigns in America last war, and cannot recollect a single instance of ill-behaviour in the provincials." And then he comes to Howe. "Gracious God! is it possible that Mr. Howe should be prevailed upon to accept of such an office! The brother of him to whose memory the much-injured people of Boston erected a monument,* employed as one of the instruments of their destruction." And so, after a few pleasant allusions to George III as an Eastern Despot and North as felonious, the letter ends "with the greatest sincerity and affection, Yours, C. Lee."

Burgoyne's reply, written on July ninth, might have been penned by Sir Charles Grandison and Dr. Johnson, in collaboration. It is painfully polite and even more painfully pompous. He had never anticipated that the "vicissitudes of human affairs" would cause them to meet as foes. It had been his pride to be Lee's friend, but Lee is in the wrong. Burgoyne himself is "no stranger to the doctrines of Mr. Locke" and looks "with reverence almost amounting to idolatry upon those immortal Whigs who adopted and applied such doctrine during part of the reign of Charles the First, and in that of James the Second." The letter is like a speech in Parliament

*In the language of the day it represented "the Genius of the Province of Massachusetts Bay in a mournful posture lamenting the fall of the hero."

on the American question, in all probability it was based on notes for a speech which he never delivered. It ends by proposing that he and Lee should meet in "the house upon Boston Neck, just within our advanced sentries, called Brown's house." But one paragraph in this letter was destined to flutter the dove-cots. Burgoyne said, "Is it then from a relief of taxes or from the control of Parliament 'in all cases whatsoever' we are in war? If for the former, the quarrel is at an end: there is not a man of sense and information in America, who does not know it is in the power of the Colonies to put an end to the exercise of taxation immediately and for ever. I boldly assert it, because sense and information will also suggest to every man, that it can never be the interest of Great Britain, after her late experience, to make another trial." Charles Stuart, Lord Bute's son, wrote home, "I have seen Burgoyne's letter to Lee, which was sent to Congress, and heard Major Bruce* say in a conference when I happened to be on duty, that General Putnam had assured him if General Burgoyne had authority from His Majesty to write the Letter, he was certain Congress would be happy to receive the terms he hinted at. I fear the General has said too much, and I think replied to Lee very improperly." Major Webb, writing to Silas Deane, says, "General Burgoyne commands on the Neck, at Roxbury. He has wrote a long letter to General Lee in which he proposes a meeting, whether this will be complied with or not, I cannot say. A certain something runs through the whole of his

*Major Samuel B. Webb, writing to Silas Deane (July 11, 1775), has an interesting note on this officer: "Major Bruce, who served two years in Portugal with Genl. Lee, told my brother Joe at the lines that it [Bunker Hill] was the hottest engagement he ever knew; even, says he, the Battle of Minden did not equal it."

letter, which shews they are sick at the stomach. He says, 'if the right of taxation is all we are contending for, he is empowered* to say Great Britain will give that up.' Why did they not say that six months ago? They must now remember that we have an undoubted right to ask for the expense we have incurred in raising an army and for the loss of the beautiful town of Charlestown, which is now a heap of rubbish. We doubt not Burgoyne writes thus so as hereafter to say that he made us generous offers, with a view to compromise matters. He is as cunning and subtle as the Devil himself, and writes as if he were on the right of the question, like a man of abilities, but his wickedness is to be seen in every sentence of his letter."

The *New York Gazette* gave a better summing-up of the letter.

> "July 8, 1775. This forenoon a trumpeter came from the Regulars army with a letter from General Burgoyne to General Lee, and was conducted blindfolded by the guards to the headquarters in Cambridge. The contents of this letter has occasioned much speculation and is variously reported, but we hear the substance of it is nothing more than this: That General Burgoyne laments being obliged to act in opposition to a gentleman for whom he formerly entertained a great veneration; but that his conduct proceeds from principles, and doubts not that General Lee is actuated by the same motive; he wishes affairs may be accommodated, and desires to have a conference with General Lee."

---

*It will be noted Burgoyne did not use this actual word.

Lee submits this proposal to the Provincial Congress of Massachusetts.

"Head Quarters, July 10th, 1775.

"General Lee presents his respects to the President and gentlemen of the Provincial Congress of Massachusetts, and submits to their perusal a letter which he yesterday received from General Burgoyne, in answer to one which was read and approved by the Delegates of this Province, and other members of the Continental Congress. He begs leave to receive their commands with respect to the proposed interview. If they approve of it, he shall be glad to accept of it; if they disapprove, he shall reject it. But if they approve of it, he must request that they will depute some one gentleman of their body to accompany General Lee, and be witness of the conversation. He desires their answer immediately, as he has engaged to inform Genl. Burgoyne by four o'clock this afternoon, whether the interview is to take place. He shall likewise be much obliged to the gentlemen if they will return the letter; but if they choose to take a copy of it, he can have no objection."

The Provincial Congress replied, diplomatically and wisely:

[Watertown, July 10, 1775]

"Sir:

"The Congress have perused the letter from Genl. Burgoyne, which you was kind enough to submit to their inspection. They can have no objection to the proposed interview, from a want of the highest confidence in the wisdom, discretion, and integrity of

Gen. Lee; but beg leave to suggest that as the confidence of the people in their General is so essentially necessary to the well-conducting of the enterprise in which we are engaged, and as a people contending for their liberties are naturally disposed to jealousy, and not inclined to make the most favorable construction of the motives of conduct which they are not fully acquainted with, whether such an interview might not have a tendency to lessen the influence which the Congress would wish to extend to the utmost of their power to facilitate and succeed the operations of war.

"The Congress, agreeable to your request, have, to prevent as far as we are able, any disagreeable consequences which may arise from the jealousy of the people on such an occasion, appointed Mr. Elbridge Gerry to attend you at the proposed interview, if you shall think proper to proceed in it; and as they do not think themselves authorized to counteract the General's inclination, they would submit it to his opinion, whether the advice of the Council of War might not be taken in a matter of such apparent delicacy.

"To the Honourable Genl. Lee."

Lee took the hint and wrote to Burgoyne:

"Headquarters, Cambridge, July 11, 1775.

"General Lee's compliments to General Burgoyne. Would be extremely happy in the interview he so kindly proposed; but as he perceives that General Burgoyne has already made up his mind on this great subject, and as it is impossible that he (General Lee) should ever alter his opinion, he is apprehensive that the interview might create those jealousies and suspicions so natural to a people struggling in the dearest of all causes, that of their liberty, property, wives, children, and their future generation. He must, therefore, defer the happiness of embracing a man whom he most sincerely loves, until the subversion of the present tyrannical Ministry and system, which he is persuaded must be in a few months, as he knows Great Britain cannot stand the contest. He begs General Burgoyne will send the letters which his Aid-de-Camp has for him—— If Gardiner is his Aid-de-Camp, he desires his love to him."

The last sentence strikes a delightfully human note.

It was as well the conference did not take place. It could only have led to a long speech in Gentleman Johnny's best parliamentary manner, besprinkled with "Good God, Sirs," with an exordium and a peroration calculated to make old Brown, had he been present with his ear applied to the keyhole, yawn his head off and call loudly for rum as a restorative.

We now come to Burgoyne the diplomatist. Nothing is too dirty for diplomacy; it will steam open despatches and regard solemn engagements as scraps of paper. But it is rather disconcerting to find Burgoyne writing to Lord North that it might be possible to bribe Lee. He begins by alluding to him as "late half-pay Major and incendiary in the King's service, at present, by a very strange progression for a man of his temper, Major-General and demagogue in the rebel army which forms the blockade of Boston." He then explains what he would have done had the proposed interview taken place. He would have cut him short in his "paltry jargon of invective"; he would have pointed out "the phrenzy of

British Colonies offering themselves to France or Spain"; and he would have proved to him that were it possible to come to an accommodation, the negotiator (Lee) "would deserve the united thanks of the whole Empire, and America herself, when her senses returned, would raise statues to his memory." He says that Lee's ruling passion was avarice, and "though he would have started at a direct bribe he might have caught at an overture of changing his party to gratify his interest." And Burgoyne, always ready with an historical precedent, thinks that the example of General Monk might have occurred to Lee. He apologizes for the mild and friendly terms in which he had written to the "incendiary," his excuse being "were he secretly bought over, the services he might do are great; and very great I confess they ought to be to atone for his offences."

Burgoyne quotes another letter from Lee from which he deduced that "the rebels are more alarmed at the report of engaging the Indians than at any other measure, and I humbly think this letter alone shows the expediency of diligently preparing and employing that engine." They proved, as we shall see, about as efficient an "engine" as the Russian "steamroller" which, so many armchair strategists argued in the fall of 1914, would, before Christmas, be steaming and rolling along the *Unter den Linden* in Berlin.

There is another interesting point made by Lee and quoted by Burgoyne. This is that "France and Spain are ready to accept the Colonies," that is to say, to recognize them. Burgoyne adds, and rightly, that if North communicated this to the Ministers of those Courts, "I take it for granted, though it should be true, they will flatly deny it." He had not been a member of the House of Commons for nothing. He ends by saying that probably the "leaders of the revolt" would be "as much averse to trust their cause to fair discussion as to the fair field: distant skirmish, ambush, entrenchment, concealment are what they depend upon in debate as in arms." The shameful Donkin took much the same view: he complained of the American "cowardliness in delighting more in murdering from woods, walls and houses than in shewing any genius or science in the art military." Burgoyne, of course, meant to be nasty, but as a matter of fact he is paying a great compliment to the American troops and their leaders. It is always very unpleasant when your enemy will not fight according to the strategical rules laid down in the works by the great writers on war. I remember once reading in an American military magazine a delightfully cynical remark on this point: "Strategy when practised by savages is treachery." "The principles of strategy are eternal": those unprincipled warriors who monkey about with them and fight according to the light of nature are iconoclasts and, even if they win, deserve the heaviest censure for not conducting warfare *à la Cocker Militaire, i. e.,* some old Prussian General von und zu Schmellfungus.

Burgoyne wrote about the same time to Lord Rochfort, lamenting the inertness and procrastination at Boston and blaming for them not so much Gage as the Admiral (Admiral Graves*) as largely responsible for "our inactivity, our disgrace and our distress." He discusses the question of evacuating Boston for New York and savagely attacks the departments at home. "At present the sick and wounded are without broth for want

*Graves was quite incompetent. He undertook nothing which did not miscarry, and did not get on well with the soldiers.

of fresh provisions and the poor ensign cannot draw his pay for less than 15 per cent. discount." Finance of any kind is a mystery to most of us, but I have no doubt this state of affairs was all to the benefit of Mr. Rigby, the Paymaster General.

We now come to a correspondence between the greatest man on the American side, George Washington, and the handsomest—I can not also say the greatest, for I fear there were no great Englishmen then in America—man on the British side, Gentleman Johnny. Washington wrote, early in August, 1775, complaining of the treatment of American officers who were prisoners of war and who had been "indiscriminately thrown into a common gaol appropriated for felons." The letter was, of course, addressed to Gage, and equally of course Burgoyne, the Polite Letter-Writer of Gage's family* was called in to answer it. I do not know if the expressive word "Shucks" had then come into existence, and if it had I do not for one moment suppose Washington would have used it; but it is difficult to refrain from doing so: Burgoyne's letter is so painfully grandiloquent. "Britons ever prominent in mercy have overlooked the criminal in the captive." "Your prisoners [*i. e.*, your officers who are our prisoners] whose lives by the law of the land are destined to the cord have hitherto been treated with care and kindness." He then proceeds to give Washington a little good advice. "Be temperate in political disquisition; give free operation to truth; and punish those who deceive and misrepresent; and not only the effects but the causes of this unhappy conflict will be removed." One has heard of people who were not born to be drowned, but "destined to the cord" is painfully pedantic.

---

*In the eighteenth century a general's "family" meant his staff.

But Burgoyne could, on occasion, unbend. Boston, although practically blockaded and, thanks to the inefficiency of the Admiral, on short commons, had its little amenities. One of them was amateur theatricals. Burgoyne wrote a farce called *The Blockade of Boston:* the Americans retaliated with another, *The Blockheads.* Washington was a character in *The Blockade,* in an unmilitary dress and with a huge wig and long sword. In January, 1776, the farce had a rude interruption. The Americans who knew exactly when the performance began, attacked the mill at Charlestown at that very moment. The alarm was given and a sergeant outside the playhouse door rushed in upon the stage, crying, "Turn out! turn out! They're hard at it hammer and tongs." He was vigorously applauded, being taken as a character in the play, until it was realized that he was in earnest—and the farce came to an abrupt end. In September, 1775, the officers gave a performance of *Zara,* Burgoyne writing the prologue. Puritans have often been a target for dramatists, and perhaps the best lines in this prologue are those to their address. Thanks to them, says Burgoyne:

Then fell the stage, quell'd by the bigots roar,
Truth fell with sense, and Shakespeare charmed no more.

He also urges the "Boston prudes—if prudes there are"—to come and see the show and be cheered up by it. It is not a very lively prologue. Prologues and Epilogues rarely are, always excepting that in which Nell Gwyn ("His late Majesty's Miss," to give her the title by which she was known after the death of the Merriest Monarch), lying upon the stage a corpse, suddenly arose and said to a scene-shifter who had offered to shift her:

Hold! Let me be, you damned confounded dog,
I am to rise and speak the Epilogue.

Prologues and Epilogues were recitations and therefore bound to be dull. If we must have a recitation, let us have, "It was Christmas Day in the Harem" (though this is not calculated to please Prudes) or the more modern "Casey at the Bat." I do not suppose there are any prudes nowadays in Boston, and if there are, I do not think Zara would give them anything except a headache. Burgoyne's prologue was spoken by Lord Rawdon, known in his day as "the ugliest man in Europe," and, judging from his portrait in the War Office, his day was entirely right. Later on he became Lord Moira and an intimate friend of the Prince Regent. In 1817 he was made Marquis of Hastings, and no doubt then appeared less ugly.

About this time Burgoyne wrote a long letter to Lord George Germain. He talks of "fatal procrastination" and says that we have crossed the Rubicon (good old Rubicon! How many times has it been crossed?) and "plunged into a most serious war, without a single requisite, gunpowder excepted, for carrying it on." Bunker Hill (he calls it Charlestown*) he speaks of as a victory which had reestablished the reputation of trained troops as against untrained, which had been rather blown upon by the affair at Lexington against "the undisciplined rabble." He is obviously a little sore about the fight put up by the colonists on Bunker Hill. They are not "one jot above the level of all men expert in the use of firearms, Corsicans, Miquelets, Croats, Tartars, moun-

*And so did Washington in a letter to Congress of July 21, 1775. Battles get various names. The Prussians call Waterloo La Belle Alliance and the French, Mont St. Jean.

taineers and borderers." He is equally severe on their leaders. Some of them, he admits, are very able, but are at the same time "the most profligate hypocrites," while Adams is "as great a conspirator as ever subverted a state." He quotes an intercepted letter in which Adams refers to "one of his tools, I conclude he means Handcock *(sic)*, as a piddling genius." Adams himself although "a profligate character," has by the exercise of his parts, availing himself of the temper and prejudice of the times, cajoled the opulent, drawn in the wary, deluded the vulgar, till all parties in America, and some in Great Britain, are puppets in his string." He is, in short, Catiline and Cromwell rolled into one. Burgoyne is more to the point and more sensible when he says the British troops have "neither bread-waggons, bat horses, sufficient artillery horses, nor other articles of *attirail* necessary for an army to move at a distance, nor numbers to keep up posts of communication and convoys, had we even magazines to be conveyed." He says that his "favourite plan" is a descent at Rhode Island. But he must not be thought to be blaming General Gage, who has "a character replete with virtue and with talents," but who is also—the censure is pleasantly wrapped up—quite unequal to the situation. Next he fires a regular broadside at the Admiral (Graves), who was, as a matter of fact, quite as incompetent as Gage, not more; that would not be possible.

"It may be asked in England, 'What is the Admiral doing?' I wish I were able to answer that question satisfactorily; but I can only say what he is *not* doing.

"That he is *not* supplying us with sheep and oxen, the dinners of the best of us bear meagre testimony; the state of our hospitals bears a more melancholy one.

"View of the attack on Bunker's Hill with the burning of Charles Town, June 17, 1775"
Engraved for Barnard's "New Complete & Authentic History of England"

"He is *not* defending his own flocks and herds, for the enemy have repeatedly plundered his own islands.

"He is *not* defending the other islands in the harbour, for the enemy in force landed from a great number of boats, and burned the lighthouse at noon-day (having first killed and taken the party of marines which was posted there) almost under the guns of two or three men-of-war.

"He is *not* employing his ships to keep up communication and intelligence with the King's servants and friends at the different parts of the continent, for I do not believe General Gage has received a letter from any correspondent out of Boston these six weeks.

"He is intent upon greater objects you will think, supporting in the great points the dignity of the British flag, and where a number of boats have been built for the enemy, privateers fitted out, prizes carried in, the King's armed vessels sunk, the crews made prisoners, the officers killed—he is doubtless enforcing instant restitution and reparation by the voice of his cannon and laying the towns in ashes that refuse his terms? Alas! he is not. British thunder is diverted or controlled by pitiful attentions and mere Quaker-like scruples; and, under such influences, insult and impunity, like righteousness and peace, have kissed each other."

The Quartermaster-General, the Adjutant-General, the Secretaries and Commissaries (but not their wives) are just as bad, and the general situation is summed up as being "a mass of inefficiencies." And then he comes to the really important part, his personal grievances. "It is hard to conceive so absolute a cypher in a military light as the youngest Major-General in this army." He is fond of this word, he has used it before, and he uses it again in a letter to Mr. Thurlow, afterward the well-known Lord Chancellor. "In regard to myself (forgive me for detaining you a moment with the mention of such a cypher) I am placed in a situation that leaves me little more than contemplation for employment, except when I am sometimes called upon to draw a pen instead of a sword." He again calls the American leaders "profligate hypocrites" and says of Adams, "he has certainly taken Cromwell for his model, and perhaps guides secret counsels with more address, and soars too high in personal ambition to incline to accommodation." But he pays a high compliment to his style and says he "appears to me to write with the conciseness of Tacitus." Which is more than Gentleman Johnny himself did. More grousing in another letter. "I seek to blame nobody. General Gage is entitled to my respect and esteem upon every principle that can commend a private character. He is amiable for his virtues, but he is not equal to his situation." The Quartermaster-General means well and is always busy, "but I am afraid his *ideas* only go to supply the army from hand to mouth." "The department of the Adjutant General is also all peace, parade, and St. James's Park." This is an excellent phrase, and might have come out of one of Burgoyne's comedies. And again he exposes the corruption at home: "General Gage told me, within this week, he had not more money in his treasurer's hands than would supply the next month's subsistence; none can possibly be got for bills, not even at 10 per cent. discount, which has been the rate at which the officers of the army have been compelled to draw for their private pay for some time past. He expected £40,000 by the *Cerberus,* being the balance of £50,000 which he was officially informed *was* issued, and of which he received ten. Not a guinea more is come. In what contractor or clerk's hands is the interest of that sum?" Meanwhile Mr. Rigby was busy at home drinking brandy and, like the poet's bird, painting his face in his agreeable way "a brighter purple." And once more Burgoyne points out that Gage was not only lacking in intelligence but also in getting it beyond what "can be obtained by a spying-glass or from common report often calculated to deceive him."

Intelligence, or information, was a weak point in many British campaigns in the eighteenth century and, perhaps, in other centuries. In Canada in 1760 the only way in which General James Murray could get it was "by giving brandy for it." I believe the same system is followed nowadays by reporters in Fleet Street, sent upon a "story." Money so expended is delicately accounted for as "Inquiry Expenses," which certainly sounds better than "10 doubles and splashes at 1/6." But the classic intelligence story of that day relates to the Carthagena Expedition. On March 5, 1740, a Council of War was held on the Admiral's ship consisting of the four principal officers of the Army and the four principal officers of the Navy, to draw up a plan of attack. The General was asked his opinion, but politely replied that "he was a Stranger in those Seas" and left it, as they say at cards, to the Admiral. But the Admiral also had "no proper intelligence."* So then, having first probably "spliced the mainbrace," they all put their heads together and with much thought and weighing of pros and cons, "drew up a scheme for—settling the shares of Plunder." After

*A cynic might say they rarely have.

all, if you have a committee meeting or a council of war, you must settle something.

General Gage returned to England in October, 1775, ostensibly to "explain the various wants for carrying on the next campaign," but really to be gently put upon some military shelf. In the Boer War this was called being "Stellenboschèd," in the European War, in the French army, the phrase was to be "Limoged." In December Burgoyne followed Gage home on leave in the *Boyne*. Captain Evelyn wrote home on his departure, "He appears from the line he has taken here to have been intended rather as a negotiator than to be active in the field. He is a man of great abilities and power of language."

Lee wrote Burgoyne a final letter, which is worth quoting in full.

"Camp on Prospect Hill, Dec. 1st, 1775.

"Dear Sir,

"As I am just informed you are ready to embark for England, I cannot refrain from once more trespassing on your patience. An opportunity is now presented of immortalising yourself as the saviour of your country. The whole British Empire stands tottering on the brink of ruin, and you have it in your power to prevent the fatal catastrophe; but it will admit of no delay. For heaven's sake avail yourself of the precious moment: put an end to the delusion: exert the voice of a brave, virtuous citizen; and tell the people at home, that they must immediately rescind all their impolitic, iniquitous, tyrannical, murderous acts; that they must overturn the whole frantic system, or that they are undone. You ask me in your letter, if it is independence at which the Americans aim? I answer, No; the idea never entered a single American's head, until the most intolerable oppression forced it upon them. All they required was, to remain masters of their own property, and be governed by the same equitable laws which they had enjoyed from the first formation of the Colonies. The ties of connection which bound them to their parent country were so dear to them, that he who would have ventured to touch them would have been considered as the most impious of mortals; but these sacred ties, the same men, who have violated or baffled the most precious laws and rights of the people at home, dissipated, or refused to account for their treasures, tarnished the glory, and annihilated the importance of the nation: these sacred ties, I say, so dear to every American, Bute and his tory administration are now rending asunder.

"You ask whether it is the weight of taxes of which they complain? I answer, No: it is the principle they combat, and they would be guilty in the eyes of God and men, of the present world, and all posterity, did they not reject it; for if it were admitted, they would have nothing they could call their own; they would be in a worse condition than the wretched slaves in the West India's Islands, whose little peculium has ever been esteemed inviolate. But wherefore should I dwell on this? Is not the case with Ireland the same as theirs? They are subordinate to the British empire; they are subordinate to the Parliament of Great Britain, but they tax themselves. Why, as the case is similar, do you begin with them? But you know, Mr. Burgoyne, audacious as the ministry are, they dare not attempt it. There is one part of your letter which, I confess, I do not understand.* If I recollect right (for I unfortunately have not the letter by me), you say that if the privilege of taxing themselves is what the Americans claim, the contest is at an end. You surely cannot allude to the propositions of North. It is impossible that you should not think, with me and all mankind, that these propositions are no more or less than adding to a most abominable oppression, a more abominable insult. But to recur to the question of Americans aiming at independence: Do any instructions of any one of the provinces, furnish the least ground for this suspicion? On the contrary, do they not all breathe the strongest attachment and filial piety to their parent country? But if she discards all the natural tenderness of a mother, and acts the part of a cruel stepdame, it must naturally be expected that their affection will cease; the ministry leave them no alternative, *aut serviri, aut alienari jubent;* it is in human nature; it is a moral obligation to adopt the latter. But the fatal separation has not yet taken place, and yourself, your single self, my friend, may perhaps prevent it. Upon the ministry, I am afraid, you can make no impression; for, to repeat a hackneyed quotation,

" 'They are in blood
Stepped in so far, that, should they wade no more,
To return would be as tedious as go o'er.'

"But if you will at once break off all connections with these pernicious men; if you will wave all con-

---

*This is the paragraph which caused the stir. It certainly is difficult to understand exactly what Burgoyne meant.

sideration, but the salvation of your country, Great Britain may stand as indebted to General Burgoyne, as Rome was to her Camillus. Do not, I entreat you, my dear Sir, think this the mad rhapsody of an enthusiast, nor the cant of a factious designing man; for, in these colours, I am told, I am frequently painted. I swear by all that's sacred, as I hope for comfort and honour in this world and to avoid misery in the next, that I most earnestly and devoutly love my native country; that I wish the same happy relation to subsist for ages betwixt her and her children, which has raised the wide arch of her empire to so stupendous and enviable a height; but at the same time I avow, that if the parliament and people should be depraved enough to support any longer the present ministry in their infernal scheme, my zeal and reverence for the rights of humanity are so much greater than my fondness for any particular spot, even the place of my nativity, that, had I any influence in the councils of America, I would advise not to hesitate a single instant, but decisively to cut the Gordian knot, now besmeared with civil blood.

"This, I know, is strong emphatic language, and might pass, with men who are strangers to the flame which the love of liberty is capable of lighting up in the human breast, for a proof of my insanity; but you, sir, unless I have mistaken you from the beginning, will conceive, that a man, in his sober sense, may possess such feelings. In my sober senses, therefore, permit me once more most earnestly to entreat and conjure you to exert your whole force, energy, and talents to stop the ministry in this their headlong career. If you labour in vain (as, I must repeat, I think will be the case), address yourself to the people at large. By adopting this method, I am so sanguine, as to assure myself of your success; and your public character will be as illustrious as your personal qualities are amiable to all who intimately know you. By your means the Colonies will long continue the farmers, planters and shipwrights of Great Britain; but if the present course is persisted in, an eternal divorce must inevitably take place. As to the idea of subduing them into servitude, and indemnifying yourselves for the expense, you must be convinced long before this of its absurdity.

"I should not, perhaps, be extravagant, if I advanced, that all the ships of the world would be too few to transport force sufficient to conquer three millions of people, unanimously determined to sacrifice everything to liberty; but if it were possible, the victory would not be less ruinous than the defeat. You would only destroy your own strength. No revenue can possibly be extracted out of this country. The army of place-men might be increased, but her circuitous commerce, founded on perfect freedom, which alone can furnish riches to the metropolis, would fall to the ground. But the dignity of Great Britain, it seems, is at stake. Would you, sir, if in the heat of passion you had struck a single drummer of your regiment, and afterwards discovered you had done it unjustly, think it any forfeiture of your dignity to acknowledge the wrong? No; I am well acquainted with your disposition, you would ask him pardon at the head of your regiment.

"I shall now conclude (if you will excuse the pedantry) with a sentence of Latin: *Justum est bellum quibus necessarium et pia arma quibus nulla, nisi in armis, relinquitur spes.* I most sincerely wish you a quick and prosperous voyage, and that your happiness and glory may be equal to the idea I have of your merits as,

"I am, with greatest truth and affection,

"Yours,

"CHARLES LEE.*

"Major-Gen. Burgoyne."

It is interesting to note that just as Burgoyne thought Lee might like to pose as the savior of his country *à la* General Monk, so Lee thought Burgoyne might assume the rôle of a Camillus. These two old friends never wrote to each other again. A convention finished Burgoyne's military career, a court-martial Lee's.

*Vol. I of the Lee Papers, published as Vol. 4 of the New York Historical Society Collections, 1871.

# CHAPTER V

## CANADA

LET us now have a mouthful of some warming cordial and go north and consider Our Lady of the Snows and the Sneezes, the coldest jewel in the British Crown. I remember reading as a boy in some such book as "Little Arthur's History of England," or perhaps it may have been "Geography without Sobs," that the name Canada had the following origin. Some old circumnavigator, having lost his way on the Ocean or Trackless Deep, landed upon its shores and asked the first "savage man" he saw, "What country is this?" Probably he did it by signs, pointing an inquiring finger to the horizon, assuming a more vacant and idiotic look than usual, and perhaps remarking, "Me not know whereabouts. You likee Rum? You tellee me." The savage, whose breakfast of raw blubber had probably disagreed with him, sourly told the mariner where to go in one expressive word, "Canada!" And, whether this is true or not, so it has remained ever since, though the French had a prettier name for it or part of it in Acadie.

England owes much to Canada. In the old days it sent us furs and cod-liver oil; in more modern times we have had from it apples, cheese and Lord Beaverbrook. And above all, Canada sent us those fine fighters who made Vimy Ridge as immortal a name as Wolfe and his men did Quebec.* But in 1775 the Canadian *habitants*

*There are two odd poetical associations with this victory. As

do not seem to have been particularly anxious to fight for anything or anybody. The Home Government had just passed the Quebec Act. So far as it is possible to understand any Act of Parliament, with its notwithstandings, contrariwises, schedules and the rest of it, it appears to be quite a nice and amiable act and certainly made, for the day, one very great concession. "For the more perfect security and ease of the minds of the inhabitants"—those who were Roman Catholics were graciously permitted to exercise their religion without let or hindrance. This created a storm in England, for Englishmen, apparently, have never been able to forget "Sister Mary, nicknamed Bee."* And it also called forth loud protests in Philadelphia. The General Congress there sent an address, signed by the President, Henry Middleton, to its "Friends and Fellow-subjects" in Quebec, showing what a preposterously rotten Act this was. The British Ministry is alluded to as "insolent" and "profligate,"† and the Act itself has a "tinselled out-

---

Wolfe came down the river on the ebb to the heights of Abraham, he recited Gray's *Elegy,* and a prize was offered for the best poem on his death. I do not know which was the best, but I think the worst must have been that which included the lines:

> He marched without dread or fears
> At the head of his bold Grenadiers.
> And what was very remarkable, nay very particular,
> He climbed up rocks which were perpendicular.

And, had this bard lived nowadays, I feel sure he would have added the line:

> How much easier his task had there been a Funicular.

*Sister, of course, of red-headed Eliza, as the poet-courtiers used to call Good Queen Bess; and "Bee" is short for "B——y."

†Perfectly true of them as individuals, with the exception of Dartmouth, who was known in the Clubs as "The Psalmsinger." He belonged to an evangelical sect called, delightfully, "Lady Huntingdon's Connection."

side" (just like a Pantomime Queen). Henry Middleton appears to have been a scholar, for he quotes "the celebrated Marquis Beccaria," and "your countryman the immortal Montesquieu." But as most of the French Canadians could neither read nor write, these stirring words left them as cold as their climate. The address also casually remarked, "Military men belong to a profession which *may* be useful, but is *often* dangerous." This is the old Standing Army Bugaboo which has so often squeaked and gibbered both in England and the United States. It has had this untoward result that whenever America or Great Britain has been confronted with war, both countries have invariably been unprepared for it and have been compelled to improvise armies at very short notice.

But it was not much use for either Henry Middleton or Sir Guy Carleton, the English Governor in Quebec, appealing to the Canadians to fight. In spite of their climate, or perhaps because of it, they were Laodicean. They showed "backwardness."* Agents were sent from Philadelphia to try to stir them up. A contemporary account says, "The Yankees have had their Emiceres among the French and made them thus lukewarm to Government besides it appears that a twelve years peace has Extinguished their martial spirit and that together with the Sweets of British Government makes them desire to live in Quiet." But some of them appeared to have listened to the "Emiceres," though they could hardly have understood them, for the prevailing idea among the French Canadians was that "the people of Boston are fighting merely to prevent the return of the

*Wolfe had a very poor opinion of the Canadians. He called them "vermin."

Stamps which they seem to think a matter of great politeness and do not wish to see them disturbed in so good a work."* The Americans, satisfied if only the Canadians would remain neutral, invaded Canada, Montreal was captured by Montgomery and Arnold was within an ace of capturing Quebec and probably would have done so but for the climate and Carleton, by far the ablest British General in North America.

Among Montgomery's troops were "The Green Mountain Boys," rioters and lawless fellows, and among the American officers was a typical backwoodsman, that picturesque character Ethan Allen, whom Carleton described as "a horse-jockey." He started a little expedition on his own with a delightful letter to the Indians. "I always love Indians and Have Hunted a Great Deal with them and know how to shute and Ambush, just like Indians and want your Warriors to come and see me and help me fight Regulars." But if they were inclined to fight on neither side, he would still continue to love them and invite them "to come and Hunt in our Woods and Pass through our Country in the Lake and come to our Joust and have Rum and be Good Friends." Allen was a native-born strategist and captured Ticonderoga in a very strategical manner, quite unthought of by Clausewitz and Jomini and the rest of the dull old bores. He went to the commandant, Captain de la Place, an old hunting friend, borrowed thirty of the garrison to help him—so he said—transport goods across the lake, made them gloriously drunk, and gave them enough money to get the rest of the garrison in the same pleasant frame of

*They were very simple folk. Benedict Arnold's men were linen-clad, "vêtu en toile": many of the Canadians thought this was "vêtu en tôle" or sheet-iron, a kind of crusaders, in fact.

body. He then demanded the surrender of the fort "in the name of the Great Jehovah and the Continental Congress." A pious man, or he would have put the Continental Congress first. When he was captured Prescott shook his cane at him. Ethan Allen retaliated by shaking his fist and replied in a phrase which would have won Burgoyne's approval that his (Allen's) fist would prove "the beetle of mortality for Prescott if he offered to strike." The British officer replied in the same strain, "You shall grace a halter at Tyburn."

Allen was sent to England in chains and when he was landed, still in chains, at Falmouth, he was much pleased with the interest his appearance aroused among the Cornish folk. He was kept a prisoner in that historic and charming castle, Pendennis, which has given its name to one of the most delightful books in the English language. He does not appear to have been badly treated while in captivity. He became known as an oddity and visitors would call upon him and give him bowls of punch.

But his capture of Ticonderoga had one very important result: some of the guns taken there were dragged through the woods and across country to Dorchester Heights, where they commanded the British fleet and had much to do with Howe's evacuation of Boston. Montgomery, who was killed in action, did not think very highly of his men from New England. They "melted away": the officers had no authority over them. His New Yorkers he described as "the sweepings of the streets." Which is very much what the Duke of Wellington said of the "scum" who helped him to beat Napoleon's marshals and then Napoleon himself.

The state of affairs in Canada naturally caused great stir in England, and Burgoyne was called in to advise.

He seized the opportunity and his pen—always handy—and drew up some "Reflections upon the War in America." He suggested that two armies should advance, one from the North in Canada, and one from the South, join at some given point, and cut the colonies in half. He makes some very interesting remarks on the Americans as soldiers.

> "Accustomed to felling of timber and to grubbing up trees, they are very ready at earthworks and palisading, and they will cover and entrench themselves wherever they are for a short time left unmolested with surprising alacrity. . . . Composed as the American army is, together with the strength of the country, full of woods, swamps, stone walls, and other enclosures and hiding-places, it may be said of it that every private man will in action be his own general, who will turn every tree and bush into a kind of temporary fortress, from whence, when he hath fired his shot with all the deliberation, coolness, and certainty which hidden safety inspires, he will skip as it were to the next, and so on for a long time till dislodged either by cannon or by a resolute attack of light infantry. In this view of the American militia, rebels as they are, they will be found to be respectable even in flight. Light infantry, therefore, in greater numbers than one company per regiment, ought to be an essential part of the general system of our army."

All this is very sensible. In military matters Burgoyne, like other commanders, never failed—on paper.

In February he was appointed to act as Second in Command to Carleton in Canada and in March, 1776, he sailed with some Brunswick troops as reinforcements for Quebec. Lord George Germain, in making arrangements for Burgoyne's departure, wrote him a letter saying that Captain Pennel, R. N., commanding the *Blonde,** would receive him with pleasure on board his ship, and added the very odd remark, "It seems he is rich and you need not fear putting him to expense." Probably this ended in the Captain and the General having many a pleasant game at cards on the voyage, just as if they had been at White's.

On arriving at Quebec, Burgoyne was placed in command of a column which advanced against Forts Chambly and St. John. His men, fresh from board-ship, were not in very good trim, but the Americans evacuated both forts, and Burgoyne issued a General Order: "The expedition on which Lieutenant-General Burgoyne has had the honour to be employed being finished by the precipitate flight of the rebels, he shall think it his duty to make a faithful report to His Excellency the Commander-in-Chief† of the zeal and activity shewn in the officers and men under his command, to surmount the difficulties of the march and come into action." This is Gentleman Johnny all over, giving his men credit in simple, soldierly, if slightly ungrammatical, language for what they had done. But it is also typical of him that he could not refrain from adding the grandiloquent phrase: "Those are principles that cannot fail to produce the most glorious effects whenever the enemy shall acquire boldness enough to put them to the proof."

Burgoyne had one talent which some of the greatest

---

*It was, I believe, an eighteenth century saying, "Soldiers and sailors prefer blondes."

†Carleton.

generals have never been able to acquire, that of winning the affection of his men. Wellington never achieved this, although his men respected him hugely. There is a story of two privates in the Peninsula, when things were not going well. One said to the other, "Well, Jack, we're in a hell of a scrape," and, as the Duke came cantering up, as though going to a meet, he added "And there's the long-nosed——* who is going to get us out of it." But Burgoyne's officers and men loved him. His good looks and his reputation for being by no means an anchorite had a good deal to do with it. Soldiers, and indeed all of us, ladies—most particularly—included, like a good-looking, well set-up man and a *bon viveur*. The grouch is never popular. He hates himself. Is it therefore astonishing that people hate him?

Lieutenant Digby, of the 53rd Foot, who served under Burgoyne at this time, compares him with Carleton, a far more able general.

> "General Carleton is one of the most distant, reserved men in the world, he has a rigid strictness in his manner which is very unpleasing and which he observes even to his most particular friends and acquaintances. . . . He was far from being the favourite of the army. General Burgoyne alone engrossed their warmest attachment. From having seen a great deal of polite life, he possesses a winning manner in his appearance and address (far different from the severity of Carleton), which caused him to be idolized by the army, his orders appearing more like recommending subordination than enforcing it. On every occasion he was the soldier's friend well

*"Term of endearment amongst sailors" (Johnson).

knowing the most sanguine expectations a general can have of success, must proceed from the spirit of the troops under his command. The manner he gained their esteem was by rewarding the meritorious when in his power, which seldom failed from the praise which they received to cause a remissness in duty to be regarded as odious and unmanly and a desire of emulation soldier-like and honourable."

"On every occasion he was the soldier's friend." This is praise which I imagine every general in any army would be proud to receive. Exactly the same words were used—by a private—of the Duke of York, second son of George III, who, though like Burgoyne not a success in the field, had with the officers of the army and the rank and file a popularity, nay, more, an affection which Wellington never won, nor, indeed, tried to win. There are other striking resemblances between John Burgoyne and Frederick Augustus, Duke of York and Albany, who was, in the word of Sir John Fortescue, "the best Commander-in-Chief who ever ruled the British army." They both were devotees of cards, racing, gambling, wine, song and (last but not least) women,—like most of us, I suppose, though some of us will not admit it.

The Americans, driven back from Quebec, had retreated to Ticonderoga, that frontier fort so famous in the old days* but now (I suppose) unknown, save as a place of pilgrimage. Burgoyne and Major-General Phillips urged Carleton to attack it. The place had been greatly strengthened by Kosciusko (whose fall caused

*When it was known by the musical name of Carillon.

Sir Guy Carleton

Freedom to emit a piercing shriek) and Carleton, probably wisely, decided not to do so. Phillips, an officer of the artillery, who had won great distinction at Minden and Warburg, in a letter to Burgoyne, October 23, 1776, speaks pretty strongly about "the sloth and changes of this atmosphere." At the Camp at Crown Point, whence he wrote, there was, he says, "neither reconnoitring post nor scout sent forward, but as the whim of a drunken Indian prevails: I have endeavoured in vain to form a small detachment to feel the pulse of the enemy, the answer is that it is wrong to teach these rebels war." And he says definitely, "I think the army should have moved forward and a trial made at Ticonderoga; had we failed in a strong feint we could but have retired, and I must think there are good chances of success from the very strong panic which has taken the rebels. But it is the humour here to suppose that it is no disgrace to retire if it is not done in the face of the enemy."

I think Phillips, who had come out with Burgoyne and was new to the country, was in the wrong. Gates at Ticonderoga had nine thousand effectives, and a boom of heavy logs had been thrown across the narrows to prevent vessels passing. Moreover light regiments of militia were on their way from New England to join him and the cold weather was setting in. It is difficult not to conclude that Carleton was right in breaking off operations. But, in his kindness of heart, he made one great mistake, and that was in his humane treatment of the American prisoners. General Waterbury, who had fought in six campaigns against the French, was treated by him, not as a prisoner but as a guest. The rest, amounting to one hundred and ten officers and men, on signing an agreement not to bear arms again unless formally exchanged, were allowed to go free. They were provided with shoes, stockings and waistcoats, and Carleton made them a friendly little speech: "My lads, why did you come to disturb an honest man in his government, that never did any harm to you in his life? I never invaded your property, nor sent a single soldier to distress you. Come, my boys, you are in a very distressing situation, and not able to go home with any comfort; I must provide you with shoes, stockings and good warm waistcoats. I must give you some good victuals to carry you home. Take care, my lads, that you do not come here again, lest I should not treat you so kindly." So enthusiastic were the released prisoners about the treatment they had received, that Gates would not let them join the garrison at Ticonderoga, but sent them to their homes. But to the Ministers in London all Americans were rebels, and Carleton got into hot water for this.

Burgoyne, who returned home early in November, before the St. Lawrence was closed by ice, was icily received by Germain, who coupled him with Carleton, for whom he had a personal dislike,* for the failure to attack Ticonderoga. But few could resist Handsome Jack, and before long he was seen riding in Hyde Park with George III, and he submitted to him his *Thoughts for Conducting the War from the Side of Canada.* This is a very important document, as the plan of campaign for 1777 was based upon it. Burgoyne sent it to Germain for transmission to the King from his house in Hertford

*Some historians say that this was due to Carleton having borne testimony against him at the Minden court-martial. This was not so, for Carleton was not a witness on that occasion. The ill-feeling was probably due to the fact that a bad man on general principles dislikes a good man; another reason was that Carleton would not promote a protégé of the Minister.

Street, February 28, 1777, after spending two months in Bath* as his physicians had pressed him to do and which he found "requisite to my health and spirits." Which, no doubt, meant the waters for his health, and a little genteel gambling for his spirits.

Let us now consider his *Thoughts.* He assumes that the enemy will be in great force at Ticonderoga, where the works can accommodate twelve thousand men; he will also have a large naval force on Lake George, to assure his retreat, and will block the roads from Ticonderoga by Skenesborough to Albany, by felling trees, breaking bridges, by other impediments—which is exactly what Schuyler did—and by fortifying strong positions. This will necessitate the King's army "carrying a weight of artillery with it." He suggests, too, that the invading army should consist of at least eight thousand regulars, artillery as proposed by General Carleton, a corps of watermen, two thousand Canadians and one thousand or more "savages." He proposes that three thousand troops should be left in Canada. Provisions and stores should be collected at Crown Point; this he regards as "one of the most important operations of the campaign because it is upon that that most of the rest will depend." This, and the recruiting of "savages" and Canadians, will, naturally, be the work of the Governor (Carleton) and it is to be "presumed that the general officer employed to proceed with the army will be held to be out of reach of any possible blame till he is clear of the province of Canada and furnished with the proposed supplies." This is perfectly natural, but it shows that Burgoyne had anticipated that Carleton might be annoyed—as indeed

*Or rather "The Bath" as it was then called.

who would not?—at being superseded in the command of the expedition. He then says that Ticonderoga would in all probability be taken early in the summer, and should then be used as a base ("place of arms") in lieu of Crown Point.

Now we come to the important part. He assumes that the chief purpose of the invading army is to *effect a junction with General Howe at Albany*. He lays stress upon this in two successive paragraphs. He also suggests the idea of an expedition, at the outset of the campaign, by Lake Ontario and Oswego to the Mohawk River as a "diversion." And finally he brings in a word, which he was to use constantly later on, *viz.*, that the general in charge of the operations, that is to say himself, should have a "latitude." By this he means that he should be at liberty to act as he may think fit, in view of possible contingencies and stress of circumstances that it is impossible to foresee so far ahead. In other words, he should be given a free hand, if necessary, and not bound by hard and fast instructions. King George approved the *Thoughts* in principle and wrote in so many words, "As Sir William Howe does not think of acting from Rhode Island into Massachusetts, *the force from Canada must join him at Albany*."

It is curious that the most sensible suggestion in Burgoyne's *Thoughts* should make a mere casual appearance at the end of them. This was that the troops in Canada should be sent by sea to join Howe. He was not enthusiastic about this idea, and remarked that it ought not to be contemplated except "upon positive conviction of necessity." George III firmly rejected it with the words: "I greatly dislike that idea." The reason no doubt was that an invasion *from* Canada, as proposed, would prevent another invasion *of* Canada. It was not so very long since Wolfe had won it from the French; to take troops away from it by sea would, so it was argued, expose it to attack.

Germain wrote on March twenty-sixth to Carleton. He begins with the interesting statement that a letter of his dated August second in the preceding year (1776) was entrusted to Captain Le Maitre, who, "after having been three times in the Gulph of St. Lawrence, had the Mortification to find it impossible to make his passage to Quebec and therefore returned to England with it."* This alone ought to have convinced this blunderer that he might as well have been in the moon as in Whitehall so far as the conduct of operations in North America was concerned. He then says he has "had the Mortification to learn that upon your repassing Lake Champlain a very considerable Number of the Insurgents, finding their presence no longer necessary near Ticonderoga, immediately marched from thence and joined the Rebel Forces in the Provinces of New York and Jersey," and had been worrying Sir William Howe. He then notifies Sir Guy as to the number of troops to be sent under Burgoyne and of those to be left in Canada, and says in so many words that it has become "highly necessary that the most speedy Junction of the two Armies† should be effected." At the end of the letter he says, "I shall write to Sir William Howe by the first Packet."

---

*When Haldimand "took over" from Carleton in July, 1778, he wrote home, "There have been no accounts from Great Britain for nine or ten months, except but what were conveyed by Rebel Newspapers."

†*i. e.,* Burgoyne's and Howe's. Washington, with extraordinary prescience wrote, July 4, 1776, "It seems beyond question that the enemy will attempt to unite their two armies, that under General Burgoyne and the one arrived here"—*i. e.,* in New York.

Sir Guy Carleton answered this on May twentieth. His letter is what soldiers call a "snorter," and I will quote bits of it, as it shows clearly what an incompetent ass Germain was. Carleton suggests that "any officer entrusted with supreme command, ought upon the spot to see what was most expedient to be done better than a great general at three thousand miles distance." The man broke for cowardice at Minden a "great general"! Splendid! He points out that Germain, snug in Whitehall, knows nothing whatever about the rigors of the winter in Canada, and as for the charge that his failure to attack Ticonderoga has set free troops to annoy Howe, he says, "If your Lordship means the affair of Trenton, a little military reasoning might prove the rebels required no reinforcement, from any part, to cut off that corps, if unconnected and alone; the force they employed upon that occasion clearly demonstrated this. Without my troubling your Lordship with any reasoning upon the matter, a little attention to the strength of General Howe's army will, I hope, convince you that, connected and in a situation to support each other, they might have defended themselves, tho' all the rebels from Ticonderoga had reinforced Mr. Washington's army." He rubs this point in so forcibly that even Germain must have been able to see it.

He says of the operations of the previous autumn:

> "In spight of every obstruction a greater marine was built and equipt; a greater marine force was defeated than had ever appeared on that Lake (Champlain) before; two Brigades were taken across and remained at Crown Point till the 2nd of November, for the sole purpose of drawing off the attention

of the Rebels from Mr. Howe and to Facilitate his victories (during) the remainder of the campaign. Nature had then put an end to ours. His winter quarters, I confess, I had never thought of covering: it was supposed, 'tis true, that was the army favoured by your Lordship, and in which you put your trust, yet I never could imagine, while an army to the southward found it necessary to finish their campaign, and to go into winter-quarters, Your Lordship could possibly expect Troops so far North should continue their operations, lest Mr. Howe should be disturbed during the winter, if that great army near the sea-coast had their quarters insulted [*i. e.,* assaulted] what could Your Lordship expect would be the fate of a small corps detached into the heart of the rebel country in that season? For these things I am so severely censured by Your Lordship."

Sir Guy then proceeds to add that Burgoyne shall have every possible assistance that he could give him. He waives the manner in which he has been treated and says that his one wish is "for the prosperity of the King's Arms." In his next letter of May twenty-second Sir Guy dots the *i*'s. He has been treated with "Slight, Disregard and Censure." This he attributes to Germain's "private Enmity."

In his reply of July twenty-fifth, "Geo. Germain," as he always signed himself, takes shelter behind the King. He is only a mouthpiece. It was the King's wishes that Burgoyne should have the command. "It would ill become my situation to enter into an ill-humoured altercation with you. . . . I think it proper to assure you that whatever reports you may have heard of my having any personal dislike to you are without the least foundation."

It is not necessary to quote any more. Briefly, Lord George had treated Sir Guy very scurvily and, when taxed with it, wriggled like the worm he was. No doubt in all countries and at all times soldiers have been so treated, when things went wrong, by the civilian ministers at home.

Burgoyne, as stated above, assumed that the chief object of this expedition was to "effect a junction" with Howe. And Germain in his letter of March twenty-sixth to Carleton said that he was going to write to Howe to this effect "by the first Packet." Howe, who saw a copy of this letter, said in a Committee of the House of Commons, "the letter intended to have been written to me by the first packet and which was probably to have contained some instructions, was never sent." The anonymous author of *Letters to a Nobleman,* obviously one of Germain's creatures, if not Germain himself, definitely charges Howe with neglecting Lord George's instructions to support the Northern Army and adds that "by that neglect he sacrificed a British army and involved his country in a degree of disgrace it never before had experienced." Howe, in answering this charge in his *Observations* upon the *Letters to a Nobleman,* repeats his denial that he ever received any such instructions. He certainly did not receive any. It is true that a despatch giving detailed instructions to Howe was duly written, but it was not sent by the first packet, or any other packet. Why?

Well, this remained a mystery until it was elucidated by Lord E. Fitzmaurice in his *Life of Lord Shelburne.* He quotes a memorandum by Lord Shelburne who wrote that, though it "might appear incredible," the explanation was as follows: "Lord George having among other peculiarities a particular aversion to be put out of his way on any occasion, had arranged to call at his office on his way to the country in order to sign the despatches; but as those addressed to Howe had not been 'fair copied' and he was not disposed to be balked of his projected visit into Kent,* they were not signed then and were forgotten on his return to town."

Sir George Trevelyan thinks that what with secretaries and clerks it is not possible that this should have happened. But the same story is told, in a slightly different form, in the Knox Manuscripts. William Knox was Under Secretary in the Colonial Department. When Burgoyne, on his return after Saratoga to England, demanded an investigation, Knox, who was told off to make the best case he could for his chief, Lord George, wrote, "There certainly was a weak place in Lord Sackville's† defence which was the want of an official communication to Howe of the plan and Burgoyne's instructions, with orders for his co-operation." After Burgoyne had been appointed and the necessary documents were being drawn up, he goes on: "When all was prepared and I had them to compare and make up, Lord Sackville came down to the office on his way to Stoneland, when I observed to him that there was no letter to Howe to acquaint him with the plan or what was expected of him in consequence of it. His Lordship stared and D'Oyly‡ started but said he would in a moment write a few lines. 'So,' says Lord Sackville, 'my poor horses must stand in the street all the time, and I shan't be to my time anywhere.' D'Oyly then said he had better go, and he would write

*Sussex, not Kent.

†The title which he got later as a reward for his blundering.

‡Deputy Secretary.

from himself to Howe and enclose copies of Burgoyne's instructions which would tell him all that he would want to know and with this his Lordship was satisfied as it enabled him to keep his time, for he would never bear delay or disappointment." This, it will be seen, is practically an elaboration of Lord Shelburne's memorandum. Lord George should have waited five minutes, for it is pretty obvious that D'Oyly forgot all about it. Howe, as we have seen, definitely denied that he had ever received any such letter, and when the question of the Inquiry came up, Knox urged D'Oyly to get a copy from Howe, "who had the original." But D'Oyly would not ask Howe for a copy, obviously because he knew that the original had never left Whitehall.

So my Lord George Germain, who ruined the chances of a magnificent British victory at Minden by *not* being in a hurry to advance against the enemy, also ruined any prospect Burgoyne might have had of being successful by *being* in a hurry—to spend a week-end in Sussex. We have some statues in London which it is hard to justify. There is one—if you want a good laugh, you should go and see it—in Camden Town of that great, that noble character, Mr. Cobden, who heartily approved of child-labor in factories because it was good for competition and kept the children out of mischief. There is another, in the Embankment Gardens, of Sir Wilfrid Lawson, who made very bad jokes in Parliament and wanted to make England dry. But we have in London no statue of Lord George Germain. He did so much to lose the American War that surely there ought to be one of him in the United States, with emblematical figures of Cowardice and Stupidity on either side of him as supporters, and a frieze showing the British Cavalry await-

Charles James Fox

Painted by Sir Joshua Reynolds. From a print in possession of Messrs. T. H. Parker, 12a, Berkeley Street, London, W. 1

ing the order to advance. On second thoughts, no. I apologize. For nobody would like to erect a memorial to a Poltroon.

Burgoyne before he sailed for Quebec was offered by King George a knighthood, that of the Bath. He wisely refused it. He was also given some very sound advice by his old friend in the House and at the gaming-table, Charles James Fox. When Gentleman Johnny remarked at Arthur's that he hoped to bring America to her senses before he returned, Fox is reported to have said, in a very Cassandra-like manner, "Burgoyne, be not over-sanguine in your expectations: I believe when next you return to England you will be a prisoner on parole."

## CHAPTER VI

### THE RIVAL FORCES

BEFORE landing with John Burgoyne at Quebec, let us consider what was the military purpose of the expedition from Canada and why was the Hudson route taken? It has been generally assumed that it was a scheme to split the rebellion in two, in other words to disunite the United States. It is all very well to talk airily of holding the line of the Hudson, and the strategical* advantages thereof. It is a very long line, and to hold it, even by a series of blockhouses, would have immobilized a very large number of troops and have required a fleet of gunboats. Germain's words were, "With a view of quelling the rebellion as soon as possible it has become highly necessary that the most speedy junction of the two armies should be effected." That is to say he wanted the troops in Canada to join Howe's army in the main theater of operations, to use a modern phrase. But, if speed was necessary, why were not the troops in Canada taken south by sea? For two reasons, first because King George (and what Majesty said † went in those days) "greatly disliked the idea," second because Whitehall was uneasy about another possible attack upon Canada. And then there was the magic of the

---

*By the way the words "strategy" and "strategical" only date back to the beginning of the nineteenth century.

†See page 112.

name Ticonderoga, a name familiar even to the gamblers at White's and the idlers in the coffee houses. Just as Belgium was destined by nature to be the cockpit of Europe, so does Ticonderoga always crop up in the history books when there was fighting in North America. In the French and Indian wars it had always been a jumping-off place for invasions of Canada by land. Germain considered it as "one of those posts necessary to possess upon the frontier in order to secure this province [*i. e.*, Quebec] from future insults." So one may safely say that the object of the expedition was to kill two birds with one stone, to get Burgoyne's force down into the fighting country and by so doing to prevent another invasion of Canada.

Burgoyne arrived in Quebec on May 6, 1777. The force he was to command consisted of about eight thousand men: four thousand British, 9th, 20th, 21st, 24th, 47th, 53rd and 62nd Regiments; three thousand Germans; one hundred and fifty Canadians, and five hundred Red Indians. He had also a large artillery train. Some critics said that he was overartilleried.

The Noble Red Man is a myth. Two people are chiefly responsible for this fable of his nobility. First Pope, with the fine passage which begins:

> Lo, the poor Indian! whose untutored mind
> Sees God in clouds, or hears Him in the wind,

and which ends:

> To be, contents his natural desire,
> He asks no angel's wing, no seraph's fire,
> But thinks, admitted to that equal sky,
> His faithful dog shall bear him company.

The other is Fenimore Cooper with the romances which have caused so many boys to dress up in war-paint and tomahawk their little sisters' dolls. The Noble Red Indian of the late eighteenth century certainly did not ask for "Seraph's Fire," unless there was any particular brand of rum of the period so called. What Mr. J. W. Steele, a great authority on the Indians, said of the descendants may equally be said of the ancestors: "Brave only in superior numbers or in ambush, honest only in being a consummate hypocrite, merry only at the sight of suffering inflicted by his own hand, friendly only through cunning and hospitable never, and above all sublimely mendacious and a liar always, the Indian as he really is to those who, unfortunately, know him, seems poor material out of which to manufacture a hero or frame a romance. Mollified by semi-annual gifts and pacified by periodical talks about the Great Father and blarney about brothers, he has only the one redeeming fact upon his record, that he has never been tamed and never been a servant. Neither has the hyena."

Those who came in contact with the Indians of Burgoyne's day give a most unpleasant account of them. The description which Hadden gives of them in their war-paint reminds one of nothing so much as that delightful creature the King in his personation of The King's Camelopard or The Royal Nonesuch! ! ! He, it will be remembered, was "painted all over, ring-streaked and striped, all sorts of colours, as splendid as a rainbow. And—but never mind the rest of his outfit, it was just wild, but it was awful funny."

Lieutenant Hadden is less delicate than Huckleberry Finn. He gives curious details, which can not be quoted, of their costume and ornaments. The Indian ladies, he says, "cover themselves with grease as a defense against the Mousqueato's and other Flies: this makes them far from tempting." They had, too, the odd notion that it was fashionable to turn their feet inward, so as to make the toes of each foot meet. Another English observer of the same date was particularly struck by the Indian style of dancing. "Antick Postures and very high Bounds that would puzzle our best Harlequins to imitate." He found their war-cries offensive, "the most horrid Song or Cry that ever I heard, the Sound would strike Terror into the stoutest Heart."

A howl went up against the employment of Indians; what Chatham said, later on, is typical. "We had sullied and tarnished the arms of Britain for ever by employing savages in our service, by drawing them up in a British line, and mixing the scalping-knife and the tomahawk with the sword and the fire-lock." He also denied that they had been employed against the French. It is rather sad to read that when Lord Bute heard of this denial he exclaimed, "Good Heavens, did Pitt really deny it? Is it possible? Why, I have here lying by me letters of his that sing Peans on the advantages we gained by employing Indians in the Canadian war."* And, as a matter of fact, America was equally guilty in this respect with Britain. The Second Provincial Congress in April, 1775, sent an address to Johoiakin Mothskin (delightful name!) "and the rest of our brethren the Indians, natives of Stockbridge," urging them to "take up the hatchet" in the cause of Liberty and empowering Colonel

*On the authority of Bute's daughter, Lady Louisa Stuart, quoted in *A Prime Minister and his Son.* There is a pleasant caricature showing a Red Indian and George III each gnawing an end of the same human thigh bone. It is entitled "The Allies—par nobile Fratrum."

Paterson to present "each of you that have enlisted in the service with a blanket and a ribbon as a testimony of our affection." News of this reached England and on July twenty-fourth Dartmouth wrote to Colonel Guy Johnson instructing him "to take such steps as may induce them [the Indians] to take up the Hatchet against His Majesty's Rebellious Subjects in America." These Stockbridge Indians were queer folk. Some of them took the very un-Indian step of asking Congress to take care of their money, lest they should spend it on strong drink. The Mohawk Indians were also approached, though it is doubtful if one argument used, the sins of papistry and idolatry as introduced into Canada, had any great weight with them. Washington himself, in July, 1775, saw a Chief of the Caghnewaga tribe, of the Montreal neighborhood, who said his people would give all the help they could; and in June, 1776, a Committee recommended that "the Indians shall be allowed £50 for any prisoner they shall take at Niagara," and in August of the same year a Mr. Edwards was empowered formally to enlist Stockbridge Indians "and to indulge them with liberty to join this [Washington's] or the Northern Army, or both, as their inclination may lead." So, as far as the employment of Indians goes, it would seem that England and America were "all square." But the Indians for whom Burgoyne had stipulated in his *Thoughts* were to prove, as we shall see, a very sorry corps, worse, in fact, at a pinch, than useless.

The Germans have very often in history been hirelings. In the eighteenth century they would be farmed out as soldiers by their overlords, just as, in more modern times, they would hire themselves out as waiters, and very good waiters too. The subsidies that England used to pay for German troops kept many a petty German court in pumpernickel, hams, sausages, sauerkraut, Rhenish wine and mistresses. The German princes were quite frank about it. The Landgrave of Hesse, in 1777, complained bitterly that a certain "Colonel M." had not lost a single man from his corps. His Hessians must remember that they were Hessians and fight to the last man. Why? Because, of course, more recruits, each worth thirty marks when recruited, and another thirty when killed, wounded or captured, would then be wanted.* And most desirable too, seeing that he (the Landgrave) had just engaged La Signora F. to come from Italy at a salary of five hundred guineas a year to—well, he does not say for what, perhaps to teach him Italian. The Duke of Brunswick was terribly distressed when a number of his soldiers were taken prisoners. He hoped that the British Government would not for one moment dream of having them exchanged and sent back to Germany—this would have a most unpleasant effect and create an unfortunate sensation. If they *must* come back, for heaven's sake let them recuperate in, say, the Isle of Wight, be joined there by other German recruits—and then sent back to fight in America. Most of the German officers could just write, knew no English and had but a smattering of indifferent French. Riedesel, for example, began a letter, *"Le courier qui prendra cette lettre avec."* As one of them said, "We are neither fish nor flesh."

They were indeed a nondescript crowd. One of them wrote that his fellow recruits were "a runaway son of

*Nothing was paid for deserters. No doubt the Hessians were sternly commanded to remember that the blackest crime of which a soldier can be guilty is desertion.

the Muses from Jena, a bankrupt tradesman from Vienna, a fringe-maker from Hanover, a discharged secretary from the Post Office at Gotha, a monk from Wurzburg, an upper steward from Meningen, a Prussian sergeant of Hussars, and a cashiered Hessian Major." It is difficult to imagine a more awkward squad.

The best thing about the Brunswickers and Hessians was their love for animals and their admiration of the American ladies, of whom one of them said, "There is scarcely one in ten who is not both beautiful and elegant." Their simplicity also is to be remarked. A certain Colonel von Heeringen, said, "Lord Stirling is not really a Lord and General Putnam is a butcher." This he could not understand. They were certainly solid troops, too solid for the backwoods, with their "haversacks, long-skirted coats, long swords, enormous canteens, grenadier caps with heavy brass ornaments, much hair-powder and pomatum and great clumsy queues." They were also stolid. Cresswell, who saw the Hessians in 1777 at New York, writes, "One of their Corporals ran the Gauntlet eight times through the Regiment, he had upwards of 2,000 lashes which he bore with the greatest resolution and firmness, not a single muscle of his face discomposed all the time. They appear to be a set of cruel, unfeeling people."

The two chief German officers with Burgoyne were General Riedesel (not forgetting Mrs. General Riedesel of whom more anon) and Colonel Breyman. The principal English officers were Major-General Phillips, a very distinguished gunner, and Brigadier-Generals Fraser and Hamilton. The Adjutant-General was Colonel Kingston, the Quartermaster-General Colonel Money. Burgoyne's aides-de-camp were Sir Francis Clark (killed at Saratoga) and Lord Petersham. Major Lord Balcarres commanded the Light Infantry and Major Acland* the Grenadiers. Phillips was second in command, so appointed by Sir Guy Carleton, who, in spite of the natural mortification he felt at being passed over in favor of Burgoyne, did, in the most loyal and self-forgetting manner, everything he possibly could to make the expedition a success. Lord North wrote to him, August 3, 1777, "All the letters from General Burgoyne and the other officers of the northern army are full of the warmest acknowledgements of the cordial, zealous and effectual assistance they have received from you." North was a gentleman; Germain was not.

At a very early date Burgoyne felt uneasy about the Canadians. On May fourteenth he wrote to Germain:

> "I cannot speak with much confidence of the military assistance I am to look for from the Canadians. The only corps yet instituted, or that I am informed can at present be instituted, are three Independent Companies of 100 men each, officered by Seigneurs of the country who are well-chosen; but they have not been able to engage many volunteers. The men are chiefly drafted from the militia, according to a late regulation of the Legislative Council. Those I have yet seen afford no promise of arms—awkward,

*The Acland family is a very good example of those county families which, from Cumberland to Cornwall, were the backbone of England. The names of such families do not very often appear in the history books. They do not buy peerages; they have never made fortunes when England has been at war; they do not cozen and cheat and swindle; they have never (they would say "Thank heaven!") produced a Waw or a Shells, they have sometimes lived hard, and sometimes drunk hard, but they have always sent their cadets into the army and their bones lie buried all over the world. The Aaronsteins and Isaacsteins who have bought many of their estates will, perhaps, in time learn to follow their example.

ignorant, disinclined to the service, and spiritless. Various reasons are assigned for this change in the natives since the time of the French government. It may partly be owing to a disuse of arms, but I believe principally to the unpopularity of their Seigneurs, and to the poison which the emissaries of the rebels have thrown into their mind."

He ends with a handsome and well-deserved compliment to Sir Guy:

"I should think myself deficient in justice and in honour, were I to close my letter without mentioning the sense I entertain of General Carleton's conduct; that he was anxiously desirous of leading the military operations out of the province, is easily to be discerned; but his deference to His Majesty's decision, and his zeal to give effect to his measures in my hands, are equally manifest, exemplary and satisfactory."

And on May twenty-sixth he writes from Montreal on the same subject (the Canadians) to Carleton, stating that the men are deserting* already and adding:

"When the plan of my expedition was framed, the ideas of Government respecting armed Canadians went to six times the number. . . . Without that dependence I have reason to believe the proportion of Regulars would have been larger. To remedy in some measure this deficiency I have to propose to your Excellency a Corvée of a thousand men to attend the expedi-

*Later on some of them who were captured at Bennington actually enlisted in Moses Hazen's Regiment, at Albany.

tion for a limited time for the purposes of labour and transport."

Carleton in his reply from Quebec of May twenty-ninth could not resist the temptation to get in a dig at the Minister who had treated him so scurvily:

"The Desertion you give me Notice of in your Letter does not surprise me, it has been the same here, and was no more than what I expected; if Government laid any great stress upon assistance from the Canadians, for carrying on the present war, it surely was not upon Information proceeding from me. Experience might have taught them and it did not require that to convince me, these People had been governed with too loose a Rein for many years, and had imbibed too much of the American spirit of Licentiousness and Independence, administered by a numerous and turbulent Faction here, to be suddenly restored to a proper and desirable Subordination."

But with the exception of Canadian and Indian, *Arcades ambo*, it was a fine army and started with every prospect of success.

The Americans began the War of Independence with no army. This may seem, and is, a drawback so far as fighting goes, but on the other hand it has its compensations. If a nation has no army it also has no preconceived, dry-as-dust, text-book ideas about Strategy and Tactics. These two branches of military study, about which thousands and thousands of books have been written, are, fundamentally, horse sense, and in that the Americans were not lacking, especially those who did not live in the towns. When you are painfully aware that the retention of your scalp and your daily dinner depend upon your ability to know instinctively when it is the right moment to come in out of the rain and upon your skill with your musket, you imperceptibly acquire a knowledge of strategy and tactics in daily life which are excellent foundations upon which to work when it comes to war. You lack discipline, of course, but the Drill Sergeant will soon put *that* right. The United States in due course got their Drill Sergeant in the shape of that excellent old German Baron von Steuben, who in himself alone was worth any number of the Hessian and Brunswick regiments which fought on the other side. The Boers in South Africa were in much the same case as the Americans, and the Boer War was not won in a month. I was told by a friend who served in it, and who may perhaps have been pulling my leg, that their *corps d'élite,* their Grenadier Guards as it were, were clad in seedy old top-coats and had on their heads even seedier toppers. But they were excellent shots.

That remarkable observer, Robert Jackson, who visited America during the war and who sized up the nations of the world, ancient and modern, from a recruiting officer's point of view, has some very sensible reflections on the "Military Character of the People of North America." Briefly—for he was a long-winded old gentleman and when on his travels was always stopping to make notes about feminine "limbs"—his remarks are that the Americans had no tactics, or knowledge of maneuver, no discipline, which they abhorred, and would rather shoot from cover than in ranks in the open. On the other hand, they were wonderfully expert marksmen, far more so than the British and Germans opposed to them. They had great knowledge of wood-craft and of the nature of their country and consequently made excellent "partizans" or "guerrillas." They were, in short, Irregulars. Wars between Irregulars and Regulars, between Common Sense and Text-Books, are always interesting to read of, and as a rule take a long time to come to an end. It took the Russians about sixty years' continuous fighting to subdue the mountaineers of the Frosty Caucasus, and I do not think it would have been safe to ask any Russian general of that day, "Is the Caucasian played out?"

But the general opinion in England at the time, in spite of Bunker Hill, was that the Americans would put up but a poor fight. Wolfe had given them a very bad character; in August, 1758, he wrote: "There is no depending on them in action. They fall down dead in their own dirt and desert by battalions, officers and all. Such rascals as these are rather an encumbrance than any real strength to an army." The Sandwich man followed suit. "They are raw, undisciplined, cowardly men." I have already quoted Charles Lee's words of warning; in another letter, written before the outbreak of hostilities to Burke, he said: "If I have any judgment the people of New England are this day more calculated to form irresistible conquering armies than any people on the face of the globe. Even the appearance of their individuals is totally changed since first I knew them. Formerly they had a slouching, slovenly air. Now every peasant has his hair smartly dressed, is erect and soldier-like in his air and gait. . . . I shall say nothing of the formidable numbers of Light Infantry, undoubtedly the best in the world, which their back provinces can produce. In short, it is my persuasion that, should the people of England be infatuated enough to suffer their misrulers to proceed in their measures, this country may scorch her fingers but they themselves will perish in the flames."

Barré, who had served (and lost an eye) in North America, said in the House he had seen as good regiments of Militia there as ever he had seen of Regulars. He also brought out the democratic nature of the Americans by a quaint anecdote; "I remember an officer of my acquaintance going to pay his respects to the commanding officer of a fort: when he came to it he sent for the barber to shave him, in order that he might clean himself and look a little smart before he waited on his Excellency. He was somewhat in a hurry, and desired the barber to make haste, for he had some business with the commanding officer of the fort. The barber said, 'Sir, you need not lose your time, you may as well disclose your business now, for I am the commanding officer.' "

The British Army has never been democratic to this extent. Which has often puzzled people. A few years ago a Member of Parliament, a native of a quarter of the globe not so very far from that island "where only man is vile," when the question of Army Agents was under discussion in the House of Commons, asked indignantly, "Is British Officer too proud, too aristocratic to go for pay to Post Office Savings Bank?" The eighteenth-century Mr. Hansard would, I think, have interpolated "Here a great roar of laughter," for I do not think we are likely to see, at all events in my time, the Officers of His Majesty's Guards queueing up outside a post-office in order to draw their pay.

The drawback of course to the American system of engaging troops was that when the men's period of service was up they melted away. But for this, and the weather, Arnold might have captured Quebec. To quote Mr. Harris Dickson, "Minute-men volunteered, quite a bunch of them. They came in a minute and stayed about a minute. Every day Washington had a different army from the one of yesterday and generally smaller." Why? Because the minute-man "hiked home." I think Washington's most amazing feat was that he created an army; apart from his services in the field he was the Carnot of the United States and did for them what Lord Kitchener by the mere magic of his name did for England.

Washington's *Official Letters to the Honourable American Congress* give us a vivid idea of his difficulties. In the earlier letters there is almost on every page an allusion to scarcity of powder, arms, tents, camp-kettles, money, clothing and blankets. The men are in a state of nakedness, he has no accurate maps, the men have to be sent to their homes without their pay, and some of them nearly mutinied for this reason; and "limited enlistment" is a curse. He writes on December 20, 1776, "Ten days more will put an end to the existence of our army." His officers, too, were a source of worry; one Brigadier was "blind and deaf," and "if I send an officer to collect the sick and scattered of his regiment, it is 10 to 1 but he neglects his duty, goes home on pleasure or business, and the next I hear of him is that he has resigned—furloughs are no more attended to than if there was no limitation of time." The militia is a "broken staff" consisting of "men just dragged from the tender scenes of domestic life, unaccustomed to the din of arms, but accustomed to unbounded freedom and no control." They not only deserted, but set a fashion in desertion. Another worry to Washington was provided by the French soldiers of fortune who came in swarms from "Old France and the Islands," hoping to get commissions. "You cannot conceive what a weight these kind of people are upon the service and upon me in particular. Few of them have any knowledge of the branches which they profess to understand and those that have are entirely useless as officers from their ignorance of the English language." And what is more, they declined to learn it. On the top of this Howe had, for once, two bright ideas. He offered sixteen dollars "bounty" to any man who would desert, and tried to get counterfeit money into circulation among the Americans, just as William Pitt did with the forged assignats in 1795, at the time of the projected expedition to Quiberon. Washington had, indeed, a very difficult task.

But Burgoyne, whom we have left sharpening his quill pen and perhaps, in his leisure, preparing Siege Operations against some Mrs. Commissary, also had his difficulties, one of them of a very serious character indeed. On May nineteenth he wrote from Montreal to General Harvey: he is much pleased with the exertions made during the winter, everything is well forward, and the troops are in health and good spirits. Sir Guy Carleton has done everything he possibly could to assist, though it is evident that "he thinks he has some cause of resentment for the general tenor of treatment he has received from some of the ministers."

He proceeds:

> "My intention is, during my advance to Ticonderoga, and siege of that post, for a siege I apprehend it must be, to give all possible jealousy on the side of Connecticut. If I can by manœuvre make them suspect that after the reduction of Ticonderoga my views are pointed that way, it may make the Connecticut forces very cautious of leaving their own frontiers, and much facilitate my progress to Albany. I mention

this intention only to Lord George and yourself, and I do it lest from any intelligence of my motions that may reach England indirectly, it should be supposed I have suffered myself to be diverted from the main object of my orders. The King and his Majesty's ministers may rest assured that whatever demonstrations I may endeavour to impose upon the enemy, I shall really make no movement that can procrastinate my progress to Albany."

He then adds the very significant paragraph:

"One thing more occurs. I had the surprise and mortification to find a paper handed about at Montreal, publishing the whole design of the campaign, almost as accurately as if it had been copied from the Secretary of State's letter. My own caution has been such that not a man in my own family* has been let into the secret. Sir Guy Carleton's I am confident, has been equal; I am therefore led to doubt whether imprudence has not been committed from private letters from England, and wish you would ask my friend D'Oyley,† to whom my very affectionate compliments, whether there is any person within the line of ministerial communication that he can suspect to be so unguarded? It is not of great consequence here, except as far as regards St. Leger's expedition; but such a trick may be of most prejudicial consequence in other cases, and should be guarded against."

Though Burgoyne tends to make light of it, probably guessing who was responsible, this was very serious in-

*i. e., staff. See Note on page 87.
†A colleague of "lownging" John Pownall.

deed. It is confirmed by Lieutenant Anburey who, writing to a friend, says: "We have more dangerous enemies at home* than any we have to encounter abroad; for all transactions that are to take place are fully known before they are given out in orders, and I make no doubt you will be as much surprised as the General was when I tell you that the whole operations of the ensuing campaign were canvassed for several days before he arrived, while he supposed that he was communicating an entire secret." In fact, everybody appears to have known the whole plan of campaign—except Sir William Howe!

How did this secret come out? Well, it is not difficult to guess. Statesmen at this date were extraordinarily casual. It is related of Lord North, that easy-going nobleman, that he mislaid a most important document. Search was made in all likely places, but in vain. Finally it was found lying on the floor of his water closet. To quote the old cliché: "Comment is superfluous." It might be added that Queen Victoria's Lord Salisbury was quite as casual as Lord North. It is told of him that when asked to return a most secret document, he replied that he thought he had left it in the pocket of an old coat which he had given away.

On the same day, May twelfth, that Burgoyne wrote to General Harvey, he also wrote to Germain reporting progress and stating his intentions:

> "The only delay is occasioned by the impracticability of the roads, owing to late extraordinary heavy rains, and this difficulty will be speedily removed, by

*General Canonge, writing of Hannibal, said exactly the same thing: "Hannibal had two enemies, Rome and Carthage."

exerting the services of the parishes as soon as the weather clears. In the mean time I am employing every means that water carriage will admit for drawing the troops and stores towards their point. I trust, I shall have vessels sufficient to move the army and stores together, and in that case, will take post at once, within sight of Ticonderoga, and only make use of Crown Point for my hospital and magazine. A continuation of intelligence from different spies and deserters, confirms the design of the enemy to dispute Ticonderoga vigorously. They are also building bowgallies at Fort George, for the defence of that Lake, etc., fortifying on the road to Skenesborough. It is consigned to the New England colonies to furnish supplies of men and provision to oppose the progress of my army, and they have undertaken the task, upon condition of being exempt from supplying Mr. Washington's main army. It is my design, while advancing to Ticonderoga, and during the siege of that post, for a siege I apprehend it must be, to give all possible jealousy on the side of Connecticut."

He then repeats what he had said in his letter to General Harvey, quoted above.

It will be remembered that Burgoyne in his *Thoughts* suggested an expedition by Lake Ontario and Oswego to the Mohawk River as a diversion.* It finally was decided that this was to be more than a "diversion," it was intended that it should join Burgoyne and Howe at Albany. Before starting with Gentleman Johnny for Ticonderoga, let us see how this diversion fared. Fort Stanwix, better known as Fort Schuyler, was the key to

*See page 112.

the Mohawk Valley and when St. Leger set out to capture it, it had a garrison of some seven hundred and fifty men under Colonel Gansevoort. St. Leger had a mixed force of British, Canadians, Germans and Indians, in all about seventeen hundred men. The Indians, amounting to seven hundred or so, were led by a chief called Thayendanegea, or Joseph Brant. Colonel Gansevoort's position was not happy. He was surrounded by "inimical Indians," his stock of powder was low, most of the beef had gone bad and many of the bullets did not "suit the fire-locks." And, a minor point, the garrison had no flag, but this was easily remedied by making one out of odd scraps of red, white and blue cloth.* His chief strength was the fort itself, a square, log-built, tough proposition, and so St. Leger found it. He arrived before it on August third—he had left Montreal in the middle of June—and the first thing he did was to send in a proclamation. The hand that drew this up was the hand of St. Leger, but the voice was the voice of Burgoyne;† witness this grandiloquent period; if the garrison would not surrender, "the messengers of justice and of wrath await them in the field; and devastation, famine and every concomitant horror that a reluctant but indispensable prosecution of military duty must occasion will bar the way to their return." No notice was taken of this, the siege began, and the Indians spent the first night yelling in the most discordant and unpleasant manner. But forts are not taken by yells.

Meanwhile General Herkimer marched one thousand

*A woman's petticoat, the soldiers' shirts and Colonel Gansevoort's military cloak all contributed to this. I think I am right in saying that it was at Fort Stanwix that Old Glory first saw service. It is a far cry from Fort Stanwix to Château Thierry.

†See page 145.

men to its relief. They walked straight into an ambush. Herkimer was wounded but, propped up against a tree and calmly smoking his pipe, continued to direct the fight. The garrison, hearing the firing, sallied out in support of Herkimer, and the Battle of Oriskany must be regarded as a draw. The fort was not relieved; on the other hand St. Leger did not take it, though he wrote a long despatch to Burgoyne, describing the rout of the relieving force, but rather evading the main issue. Herkimer was a gallant, pious soldier. He died a few days later, reading the Bible and smoking his pipe to the end. Congress resolved to erect a monument to his memory. I believe that this has not yet been done.

St. Leger now sent an officer to parley with Gansevoort and, the wish being father to the thought, announced, "General Burgoyne is now in Albany." He anticipated matters. Burgoyne certainly *was* in Albany some weeks later—but as a prisoner. Negotiations were broken off, the siege was continued, but suddenly on August twenty-second St. Leger and his men made their way back to Oswego, defeated, not on the battle-field but by Dame Rumor. It arose in this way. One John Joost Schuyler, known as Hon-Yost (which I suppose is the right pronunciation of his name), half-gipsy and half-idiot, had been captured while spying for St. Leger—to employ an idiot as a spy is the act of an idiot—and had been promised his life by Arnold provided he would spread tales among St. Leger's Indians that the Americans were coming in great force. The Indians, who had that reverence for idiots which they so often inspire,* asked Hon-Yost how many Americans there were? He

*Germain, for instance, had his admirers.

pointed vaguely to the leaves of the trees and probably made a sound like a million. In any case it was good enough for the Red Men, and they returned to their wigwams. St. Leger returned to Montreal. He stopped on the way at Oswego to write a lengthy despatch to Burgoyne. In this he blamed everybody but himself. His miscarriage was due to the "slackness of the Messasagoes," the toughness of the sod-work of the fort, false news that Burgoyne's army was cut to pieces, and the treachery of the Indians, who "seized the officers' liquor and cloaths." The real truth seems to be that St. Leger was not equal to his task.

# CHAPTER VII

## PAPER WARFARE AND TICONDEROGA

LADIES first. Before proceeding with John Burgoyne, let us devote a little space to Frau Generalin, or Mrs. General, Baroness Riedesel. She was a very remarkable character, more so than her husband. He, when quite a boy, was with the Hessians, who, in their Hessian boots, fought for England in the Seven Years' War. Like Lord George Sackville, he was at Minden. Unlike Lord George Sackville his gallantry and intelligence in that battle won him the approval of the Duke of Brunswick. He was, too, a thrifty fellow, and while in North America saved fifteen thousand thalers out of his forage allowance. The *Letters and Reports* of this couple were first published in Berlin in 1800. They cover the period 1776 to 1783, and give a lively picture of military life at this time. But the General is not so lively as his wife. Doctor Johnson is supposed to have said, "A man who does not mind his belly will not mind anything." This was the General's motto; he is always talking of food and of the price of food. When on board ship on his way to England in March, 1776, he mentions, with contempt, the English breakfast of tea and bread-and-butter. But he notes with approval that at dinner six toasts were nightly drunk, ranging from a Health to His Majesty King George III to "A Good Voyage to America." He drank nothing but wine on the voyage, nor can one blame him, for he speaks of the water as *stinkend.* When he reached Canada the first thing he did was to grumble that though there was plenty of meat and fowls and milk, there were no vegetables.

His wife is much more entertaining. She went with her three children from Wolfenbuttel to England, intending to follow her husband to Quebec, in spite of the fact that she had been told that there was nothing to eat there but horse-flesh and oats. There are curious little notes about her life in England. In London she finds everything very dear, including the Queen's oculist, who charged her three guineas for putting something into her eyes which hurt them horribly. She sees the King and Queen in St. James's Park, where, daily, thousands of people would take the air. But Bristol, to which she paid a visit, is not so pleasant. Looking out of the window of her lodgings she sees two sailors "stripped to the buff" (what *is* one's buff?) "pounding each other." And worse was to come. Her foreign dress excited remark, and very unpleasant remark too. When she took her walks abroad the simple, light-hearted Bristolians would follow her, point at her with the finger and pronounce the brief, yet damning, verdict: "French whore." This is, I believe, what they call in this engaging city, treating people "Bristol fash," *i.e., à la mode de Bristol.*

But a great honor awaited her when she got back to London. Lady George Germain presented her at court, the Queen asked her in a queenly way if she liked sea-voyages and the King kissed her, "At which I became fiery red, it was so sudden." When she reaches Canada she is very critical about the ladies' clothes, for they wore badly-cut and dirty dresses. She also gives interesting

The Baroness Riedesel

details about their petticoats, vests and other intimate garments which I will briefly dismiss as *lingerie,* trusting that this is the right word. She took her three children with her and there is a charming touch when the General, travel-stained and begrimed, first met them. One of the little girls, who had no recollection of her father but was very familiar with a portrait of him all shining and resplendent in uniform, burst into tears, with, "No, no, this is a nasty papa, my papa is pretty."

Mrs. General liked bear's flesh, and notes the interesting fact that the smell of burning cedar-branches keep away flies but is also, so she had been told, a frequent cause of miscarriages. One has heard of *Desire under the Elms,* but Miscarriage under the Cedars is quite a new idea.

The Baroness evidently did not like Burgoyne; she says that he "lost his head," which is not true, and to anticipate matters she notes with pain that just before the surrender "he was very merry and spent the whole night singing and drinking and amusing himself with the wife of a Commissary who was his mistress and, who like him was fond of champagne." Another German, von Eelking, corroborates this: he says, practically, "There was a sound of revelry by night," champagne flowed like water and "by the General's side sat the beautiful wife of a Commissary who was his mistress." And a Brunswicker complained that Burgoyne was inordinately fond of "rattle-snake soup." This does not sound like a delicacy, but Germans have always had odd tastes in the way of food, witness the German baron in Smollett who thought asafetida excellent.

If anybody feels inclined to blame Handsome Jack for this philandering, let me tell him a story which, I think, has never before appeared in print, of one of the possible reasons why Napoleon lost Waterloo, a riddle which has puzzled military historians from 1815 onward to the present day. A friend of mine, visiting the battlefield many years ago, got into conversation with an aged Belgian peasant. He assured my friend with pride that the real reason the Emperor did not win the battle was that he had spent the hours before the action, not in making preparations for his first (and last) encounter with the "Sepoy General," but in chatting and gallivanting with the speaker's grandmother. The Belgian troops did not behave well at Waterloo. They showed an anxiety, laudable in citizens, but less laudable in soldiers, to know from personal observation what was happening in Brussels, so hurriedly went there to see. But we must not forget that an Englishman of some standing in John Company's service, Mr. Josh Sedley, thought it would be even better to leave Brussels altogether. Whatever the Belgians may have done, or not done, at Waterloo, this excellent lady amply atoned for her fellow countrymen's shortcomings. I would also adduce in Burgoyne's defense that Blucher, better known as Marshal Forward, when on his way to Paris, stopped at an inn, the obsequious landlord of which asked if His Excellency wanted anything. His Excellency briefly replied, "A wench." Moreover a French officer said after Vittoria to the Duke of Wellington, who was himself by no means indifferent to female charms, *"Le fait est, Monseigneur, que vous avez une armée, mais nous sommes un bordel ambulant."*

But let us leave Burgoyne the lady-killer and return to Burgoyne the soldier.

Even in those days propaganda was not unknown, and

Burgoyne produced a thundering specimen of it. It is worth quoting in full, because then one can thoroughly appreciate the delightful parody of it from the American side. Here is his manifesto, or proclamation, which was dated June twentieth at Putnam's Creek.

"By John Burgoyne, Esq.

"Lieutenant General of His Majesties Armies in America, Col. of the Queen's regiment of Light Dragoons, Governor of Fort William in North Britain, One of the representatives of the Commons of Great Britain in Parliament and Commanding an army and fleet employed in an expedition from Canada.

"The forces intrusted to my command are designed to act in concert and upon a common principle with the numerous armies and fleets which already display in every quarter of America the Power, the Justice (and when properly sought) the Mercy of the King. The cause in which the British armies are exerted, applies to the most affecting interest of the human heart, and the military servants of the crown, at first called forth for the sole purpose of Restoring the rights of the Constitution, now combine with love of their Country, and duty to their Sovereign, the other extensive incitements which spring from a true sense of the general privileges of mankind. To the eyes and ears of the temperate part of the public, and to the breasts of the suffering thousands in the Provinces, be the melancholy appeal, whether the present unnatural Rebellion has not been made a foundation for the completest system of tyranny that ever God in his displeasure suffered for a time to be exercised over a froward and stubborn generation. Arbitrary Imprisonment, confiscation of property, Persecution and torture unprecedented in the Inquisition of the Romish Church are amongst the palpable enormities that verify the affirmative. These are inflicted by Assemblys and Committees, who dare to profess themselves friends to Liberty, upon the most quiet subjects, without distinction of age or sex, for the sole crime, often for the sole suspicion, of having adhered in principle to the Government under which they were born, and to which, by every tie, Divine and human, they owe allegiance. To consummate these shocking proceedings, the profanation of religion is added to the most profligate prostitution of common reason; the consciences of men are set at naught, and multitudes are compelled, not only to bear arms, but also to swear subjection to an usurpation they abhor. Animated by these considerations, at the head of troops in the full power of health, discipline and valour, determined to strike when necessary and anxious to spare when possible, I, by these presents, invite and exhort all persons, in all places where the progress of this army may point (and by the blessing of God I will extend it), to maintain such a conduct as may justify in protecting their Lands, Habitations and Families. The intention of this address is to hold forth security, not degradation, to the country. To those whom spirit and principle may induce to partake in the glorious task of redeeming their countrymen from dungeons, and re-establishing the blessings of Legal Government, I offer encouragement and employment, and upon the first intelligence of their associating, I will find means to assist their undertakings. The domestic, the industrious, the infirm and even the timid inhabitants I am desirous to protect, provided they remain quietly in their houses, that they do not suffer their cattle to be removed, nor their corn or forage to be secreted or destroyed; that they do not break up their bridges or roads, nor by any other acts, directly or indirectly, endeavour to obstruct the operations of the King's troops, or supply or subsist those of the enemy: every species of provision brought to my camp will be paid for at an equitable rate and in solid coin. The consciousness of Christianity, my Royal Master's Clemency, and the honour of soldiership, I have dwelt upon in this invitation, and wished for more persuasive terms to give it impression; and let not people be led to disregard it by considering their distance from the immediate situation of my camp. I have but to give stretch to the Indian forces under my direction (and they amount to thousands) to overtake the hardened enemies of Great Britain and America. I consider them the same wherever they may lurk. If notwithstanding these endeavours, and sincere inclinations to effect them, the phrensy of hostility should remain, I trust I shall stand acquitted in the eyes of God and men in denouncing and executing the vengeance of the State against the wilful outcasts. The messengers of Justice and wrath await them in the field: and Devastation, famine and every concomitant horror that a reluctant, but indispensable prosecution of military duty must occasion, will bar the way to their return."

Though I like and admire John Burgoyne, Horace Walpole was right when he called this fustian a "rhodomontade in which he almost promises to cross America in a hop, step and a jump." He also alludes to the writer of it as General Hurlothrombo and General Swagger. An anonymous pamphleteer of the day puts it well: "General Burgoyne shone forth in all the tinsel splendor of enlightened absurdity." Gentleman Johnny would have been better employed in making arrangements for his supplies from Canada than in writing such high-falutin bosh. But as stated above, this manifesto had one delightful result, the counterblast and parody by Francis Hopkinson.*

"Most high, most mighty, most puissant and sublime General.

"When the forces under your command arrived at Quebec in order *to act in concert and upon a common principle with the numerous fleets and armies which already display in every quarter of America the justice and mercy of your King,* we, the reptiles of America were struck with unusual trepidation and astonishment. But what words can express the plenitude of our horror when the *Colonel of the Queen's regiment of light dragoons* advanced towards Ticonderoga. The mountains shook before thee, and the trees of the forest bowed their lofty heads—the vast lakes of the North were chilled at thy presence, and the mighty cataracts stopped their tremendous career and were suspended in awe at thy approach.—Judge, then, *oh ineffable*

---

*Author of that delightful lyric, *My Generous Heart Disdains,* of which one stanza runs:

Shall a girl's capricious frown
Sink my noble spirits down?
Shall a face of white and red
Make me droop my silly head?

As good as anything by George Wither, whose *Lover's Resolution* perhaps suggested it.

*Governor of Fort William in North Britain,* what must have been the terror, dismay and despair that overspread this paltry Continent of *America* and us its wretched inhabitants. Dark and dreary, indeed, was the prospect before us, till, like the sun in the horizon, your most gracious, sublime and irresistible proclamation opened the doors of mercy, and snatch'd us, as it were, from the jaws of annihilation.

"We foolishly thought, blind as we were, that your gracious master's fleets and armies were come to destroy us and our liberties; but we are happy in hearing from you—and who can doubt what you assert? that they were *called forth for the sole purpose of restoring the rights of the constitution to a froward and stubborn generation.*

"And is it for this, Oh sublime *Lieutenant General,* that you have given yourself the trouble to cross the wide Atlantic, and with incredible fatigue traverse uncultivated wilds? And we ungratefully refuse the proffer'd blessing?—To restore the rights of the constitution you have called together an amiable host of Savages and turned them loose to scalp our women and children, and lay our country waste—this they have performed with their usual skill and clemency, and we yet remain insensible of the benefit and unthankful for so much goodness.

"Our Congress have declared independence, and our Assemblies, as your highness justly observes, have most *wickedly* imprisoned the avowed friends of that power with which they are at war, and most *profanely* compelled those, whose consciences will not permit them to fight, to pay some small part towards the expences their country is at in supporting what is called a necessary defensive war. If we go on thus in our obstinacy and ingratitude, what can we expect but that you should, in your anger, *give a stretch to the Indian forces under your direction, amounting to thousands, to overtake and destroy us;* or, which is ten times worse, that you should withdraw your fleets and armies and leave us to our own misery, without compleating the benevolent task you have begun, in *restoring to us the rights of the constitution.*

"We submit—we submit, most puissant *Colonel of the Queen's regiment of light dragoons, and Governor of Fort William in North Britain!* We offer our heads to the scalping-knife and our bellies to the bayonet. Who can resist the force of your eloquence? Who can withstand the terror of your arms? The invitation you have made in the *consciousness of christianity, your royal master's clemency, and the honor of soldiership,* we thankfully accept. The blood of the slain, the cries of injured virgins and innocent children, and the never-ceasing sighs and groans of starving wretches, now languishing in the gaols and prison-ships of New-York, call on us in vain whilst your sublime proclamation is sounded in our ears. Forgive us, oh our country! Forgive us, dear posterity! Forgive us, all ye foreign powers who are anxiously watching our conduct in this important struggle, if we yield implicitly to the persuasive tongue of the most elegant *Colonel of her Majesty's regiment of light dragoons.*

"Forbear then, thou magnanimous *Lieutenant General!* Forbear to denounce vengeance against us.—Forbear to *give a stretch* to those *restorers of constitutional rights, the Indian forces under your direction.*—Let not *the messengers of justice and wrath await us in the field, and devastation, famine, and every concomitant horror* bar our return to the allegiance of a Prince who, by his royal will, would deprive us of every blessing of life, with all possible clemency.

"We are *domestic,* we are *industrious,* we are *infirm and timid,* we shall *remain quietly at home and not remove our cattle, our corn or forage,* in hopes that you will come at the *head of troops in the full powers of health, discipline, and valour,* and take charge of them for yourselves. Behold our wives and daughters, our flocks and herds, our goods and chattels,—Are they not at the mercy of our Lord the King, and of his *Lieutenant General, Member of the House of Commons, and Governor of Fort William in North-Britain?*"

This caused great mirth not only in America but also in London. Horace Walpole wrote to the Countess of Upper Ossory: "I have never seen more humour, nor better kept up. It is as much admired as it deserves." This is praise from Sir Hubert Stanley, for Horace Walpole for all his old-womanish love of gossip and scandal, was a fairly sound critic. There was also a parody, in Hudibrastic verse, published in the *New York Journal.* The most spirited lines in it deal with the Indian threat:

If any should so hardened be
As to expect impunity
Because *procul a fulmine,*
I will let loose the dogs of hell,
Ten thousand Indians, who shall yell,
And foam and tear, and grin and roar,
And drench their maukesins in gore;
To these I'll give full scope and play
From Ticonderog to Florida;

They'll scalp your heads, and kick your shins,
And rip your guts, and flay your skins,
And of your ears be nimble croppers
And make your thumbs tobacco-stoppers.

Burgoyne also addressed the Indians in a speech of terrible pomposity which must have given the unhappy interpreter a very bad half-hour while he was translating it. He begins by flattering them, they are too sagacious and too faithful to be deluded or corrupted, except for "the refuse of a small tribe" who had been led astray by the specious allurements and insidious promises of the rebels. But he tells them that there are certain laws and customs of war to which they must conform.

> "I positively forbid bloodshed when you are not opposed in arms.
>
> "Aged men, women, children, and prisoners must be held sacred from the knife or hatchet, even in the time of actual conflict.
>
> "You shall receive compensation for the prisoners you take, but you shall be called to account for scalps.
>
> "In conformity and indulgence to your customs, which have affixed an idea of honour to such badges of victory, you shall be allowed to take the scalps of the dead, when killed by your fire, and in fair opposition; but on no account, or pretence, or subtlety, or prevarication, are they to be taken from the wounded or even dying; and still less pardonable, if possible, will it be held to kill men in that condition, on purpose, and upon a supposition, that this protection to the wounded would be thereby evaded."

This is all to John Burgoyne's credit: at all events it was well meant. Horace Walpole made fun of it, and a greater than Horace Walpole, Edmund Burke, guyed it in the House of Commons. He imagined a riot on Tower Hill and the Keeper of His Majesty's lions* addressing the animals in his charge: "My gentle lions, my humane bears, my sentimental wolves, my tender-hearted hyenas, go forth: but I exhort ye as ye are Christians and members of a civilised society, to take care not to hurt man, woman or child." The fat and lethargic Lord North, when he heard this, was, so Horry tells us, "almost suffocated with laughter."

"An Old Chief of the Iroquois" must have astonished Burgoyne by the brevity of his reply; or perhaps the interpreter was tired, he certainly had every reason to be. The Chief "in a few well-chosen words," as they always say in the papers, remarked:

> "I stand up in the name of all nations present, to assure our father, that we have attentively listened to his discourse. We receive you as our father, because when you speak, we hear the voice of our great father beyond the great lake.
>
> "We rejoice in the approbation you have expressed of our behaviour.
>
> "We have been tried and tempted by the Bostonians; but we have loved our father, and our hatchets have been sharpened upon our affections.
>
> "In proof of the sincerity of our professions, our whole villages able to go to war, are come forth. The old and infirm, our infants and wives, alone remain at home.
>
> "With one common assent we promise a constant

*In the eighteenth century the Tower of London was to Londoners what the Zoo is nowadays.

obedience to all you have ordered, and all you shall order; and may the Father of Days give you many, and success."

*(Loud and prolonged grunts)*

The Indians were led by La Corne St. Luc, a French-Canadian who had fought under Montcalm. When Canada became by conquest a British colony, he became a British subject, and helped to capture Ethan Allen, and was in his turn taken prisoner. When he was exchanged in April, 1777, he returned to Canada, furious against *"ces gueux."* He was an eager advocate of the employment of the Indians and went so far as to say. *"Il faut brutalizer les affaires."* He must therefore have listened with disgust to Burgoyne's commands in his speech, and Burgoyne was to find him a nuisance rather than a help, and later on a traitor.

On June thirtieth Burgoyne issued a General Order:

> "The army embarks tomorrow, to approach the Enemy. We are to contend for the King, and the constitution of Great Britain, to vindicate Law, and to relieve the oppressed—a cause in which his Majesty's Troops and those of the Princes his Allies, will feel equal excitement. The Services required of this particular expedition are critical and conspicuous. During our progress occasions may occur in which, nor difficulty, nor labour, nor Life are to be regarded. This Army must not Retreat."

Ticonderoga, though it had been strong enough to keep Carleton off the previous fall, was in rather a poor way the following spring. The American officer, John Paterson, who had been sent there to make an inspection, reported on May second that the garrison, then not quite two thousand men "sick and well," had few blankets, while many of them had neither shoes nor stockings. Clothing, provisions and reinforcements were badly needed. But it was no use for St. Clair, in command at Ticonderoga, to call for reinforcements—there was no food for them. The tents were bad, the powder magazines so rotten that fifty pounds of it a week got damaged, and there was no paper for cartridges. The batteaux would not float for want of pitch and tar; everything had been neglected. To defend the works required, St. Clair estimated, ten thousand men. Of the two thousand he had many were mere boys, and there was only one bayonet for every ten men. Paterson was a shrewd observer. He reported, "We have had no late intelligence from Canada, but from their seeming supineness it is generally believed they are meditating and preparing for some important stroke." On the other hand, it should be mentioned, in St. Clair's defense, that in June he was assured by Congress that the British would transport most of the troops in Canada by water to help Howe to take Philadelphia, and that the movement on Ticonderoga would only be a feint. "This the Board of War had received from reliable authority." *(The St. Clair Papers.* Annotated by W. H. Smith, 1882.) Matters were not made any easier by the fact that Schuyler, in command of the Northern Department, was not popular with the New Englanders. He was an aristocrat* and a disciplinarian; Gates was constantly intriguing against him. On June fifteenth a British spy was captured, and St. Clair learned that Ticonderoga was shortly to be attacked.

---

*His mother was a Van Cortlandt, and his wife a Van Rensselaer.

It was a fine flotilla that on July first, "the day being fine," took Burgoyne and his troops over Lake Champlain: Indians in their birch canoes each containing twenty to thirty, barges packed full with red-coats, music and drums perpetually playing, gun-boats, the frigates *Royal George* and the *Inflexible* as escorts, and Burgoyne, Phillips and Riedesel each in his pinnace—to the American scouting vessels it must have seemed a veritable British Armada. A contemporary American ballad puts it picturesquely, if roughly:

> Burgoyne, the King's commander
> From Canada set sail;
> With full eight thousand reg'lars
> He thought he could not fail.
> With Indians and Canadians
> And his cursed Tory crew
> On board his fleet of shipping
> He up Lake Champlain flew.

The troops landed a few miles short of Ticonderoga, and the Indians celebrated it by getting drunk.

General St. Clair, as stated above, was in command at Ticonderoga, with about two thousand effectives. But what really commanded Ticonderoga and also Fort Independence on the opposite shore of the lake, here little wider than a river, was Sugar Loaf Hill, a crag rising precipitously to a height of six hundred feet. So steep was it, in fact,* that the Americans had not thought to fortify it, or to occupy it, although an intelligent officer in the garrison, John Trumbull, had shown by actual experiment that a shot fired from a twelve-pounder in the

*In an old map of 1776 it is described as "Supposed inaccessible for carriages."

fort could and did reach Sugar Loaf Hill. The converse of course held good, but nothing was done. Gates was actually present when this shot was fired, so the blame was his, not Schuyler's nor St. Clair's.

General Phillips saw possibilities here: he observed, "Where a goat can go a man can go, and where a man can go he can haul up a gun." Lieutenant Twiss, the commanding engineer, constructed a road of sorts, guns were manhandled up, hoisted from tree to tree by ropes, Phillips urging the work forward "with the same vehemence with which he drove his artillery at Minden, where he broke fifteen canes over the horses," and Sugar Loaf Hill had its name changed to Fort Defiance.

A Council of General Officers was held and it is significant that St. Clair, who presided, mentioned as forming part of the garrison "about 900 militia that have joined us, and *cannot stay but a few days*." It was unanimously decided that Ticonderoga, now a trap rather than a fort, must be evacuated. This was done, it was obviously the only thing to do, on July sixth, and the British occupied it. When the news reached London on August twenty-second, King George ran into the Queen's room, crying, "I have beat them! beat all the Americans." Walpole wrote; "I hear Burgoyne has kicked Ticonderoga into one of the lakes—I don't know which, I am no geographer."

The King wanted to bestow "the vacant Red Ribbon," *i.e.*, the Order of the Bath, on Burgoyne, and Lord Derby was approached in the matter. Burgoyne apparently had told his wife's nephew that he had "a strong objection to the honor above mentioned," so the matter was dropped.

The loss of Ticonderoga, which had been regarded

as a kind of Gibraltar, was a great blow to the Americans, and there was a general demand for a public inquiry. Schuyler, writing on the ninth of July from Fort Edward to the Council of Safety of the State of New York, began: "What could induce General St. Clair and the general officers with him to evacuate Ticonderoga, God only knows." Many accused St. Clair of treachery, and the same charge was brought against Schuyler. John Adams said that they would never be able to defend a post until they shot a general. Even Washington, as a rule imperturbable, seems to have been slightly upset. He wrote to Schuyler, "It is an event of chagrin and surprise, not apprehended nor within the compass of my reasoning: this stroke is severe indeed and has distressed us much." Probably it was to the American cause a blessing in disguise. St. Clair put it well when he said, "We have lost a post but saved a province." Had Burgoyne been held up there any length of time, had he found it necessary, as he had anticipated, to lay formal siege to it, it is quite possible that a relieving army would have driven him back over the Lake to Canada, with his force more or less intact, and with sea power ready to transfer it to some other point. As it was, he set out through the woods and swamps on the route which led him ultimately to the Convention of Saratoga.

It is rather curious that, before Burgoyne started through this maze of woods, there should have been published in *The Gentleman's Magazine* in London, a detailed account of the Military Geography of the country. There is a very significant passage, evidently written from first-hand knowledge:

"The American woods have in some places a great

deal of underwood, in other parts none at all. The difficulties of making roads in such situations may be reduced to three. First, the trees in general, in their natural state, are very close to each other. In the second place, fallen trees, lying in all directions, some sound, blown down by winds, others in a rotting state, are as plenty as lamp posts upon a highway about London, and frequently as thick as the lamps upon Westminster bridge; these being irremoveable, and almost innumerable, the road is continually upon the turn to one side or the other, to get clear of them. In the third place, about every two or three miles, probably, there is a bridge to be made, twenty, thirty, or forty feet high, and twice or three times as long, over a creek, or rather a great gutter, between two hills, and the avenues, when the ground is very high, want levelling. The sum of the perplexities must be charged to the account of swamps."

What an admirable country through which to retreat, and what a difficult country through which to pursue! I suppose that, but for the railway, the same might be said of it at the present day.

## CHAPTER VIII

### JENNY McCREA AND BENNINGTON

WHILE Burgoyne and his little navy commanded by Captain Lutwidge, broke the boom across the narrows and sailed to Skenesborough, which the Americans evacuated, Fraser and Riedesel pursued St. Clair and his troops and overtook them at Hubbardton, where there was a brisk rear-guard action which may be regarded as drawn, as St. Clair got safely away to Fort Edward. It would have been a success for the British but for the slowness of the Germans; they arrived two hours late, singing psalms, with the exception of Riedesel, who was cursing and swearing at their dilatoriness. Anburey remarks, "In this action I found all manual exercise* is but an ornament." Lamb in his *Memoirs of His Own Life* says very much the same thing. "In fighting in the woods the battalion manœuvring and excellency of exercise were found of little value: to prime, load, fire and charge with the bayonet expeditiously were the chief points worthy of attention." Fraser undoubtedly realized this: the stolid Brunswickers certainly did not. Burgoyne himself was all for the "Bayonotte": in his own words "the onset of Bayonets in the hands of the Valiant is irresistible."

Lord Balcarres, in command of the light infantry, had thirty balls shot through his jacket and trousers, but

*i. e., drill according to the drill-books.

only had his hip grazed by one of them. The American Colonel Francis was killed. At the same time Lieutenant-Colonel Hill and the 9th Regiment had a spirited action near Fort Anne which resulted in the Americans retreating to Fort Edward, burning Fort Anne before they did so. On July tenth Burgoyne issued a General Order thanking the troops in general and Fraser in particular, and announcing that on the following Sunday "a Feu de joy will be fired with cannon and small arms at Ticonderoga, Crown Point and the camp at Skenesborough."*

Harder work lay before the English troops. From Fort George to Fort Edward was only twenty miles, but the way lay through thick forest and over swamps and streams. Schuyler had a thousand men employed cutting down trees so that they lay "every which way" over what rough tracks there were, and all the bridges were destroyed. It finally took Burgoyne's soldiers—pioneers now rather than fighting men—twenty days to cover these twenty miles. Forty bridges had to be constructed, mostly over marsh land; one of these bridges was two miles long. Neilson writing in 1844 said, "Many of the logs of these bridges remain entire even to this day." Fort Edward could only by courtesy be called a fort. Schuyler, Arnold and Lincoln agreed that it should be evacuated, and that the American troops should cross the Hudson and take up a position near Stillwater, thirty miles north of Albany. By July thirty-first this was done. Washington ordered up strong reinforcements.

The question now arises, why did Burgoyne choose this arduous route? He could from Skenesborough have gone back to Ticonderoga, along Lake George to Fort George whence there was a direct road to Fort Edward.

*Now Whitehall.

Instead of this he laboriously made his way to Fort Anne and Fort Edward through the difficult country already mentioned. His own excuse was that "a retrograde movement" back to Ticonderoga would have depressed his men. The real reason was that Skene (of whom more anon)—Colonel Skene by courtesy—wanted a good road made through his property at the public expense. Skene, next to Germain, was Burgoyne's evil genius.

In his despatch of July eleventh to Germain, Burgoyne says that his "manifesto" has had a great effect (chiefly, it is to be feared, in provoking mirth), but he hints that he is beginning to get uneasy about the Indians: "Your Lordship will have observed I have made no mention of the Indians in the pursuit from Ticonderoga. It is not possible to draw them in many respects from the plunder of that place, and I confidentially acknowledge this is not the only instance in which I have found (them) little more than a name. If, under the management of their conductors, they are indulged, for interested reasons, in all the caprices and humours of spoiled children, like them they grow more unreasonable and importunate upon every new favour; were they left to themselves, enormities too horrid to think of would ensue; guilty and innocent, women and infants, would be a common prey." He also points out that he was tied down by his instructions: "Your Lordship will pardon me if I a little lament that my orders do not give me the latitude I ventured to propose in my original project for the campaign, to make a real effort instead of a feint upon New England. As things have turned out, were I at liberty to march in force immediately by my left, instead of to my right, I should have little doubt of subduing before winter the province where the rebellion originated."

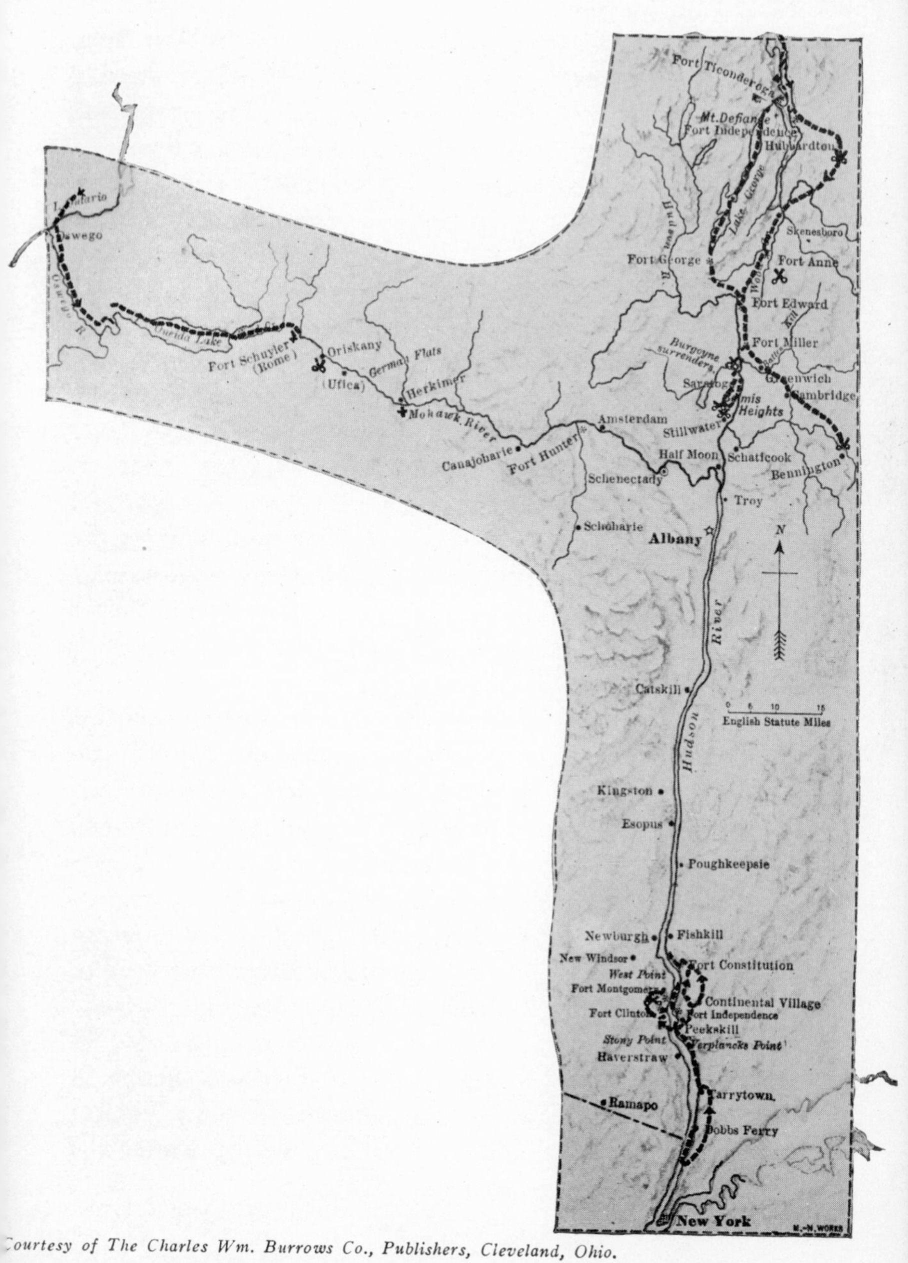


*Courtesy of The Charles Wm. Burrows Co., Publishers, Cleveland, Ohio.*

Map of the line of the Hudson, July-October, 1777

From Avery's "History of the United States"

On July eleventh Burgoyne also wrote to Carleton asking him to garrison Ticonderoga, a point which does not appear to have been taken into consideration before the campaign began, though Burgoyne had assumed that Canada would supply the troops. In a letter, July second, to Howe, he wrote: "Ticonderoga reduced, I shall leave behind me proper engineers to put it in an impregnable state, and it will be garrisoned from Canada, where all the destined supplies are safely arrived. My force therefore will be left complete for future operations." But Sir Guy found himself not in a position to do this, so Burgoyne had to leave nine hundred and ten rank and file there which, as he says, left his situation "a little difficult."

He was justified in his uneasiness about the Indians. It was at this time that the dreadful tragedy of Miss Jane McCrea was enacted. Briefly, Miss McCrea was engaged to a provincial officer in Burgoyne's army called Jones, and while on her way to the British camp to see her fiancé was killed, if not by, certainly while in the charge of, two Indians. The official version drawn up by Gates in a letter to Burgoyne is as follows:

> "That the savages of America should in their warfare mangle and scalp the unhappy prisoners who fall into their hands is neither new nor extraordinary; but that the famous Lieutenant-General Burgoyne, in whom the fine gentleman is united with the soldier and the scholar, should hire the savages of America to scalp Europeans and the descendants of Europeans, nay more, that he should pay a price* for each scalp so

*Gates, who perhaps had heard that Burgoyne had alluded to him

barbarously taken, is more than will be believed in England until authenticated facts shall in every gazette convince mankind of the truth of this horrid tale. Miss McCrea, a young lady lovely to the sight, of virtuous character and amiable disposition, engaged to be married to an officer in your army, was with other women and children taken out of a house near Fort Edward, carried into the woods, and their scalped and mangled in the most shocking manner. . . . The miserable fate of Miss McCrea was partly aggravated by her being dressed to receive her promised husband; but met her murderers employed by you."*

Burgoyne answered this with an indignation which makes his style even more inflated than usual. "I condescend to inform you that I would not be conscious of the acts you presume to impute to me for the whole continent of America, though the wealth of worlds were in its bowels and a paradise on its surface." He then proceeds to give his version of the tragedy.

"Respecting Miss McCrea, her fall wanted not the tragic display you have laboured to give it, to make it as sincerely abhorred and lamented by me, as it can

---

as "that old midwife," called Burgoyne, in conversation, "the polite Macaroni because he paid for scalps." As a friend of mine (Mr. D. C. Mearns) has wittily put it, "Gates resented scalps in his Macaroni." In the eighteenth century, by the way, the Macaroni was what we call a dandy. Sheridan's Sir Benjamin Backbite has a pleasant allusion to them in the *School for Scandal* in his epigram on Lady Betty Curricle's ponies:

> Sure never were seen two such beautiful ponies.
> Other horses are clowns, but these Macaronies.
> To give them this title I'm sure can't be wrong,
> Their legs are so short, and their tails are so long.

For the "Macaroni's knapsack" described by Burgoyne see page **331**.

*Gates was very proud of this letter: he showed it to General Lincoln and to Wilkinson and when they suggested it was rather personal exclaimed, "By God! I don't believe either of you can mend it."

possibly be by the tenderest of her friends. The fact was no premeditated barbarity, on the contrary two chiefs who had brought her off for the purpose of security, not of violence to her person, disputed who should be her guard, and in a fit of savage passion in the one from whose hands she was snatched, the unhappy woman became the victim. Upon the first intelligence of the events, I obliged the Indians to deliver the murderer into my hands, and though to have punished him by our laws and principles of justice would have been perhaps unprecedented, he certainly would have suffered an ignominious death, had I not been convinced by circumstances and observation beyond the possibility of a doubt, that a pardon under the terms I prescribed and they accepted, would be more efficacious than an execution to prevent similar mischiefs."

Burgoyne was attacked not only in America, but at home over this sad affair. In 1779 in the Committee of the House of Commons he was fully vindicated by the Earl of Harrington, who was a member of the expedition as Captain in the 29th Foot. He stated that when the news of the murder of Miss McCrea was received General Burgoyne repaired immediately to the Indian camp, threatened the culprit with death, insisted that he should be given up, "and there were many gentlemen of the army, and I own I was one of the number, who feared that he would put that threat in execution. Motives of policy, I believe, alone prevented him from it; and if he had not pardoned the man, which he did, I believe the total defection of the Indians would have ensued, and the consequences, on their return through Canada, might have been dreadful; not to speak of the weight they would have thrown into the opposite scale, had they gone over to the enemy, which I rather imagine would have been the case." Mr. J. P. Baxter in his invaluable work, *The British Invasion from the North,* proves, it would seem conclusively, that Miss McCrea was not scalped, but met her death when the Indians in whose charge she was, were fired on by a party of Americans who were pursuing them. So her death may be said to have been a pure accident. Poor Jenny McCrea gave rise to other disputes. One poet described her as having "clustering curls of soft blonde hair": another said it was "darker than a raven's wing." One, perhaps both, must have been using poetic license.

This Miss McCrea business was bad enough in all conscience, but worse was to come, and that was the Battle of Bennington. The real culprit here was the German Colonel Baume, and after him Skene. Burgoyne wanted supplies, Riedesel wanted horses for his dragoons, and Bennington was reported by Skene to be a depôt for horses and supplies in general. Colonel Baume was given by Burgoyne detailed written, supplemented by verbal, instructions. He was sent "to try the affections of the country, to disconcert the councils of the enemy, to mount the Riedesel's dragoons and to obtain large supplies of cattle, horses and carriages." He was told exactly how he was to do this: he was also told "Colonel Skeene [sic] will be with you as much as possible in order to assist you with his advice, to help you to distinguish the good subjects from the bad, to procure you the best intelligence of the enemy, and to choose those people who are to bring me the accounts of your progress and success." Skene appears to have been a kind of eighteenth-century country squire only, if possible, rather more stupid. In the Stopford-Sackville Manuscripts there is a letter from Canada quoted in which it is said of him: "*M. Skeene assura le Général Burgoyne que s'il vouloit lui donner 500 hommes il répondrait de battre les rebelles et de rapporter beaucoup de vivres et surtout des chevaux pour les dragons allemands.*" He was a rustic optimist; he was always sending the most hopeful letters to Dartmouth: "The Americans want confidence in their officers and their officers want confidence in them." "The country is coming in fast in reply to Burgoyne's manifesto." To Burgoyne this cheerful marplot remarked: "All you have to do is to scatter plunder on your march and then the rebels will be so busily engaged in collecting* it that you need have no fear of any attack." I can only trace one sensible remark of his, to wit, "This wooded country is of such a nature that it is impossible for the General to fix the Rebels in a body": that is to say, these rascally rebels would not come out into the open, line up as in the drill-books and be heavily defeated as in the text-books. Skene adds the ominous words, "Therefore the duty must be done by detachment." It is hardly necessary to add that when you have an army strictly limited in numbers opposed to an army growing in numbers daily, the more you send out detachments, the more you are asking for disaster.

Baume set out from Fort Anne with about five hundred men, mostly Germans. His rate of progress was slow, and no wonder. Burgoyne's British soldiers each carried a knapsack, a blanket, a haversack, a canteen for water, a hatchet and part of his kit: with his musket and sixty rounds of ammunition all this weighed about sixty

*In the early days of the European War the same thing was said of the German Uhlans in Belgium.

pounds. The Germans were in even worse case. Each Brunswick dragoon wore huge jack-boots, stiff leather breeches, huge gauntlets and a hat heavy with feathers. From the back of his head protruded a long peruke. By his side trailed a broadsword weighing about twelve pounds, over his shoulder was slung a heavy carbine, and he carried his quotum of flour with which to make bread. The Americans were in their shirt-sleeves. Stedman goes so far as to say of Riedesel's dragoons, "Their very hats and swords weighed very nearly as much as the whole equipment of one of our [British] soldiers," an exaggeration of course, for it is impossible to conceive a hat weighing forty-eight pounds—even Dame Fashion has not yet dared to go to such lengths, or rather weights. *Il faut souffrir pour être belle,* but not to this extent.

The credit of the American victory at Bennington, then famous for its Catamount Tavern where the Green Mountain Boys would hold convivial meetings, belongs to Stark, whom we have already met on Breed's Hill. On his way to Bennington he received orders from Schuyler to take his men to the left bank of the Hudson. Sore (like Arnold) at having been passed over for promotion, he politely declined to do so, and was censured. A few weeks later he was thanked by Congress and made a brigadier-general in the American Army. He had with him in all about eighteen hundred men. On August fourteenth* Baume and his troops, plunging heavily through the woods, accompanied by two field guns, came into touch with Stark's men. The poor simple

*Burgoyne seems to have been confident of success for on this very day he wrote to Baume a letter (which fell into Schuyler's hands) requesting him to send along all captured cattle, wheat and flour that could be spared.

German thought at first, thanks to the idiot Skene, that they were friends come to join him. When they opened fire, even Skene perceived that they were not friends. Baume entrenched himself upon a hill and sent back word to Burgoyne. Breymann, another German officer with more Germans, was sent to reinforce Baume. He also took two field guns with him; his rate of marching was half-a-mile an hour and, in addition, his guide lost his way. On the fifteenth it rained hard* and neither side made a move, except Breymann, if half-a-mile an hour can be called movement. On the sixteenth, a bright clear day, Stark attacked Baume in front and rear. As he gave the word to advance, he added the historic words: "My men, there are your enemies the red-coats and the tories: we must conquer them or to-night Molly Stark will be a widow." It is painful to have to add that some iconoclast has coldly pointed out that Mrs. Stark was really called Bessie: perhaps Molly was a pet name, or perhaps he was thinking of somebody else; in any case, in the heat of action such mistakes are comprehensible. (Another iconoclast, by the way, has tried to argue that the dying Nelson never said "Kiss me, Hardy," but "Kismet, Hardy.") There were certainly two famous Mollies (delightful name!) in North American history of this day. One was Molly Brant, the Mohawk maiden whom Sir William Johnson married when he settled among the tribe, the other was Molly Pitcher, better known as Captain Molly. She was at Fort Clinton when it was captured by the British in October, 1777, and fired the last gun on the American side. She was also at Monmouth, and Washington, for her bravery, made

*At this date there was always difficulty with the powder and cartouche boxes in heavy rain.

her a sergeant. Later she took up her abode near West Point. It is rather painful to read that in April, 1787, an official letter was sent to Major-General Henry Knox, Secretary of War:

> "Sir,
>
> "I am informed by the woman that takes care of Captain Molly that she is much in want of Shifts. If you think proper to order three or four, I shall be glad."

There have been similar warriors in the British Army, notably Old Mother Ross, that mistress of "maroding" (as she called marauding), Hannah Shell, and the quarrelsome Doctor James Barry who fought a duel at the Cape, rose to be Inspector-General of Army Hospitals, and who after his, or rather her, death in 1865 proved to be a woman.

To return to Bennington, the Indians and Canadians vamoosed, the Germans put up a brave fight until their ammunition ran out, Colonel Baume was killed, and Colonel Breymann was too late. "Our People," Stark reported, "behaved with the greatest spirit and bravery imaginable: had they been Alexanders or Charleses of Sweden they could not have behaved better; the action lasted two hours at the expiration of which time we forced their breastwork at the muzzle of their guns, took two pieces of brass cannon, with a number of prisoners." Stark said "it was the hottest action I ever saw in my life" and he had been on the Plains of Abraham with Wolfe and, as we have seen, at Bunker Hill.

New Hampshire was delighted, and justly so. The General Assembly formally thanked Stark and "resolved unanimously, that the Board of War of this State be, and hereby are, directed in the name of this Court, to present to the Honourable Brigadier General Stark, a compleat suit of Clothes becoming his Rank, together with a piece of linen; As a Testimony of the high sense this Court have of the great and important Services rendered by that brave Officer to the United States of America." Hadden, who is the authority for this curious statement, adds that among the British "it was remarked upon the above reward That either the General was Stark naked or Congress stark mad." Armies are always full of rumors ("shaves" as they used to call them) and stories, and it was said at the time that the real reason of Breymann's slowness was that he and Baume were not on the best of terms, and that he was heard to say when he heard the firing, "We will let them get warm before we reach them," and that he halted to let his men "cook their kettles." Such stories are always interesting—gossip invariably is—but as a rule they must just be taken as stories.

Most battles inspire poets. Bennington inspired several, including William Cullen Bryant. But it is doubtful if bard was ever worse inspired than the gentleman who wrote:

> Each soldier there had left at home
> A sweetheart, wife, or mother,
> A blooming sister, or perchance,
> A fair-haired, blue-eyed brother.

But perhaps I am prejudiced and bilious and hypercritical owing to the fact that Bennington was a very serious setback for John Burgoyne. Horace Walpole flippantly said of it, "General Burgoyne has had bad sport in the woods." In the Knox Manuscripts there is a story told of Thurlow, then attorney-general, who asked what was Burgoyne's reason for sending Germans to Bennington instead of English, "for that seemed the first cause of his capture." Knox explained that "the Brunswick troops happening to be on Burgoyne's left as the Hessians [at Trenton] were upon Howe's, they were of course the corps to be detached on that side." The gruff old lawyer, missing the military point by miles, exclaimed, "So because one damned blockhead did a foolish thing the other blockhead must follow his example." Skene, the intelligence (!) officer and interpreter, must take most of the blame for this defeat. "He acted like a —— showing his powers to every man who pretended to be friendly, among which number were many of the rebel soldiers, who, to remove doubts, took the oaths of allegiance and were told to wear white papers in their hats, that being the distinguishing mark of friends; to crown the folly of this farce they were permitted immediately to return, in fact to join their respective corps in the rebel army." (Hadden.)

Burgoyne, though, like the good fellow he was, he does not mention Skene by name, points pretty clearly to him in his despatch of August twentieth:

> "It appears that Lieutenant-Colonel Baume, not having been able to complete his march undiscovered, was joined at a place called Sancoix Mills, about four miles short of Bennington, by many people professing themselves to be Loyalists. A provincial gentleman of confidence who had been sent with the detachment, as knowing the country and the character of the inhabitants, was so incautious as to leave at liberty such as took the oath of allegiance.

"His credulity and their profligacy caused the first misfortune. Colonel Baume was induced to proceed without sufficient knowledge of the ground. His design was betrayed; the men who had taken the oaths were the first to fire upon him; he was attacked on all sides. He shewed great personal courage, but was overpowered by numbers."

Burgoyne also issued a General Order dealing with the Bennington disaster: the failure was not due to any want of gallantry on the part of either officers or men but to "the credulity of those who managed the department of intelligence and who suffered great numbers of the rebel soldiers to pass and repass and perhaps count the numbers of the detachment, and upon an ill-founded confidence induced Lieut-Col. Baume to advance too far to have a secure retreat." A secondary cause was Breymann's slowness: he and his men, thanks to bad weather, bad roads, tired horses and other impediments "could not reach twenty-four miles from eight in the morning of the 15th, to four in the afternoon of the 16th."

In his confidential letter of the same date as his despatch (August twentieth) to Lord George Germain, Burgoyne is more explicit. It is obvious that he is getting uneasy. Fort Stanwix still holds out, the Loyalists are not rising as was expected, he has four hundred with him, not half of them armed and the rest "trimmers" waiting to see what would happen. "Wherever the King's forces point, militia to the amount of three or four thousand assemble in twenty-four hours, they bring with them their subsistence, etc., and, the alarm over, they return to their farms. The Hampshire Grants in particular, a country unpeopled and almost unknown in the last war, now abounds in the most active and most rebellious race of the continent, and hangs like a gathering storm upon my left." A fine phrase, this last, and John Burgoyne the poet must have smacked the thigh of John Burgoyne the general as he penned it. The rest of this letter is very significant. He has only received one letter from Howe, with the astonishing news that "his intention is for Pennsylvania,"* and that Sir Henry Clinton remained in command at New York and would act as occurrences might direct. Poor Burgoyne goes on:

> "No operation, my Lord, has yet been undertaken in my favour: the highlands have not even been threatened. The consequence is that Putnam has detached two brigades to Mr. Gates, who is now strongly posted near the mouth of the Mohawk River, with an army superior to mine in troops of the Congress, and as many militia as he pleases. Had I a latitude in my orders, I should think it my duty to wait in this position, or perhaps as far back as Fort Edward, where my communication with Lake George would be perfectly secure, till some event happened to assist my movement forward, but my orders being positive to 'force a junction with Sir William Howe' I apprehend I am not at liberty to remain inactive longer than shall be necessary to collect twenty-five days provisions and to receive the reinforcement of the additional companies, the German drafts and recruits now (and unfortunately only now) on Lake Champlain."

This puts Burgoyne's view of the situation quite

*This reminds one of the old song, "I'm off to Philadelphia in the morning." Howe captured Philadelphia. But Franklin expressed it much better: he said Philadelphia captured Howe.

clearly: he had received definite orders and he thought it his duty not to deviate in any way from them. He had not, he continues, foreseen that he was to be "left to pursue my way through such a tract of country and hosts of foes, without any co-operation from New York."

The army was as astonished as Burgoyne. Everybody knew the object of the expedition was to join Sir William Howe at Albany. Anburey writes: "You can easily conceive the astonishment it occasioned when we were informed that General Howe's army had gone to Philadelphia, and it was the more increased as we could not form to ourselves any idea how such a step would facilitate or effect a junction."

The ineffable Germain comments (Knox Manuscripts) on Burgoyne's letter: "I am sorry to find that Burgoyne's campaign is so totally ruined: the best wish I can form is that he may have returned to Ticonderoga without much loss. His private letter to me, 20th of August, contains nothing material about the affair near Bennington, but what alarms me most is that he thinks his orders to go to Albany to force a junction with Sir William Howe are so positive that he must attempt at all events the obeying them." This scoundrel was evidently already preparing his defense. He knew that if it came to a plain Yes or No he could not say—or rather he could not prove, for he would have told any lie—that Howe had been instructed to go north to meet Burgoyne: so, in place of this, he is evidently going to plead, if necessary, that Burgoyne had totally misunderstood his instructions, and was given a free hand, or a "latitude" as the General says himself, to retreat toward Canada. Meanwhile where was the lethargic Howe? Why, gone, not north to join forces with Burgoyne, but south, away from him.

We know that, thanks to Germain, Howe never got instructions to go north from New York to meet Burgoyne, but why did he go south? It was not characteristic of him to go anywhere, except calling on ladies. His lethargy is well summed up by a contemporary rhymester who addressed him:

> Awake, awake, Sir Billy,
> There's forage in the plain.
> Ah! leave your little filly,
> And open the campaign.
>
> Heed not a woman's prattle
> Which tickles in the ear,
> But give the word for battle
> And grasp the warlike spear.

He was fond of fillies. In Boston he "found a Cleopatra." Judge Jones, the Loyalist historian, wrote of him: "Nothing seemed to engross his attentions but the faro table, the playhouse, the dancing assembly and, last but not least, Mrs. Loring." Howe met her first in 1775. She went a-soldiering with him and was known in the British Army as "the Sultana." Like Howe (and Burgoyne) she was a confirmed gambler, and thought nothing of losing three hundred guineas at a sitting. This "illustrious courtesan," as the Judge calls her, had a husband Joshua, who was made a Commissary of Prisoners, as a slight token of Sir William's esteem for him—and his wife. Joshua was in fact a *mari complaisant*. (According to a document in the American Manuscripts in the Royal Institution it was Loring who in February, 1782, signed the proposal for the exchange of Burgoyne for an equivalent of one thousand and forty-seven rank and file. At the same time Brigadier-General

General Horatio Gates
Painted by Gilbert Stuart

O'Hara was valued at two hundred rank and file. Which is another injustice to Ireland, another blow at O'Hara.)

In New York also Howe missed a chance. He had a lingering lunch with a beauty, Mrs. Lindley Murray, who, with "crafty hospitality" entertained him with pleasant and, in view of her name, one can assume highly grammatical, chat, while Putnam got away, I had almost added "with it." It was said at the time that "Mrs. Murray"—and her Madeira—"saved the American Army."

Why then did this lethargic, pleasure-loving General go south? Well, this remained a mystery until 1860, when Mr. G. H. Moore brought out in New York an extraordinarily interesting book, *The Treason of Charles Lee.* This contains a reproduction of a document, endorsed by Henry Strachey, then Secretary to the Royal Commissioners, the brothers Howe, "Mr. Lee's Plan—March 29, 1777." Lee, then a prisoner in British hands, thought it consistent with his honor—it was certainly consistent with his dishonor—to advise Howe what steps he should take to defeat the Americans with whom this double-traitor had joined forces. He writes that he thinks himself "not only justifiable but bound in conscience to furnish all the lights I can to enable 'em to bring matters to a conclusion in the most compendious manner and consequently the least expensive* to both Parties." He goes on to suggest that Howe should turn his attention southward and send troops up the "Patomac" to occupy Alexandria and up "Chesepeak" Bay to seize Annapolis. He should then issue proclamations of pardon "and I will answer for it with my life that all the

*Characteristic of him, for gold was his god.

Inhabitants of that great tract southward of the Patapisco and lying betwixt the Patomac and Chesepeak Bay, and those on the eastern Shore of Maryland will immediately lay down their arms."

Mr. Manners Chichester, the author of the life of Charles Lee in the *Dictionary of National Biography,* seems dubious as to the authenticity of this document. But there can be no question about it. The Sixth Report of the Royal Commission on Historical Manuscripts published in 1877 says: "During the last illness of the late Sir Henry Strachey (the second baronet) some of the most important of the first Sir Henry Strachey's American documents were withdrawn from the library of Sutton Court, conveyed to the United States and there sold. One of the writings thus taken from a muniment room in Somersetshire was that remarkable document which soon after it had come by purchase into the possession of Mr. G. H. Moore, an American scholar, was published in facsimile at New York."

Howe in his *Narrative* says: "I therefore agreed with the Admiral to go up Chesapeak Bay, a plan which had been preconcerted"—he does not say by whom. Howe does not seem to have worried much about Burgoyne. He wrote casually, July thirtieth, to Sir Henry Clinton: "If you can make any diversion in favour of General Burgoyne's approaching Albany, with security to King's-Bridge, I need not point out the utility of such a measure." He had certainly not received, as we know, any instructions to join Burgoyne, but when, after he returned home, he was asked why he did not do so on his own initiative, his answer was very feeble:

"Would not my enemies have insinuated that,

alarmed at the rapid success which the honourable General [Burgoyne] had a right to expect when Ticonderoga fell, I had enviously grasped a share of that merit which would otherwise have been all his own? And let me add, would not Ministers have told you, as they truly might, that I had acted without any orders or instructions from them; that General Burgoyne was directed to force his own way to Albany, and that they had put under his command troops sufficient to effect the march? Would they not have referred you to the original and settled plan of that expedition (which is amongst the papers on your table*) to prove that no assistance from me was suggested? And would they not readily have impressed this House with the conclusion that, if any doubt could have arisen in their minds of the success of such a well-digested plan, they should, from the beginning, have made me a party to it, and have given me explicit instructions to act accordingly?"

All this, of course, must have been most unpleasant for Germain, and must have made him wish that he had never heard of Sussex, but it does not clear Howe of the charge of lack of intelligence. He had shown great, almost suspicious lack of it when he evacuated Boston and left an enormous quantity of military stores behind him. He was extraordinarily indolent. In the early stages of the war Washington was called Fabius Cunctator, but if ever there was an Arch Cunctator it was Howe. Some writers have thought that he was unfaithful to his trust, but this is difficult to prove. He and his brother were commissioners to bring about peace if possible: it is

*i. e., in the House of Commons.

difficult to fight with a sword in one hand, an olive-branch in the other. He certainly does not seem to have been enthusiastic in the cause for which he was fighting. Save when on the actual battle-field, he had rather less energy than a slug. Lee sums him up admirably: "He shut his eyes, fought his battles, drunk his bottle, had his little whore, received his orders from North and Germain, one more absurd than the other, shut his eyes and fought again." As regards his move southward the truth undoubtedly was that, like other people,* he had been impressed by Charles Lee and therefore followed his suggestion. The army in general was stupefied by Howe's move. Sir Henry Clinton wrote: "I owe it to truth to say there was not I believe a man in the army except Lord Cornwallis and General Grant who did not reprobate the movement to the southward and see the necessity of a co-operation with General Burgoyne." William Knox (in the American Department) wrote (Knox Manuscripts): "People here are greatly puzzled by General Howe's conduct." He quotes the casual Germain as saying: "I am sorry the Canada army will be disappointed in the junction they expect with Sir William Howe, but the more honour for Burgoyne if he does the business without any assistance from New York." Knox also quotes a certain Henry White: "The expedition to Chesapeak Bay is the real occasion of all the mischief that has happened: had it been left to the Congress they could not have planned a more destructive measure to the King's affairs; and it was foreseen and foretold by every man of sense who was well acquainted

*For example, Washington, who offered to exchange six field officers for Lee.

with the country. This unaccountable movement is well deserving a national enquiry."

Anburey very shrewdly remarks: "I am too much afraid that those at the head of affairs too implicitly credited every report and are continually led away by the false information of men who are interested in the deception and are profiting by the common calamities of England and America." He also says that a Major Browne, who had been on Washington's staff, told him, when a prisoner, that when Washington was informed that Howe had gone to the Chesapeak, "he did not believe it: he dreaded nothing so much as General Howe's army going up the North River." Charles Lee, in fact, traitor though he was to America, did her unintentionally a good turn. Anburey's last comment (November, 1777) on this affair is: "That some great error has been committed, either unintentional or designed, must be evident to everyone—where to fix it, is impossible to say. But time, that great discloser of secrets will no doubt reveal this." He was right. Time—and Mr. G. H. Moore—did reveal it, in 1860, at New York, the very place where "Mr. Lee's Plan" was drawn up. Lee's mainspring seems to have been jealousy of Washington. When he was taken prisoner by Colonel Harcourt he had just begun a letter: "My dear Gates: *Entre nous* a certain great man is most damnably deficient." The best that can be said for him is that he saw that the Americans would make good soldiers, and that the British would have to forget a lot when they came to fight in the forests of North America. "It is very possible for men to be clothed in red, to be expert in all the tricks of the parade, to call themselves regular troops and yet, by attaching themselves principally or solely to the tinsel and show of war, to be totally unfit for real service. If they can acquit themselves tolerably in the puerile reviews exhibited for the amusement of royal masters and misses in Hyde Park or Wimbledon Common it is sufficient."

Mercy Warren, *née* Otis, wife of James Warren, summed Lee up well: "Without religion or country, principle or attachment, gold was his deity and liberty the idol of his fancy; he hoarded the former without taste for its enjoyment, and worshipped the latter as the patroness of licentiousness rather than the protectress of virtue." The best that can be said for him is that he had an amusing and vitriolic pen.* After his court-martial he had a war of words with a Member of Congress, Mr. William Henry Drayton. One can not but smile when one reads in one of his letters to this gentleman: "You tell me the Americans are the most merciful people on the face of the earth: I think so too, and the strongest instance of it is that they did not long ago hang you up." But savage humor does not excuse treachery, so let us leave Charles Lee. Briefly, he double-crossed his native land and also the land of his adoption.

It should be added that at the time Howe's movements were put down by some to jealousy. In the Dartmouth Manuscripts an anonymous correspondent is quoted as saying: "Howe's conduct since he has had command of the army has been a heap of blunders and ridiculous delays: he has always been jealous of the superior military capacity of Burgoyne and Clinton, and has made a sacrifice of the former by disabling the latter from making any diversion in his favour, having left him barely enough troops to defend New York and Staten Island."

*The only possible argument in favor of the idiotic theory that he was Junius.

This can not be substantiated. Howe's mind was far too torpid to be moved by jealousy. He lacked ideas. Lee gave him one, and he jumped at it. His lethargy continued when he proceeded to put Lee's plan into execution. He embarked his troops at New York on July fifth; kept them in transports till the twenty-third; reached the entrance of Delaware Bay on the thirtieth; and beat down the coast and up Chesapeake Bay until August twenty-third. Britannia has rarely ruled the waves in so leisurely a manner; she should have been represented carrying, not a trident, but a fan on this particular expedition.

# CHAPTER IX

## SARATOGA

"THE army must not retreat." So Burgoyne had said, and it is very evident, if you look at any portrait of him in profile in the books of his day, why he would not retreat. He has the jowl of a prize-fighter, he is a regular Gentleman Jackson. The painter Ramsay was right to take a front view of him; in that charming portrait there is little hint of the set and dogged jaw that you see in the old prints.

So on September fourteenth Burgoyne and his army crossed the Hudson by a bridge of boats and encamped "on the heights and in the plains of Saratoga." In short, as the old saying is, he burned his boats, and definitely committed himself to an advance at all costs. It was just before this date that Mrs. General Riedesel observed with surprise that the wives of the officers were beforehand informed of all the military plans. Like Corporal Brewster she adds: "This would not have done for the Dook," her duke being Ferdinand of Brunswick, under whom her husband had served in the Seven Years' War.

The Americans were at Stillwater. Let us now briefly consider General Gates. He was, in two words, an intriguer and a humbug. Also, he wore spectacles. A godson of Horace Walpole—hence his name, Horatio—he had served under Prince Ferdinand, was with Braddock (who carried military pride to such heights that he thought it cowardly to take cover) and, having married an English lady of fortune, bought an estate in Berkeley County, Virginia, which he called (it sounds rather like a road-house) "Traveller's Rest." But Mrs. Gates did little to make it so. Charles Lee describes her, with some acerbity, as "a tragedy in private life, a farce to all the world." He also pleasantly alludes to her as a Medusa. Gates got great credit,* which should have been Schuyler's and Arnold's, for the operations which led to the Convention of Saratoga, but in later life he lost his military reputation. At Camden, when the militia broke and fled, he exclaimed, with burning indignation, "I will bring the rascals back with me into line." He pursued the rascals, and such was his zeal that he is said not to have drawn rein until he was over sixty miles from the battle-field. The best that can be said for him as a soldier is that he had some considerable insight into Burgoyne's character. Writing of him on October fourth to the American General Clinton, he said: "Perhaps Burgoyne's despair may dictate to him to risque all upon one throw; he is an old gamester, and in his time has seen all chances. I will endeavour to be ready to prevent his good fortune, and, if possible, secure my own."

To be able to read your opponent's character has ever been one of the marks of a good general. The classic case is that of General R. E. Lee, of whom it was well said, "Lee read McClellan like an open book." Before the European War the German Staff had character-sketches of all the generals it was likely to meet in the

---

**e. g.*, in a contemporary British epigram:

"Burgoyne, alas, unknowing Future Fates
Could force his way through woods, but not through Gates."

field. Some of these pen-portraits would have been interesting reading—to the subjects of them.

Gates owed his appointment to succeed Schuyler to intrigue and to the fact New England did not like New York, which was too aristocratic; Vons and Vans always are. He arrived on August nineteenth with a commission in his pocket making him Commander-in-Chief of the Northern Department and he seems to have treated Schuyler with a certain hauteur; Schuyler, a true patriot and a thorough gentleman, took no notice of it. At the same time there arrived Benedict Arnold, a far better fighting general than Gates (although indeed a "Damaged Soul," to quote Mr. Gamaliel Bradford), and Morgan's Riflemen, the most famous corps of the Continental Army, all of them crack shots.

Burgoyne's troops were beginning to feel the pinch. Food for the men and forage for the horses were running short, and the soldiers were lightly clad, their winter-clothing having been sent back to Ticonderoga in anticipation of a walk-over to Albany. It was at this time that Major Acland and his wife, Lady Harriet, were nearly burned to death, owing to a "restless" Newfoundland dog—the British camp, quite apart from Mrs. Commissary, was full of pets—upsetting a candle in their tent.

The first of the Saratoga battles took place on September nineteenth. It is known as Freeman's Farm, Bemis's Heights or Bemus's Heights. Other variants are "Behmus" and "Braemus." The Baroness goes bravely for "Bimese's." The American position, chosen by Arnold, had been fortified by Kosciusko. Wilkinson, Gates's aide-de-camp, says that the battle was an accident, and that neither general contemplated an attack. This is wrong. Burgoyne knew where Gates's camp was—

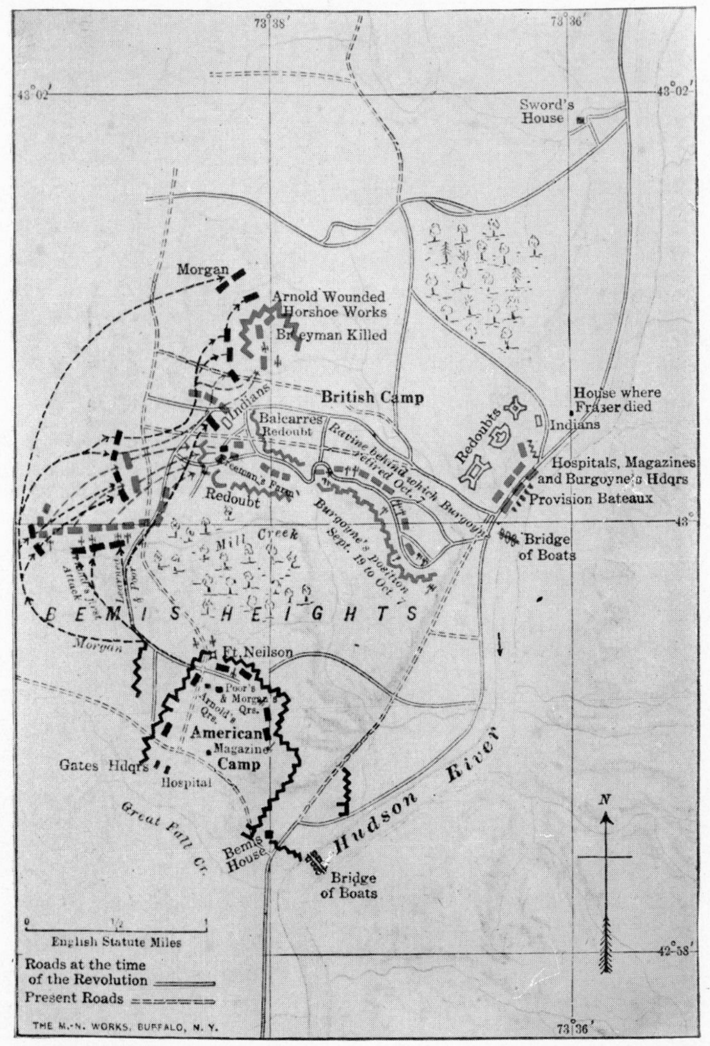


*Courtesy of The Charles Wm. Burrows Co., Publishers, Cleveland, Ohio.*

Map of Bemis Heights, October 7, 1777

From Avery's "History of the United States"

four miles away—and deliberately advanced upon it in three columns, leading the center himself, the right wing being commanded by Fraser, the left and the artillery by Riedesel and Phillips. Gates wanted to stay in his earthworks, in the rear of which he had the baggage-wagons all packed ready for the retreat which he evidently anticipated. It was the Damaged Soul, Arnold, who was all for action.

There was heavy fighting from two in the afternoon to sunset. On the British side the 20th, 21st and 62nd Regiments, immediately under the command of Burgoyne, particularly distinguished themselves. Each side went at it, hammer and tongs. "Such an explosion of fire," writes Digby, "I never had any idea of before, and the heavy artillery joining in concert like great peals of thunder, assisted by the echoes of the woods, almost deafened us with the noise." And in addition to the usual battle din could be heard Morgan's "turkey-call," the instrument normally used to decoy turkeys, but employed by him to collect his riflemen, who, perched up in trees, did deadly work as snipers, picking out the British officers by their uniforms. Burgoyne ended his despatch to Germain: "Just as the light closed, the enemy gave ground on all sides, and left us completely masters of the field of battle, with the loss of about 500 men on their side, and, as supposed, thrice that number wounded."* He wrote to Brigadier-General Powell at Ticonderoga: "We have had a smart and very honourable action and are encamped on the front of the field, which must demonstrate our victory beyond the power of even an American newspaper to explain away."

---

*It is curious that Creasy, who rightly includes Saratoga in his *Fifteen Decisive Battles of the World,* though he devotes many pages to the previous operations, dismisses this action in four lines.

As a matter of fact, gallantry apart, it was, as a victory, nothing to write home or to Ticonderoga about. The youthful Digby puts it better when he calls it "a dear-bought victory, if I can give it that name as we lost many brave men." Wilkinson uses a picturesque phrase; writing on the twentieth, he says: "The enemy have quietly licked their sores this day." He adds the very interesting statement, which he says he got later from General Phillips: "Burgoyne had intended to renew the attack on the 20th, but Fraser, saying that the grenadiers and light infantry wanted a rest, persuaded him to put it off." It is enormously to Burgoyne's credit that, Fraser being dead, he never said a word of this when he was defending himself against those who attacked him, with more than Indian craft, at home. Meanwhile Clinton's letter that he intended to move against the highlands arrived, and Burgoyne decided to wait. Wilkinson was of opinion that, had he attacked at once, he would probably have obtained a decisive victory.

During the action Gentleman Johnny was in the thick of it, thoroughly enjoying it, we may be sure. "General Burgoyne during this conflict behaved with great personal bravery. He shunned no danger; his presence and conduct animated the troops, for they greatly loved the General. He delivered his orders with precision and coolness and in the heat, danger and fury of the fight maintained the true characteristics of the soldier, serenity, fortitude, and undaunted intrepidity." This is a fine testimonial from a soldier (Lamb), and Digby says much the same: "General Burgoyne was everywhere and did everything that could be expected from a brave officer." The men were half-frozen and "sleep was a stranger to us, but we were all in good spirits and ready to obey with cheerfulness any orders the general might issue before morning dawned." Burgoyne never got his Order of the Bath, but this love of his men for him for his gallantry is far better than any distinction or decoration.

Clinton's letter was dated September twelfth. In it he said that in ten days he intended to attack Fort Montgomery. Burgoyne received it on September twenty-first. In his despatch he says: "I continued fortifying my camp and watching the enemy whose numbers increased every day. I thought it advisable on the 3rd of October to diminish the soldiers' ration in order to lengthen out the provisions, to which measure the army submitted with the utmost cheerfulness. The difficulties of a retreat to Canada were clearly foreseen, as was the dilemma, should the retreat be effected, of leaving at liberty such an army as General Gates's to operate against Sir William Howe."

The following paragraph is significant.

> "This consideration operated forcibly to determine me to abide events as long as possible, and I reasoned thus. The expedition I commanded was evidently meant at first to be *hazarded*. Circumstances might require that it should be *devoted*. A critical junction of Mr. Gates's force with Mr. Washington might possibly decide the fate of the war; the failure of my junction with Sir Harry Clinton, or the loss of my retreat to Canada, could only be a partial misfortune."

Some historians have argued that it was Burgoyne's vanity which now operated to dissuade him from giving the order for a retreat to Canada. This is not altogether fair. Obstinacy, a regular John Bullish obstinacy, perhaps. But we must remember that, as he so often said himself, there was no "latitude" in his instructions. Had he retreated to Canada—probably the best course he could have taken—Germain, that authority on not advancing, would have pounced upon it. Burgoyne's orders were to get to Albany and he thought it his duty, at all hazards, to try to do so. He knew by now that St. Leger had failed, and he must have realized that there was no likelihood of Howe advancing to Albany to meet him. And the word he uses, "devoted," or, as we would say nowadays, "sacrificed," shows pretty clearly that he understood that, if the Government at home wanted a scape-goat, they would look for it, not in Whitehall, which has never produced one, but in the woods on the banks of the Hudson River. Generals and admirals may—in the eighteenth century—have made mistakes, but ministers—why, the very idea is preposterous. Which is evident from the fact that it was Byng and not Newcastle who faced the firing-party. You can always get a new general or a new admiral: statesmen are rare.

On the twenty-seventh of September Burgoyne had sent Captain Scott, and on the following day Captain Campbell, with letters in duplicate to Clinton, urging him to cooperate with him. Campbell arrived on the fifth of October, Scott on the ninth. Clinton sent home to Whitehall an account of his "Conversation with Captain Campbell sent by General Burgoyne to me."

> "He said he was desired by General Burgoyne to tell me that the General's whole army did not exceed 5,000 men; that the consequences of the battle on the 19th were the loss of between five and six hundred men; that the enemy were within a mile and a half of

him; that he knew not their number for certain, but believed them to be twelve or fourteen thousand men; that there was besides that a considerable body in his rear. That he wished to receive my orders whether he should attack, or retreat to the lakes; that he had but provisions to the 20th of this month; and that he would not have given up his communications with Ticonderoga, had he not expected a co-operating army at Albany. That he wished to know my positive answer, as soon as possible, whether I could open a communication with Albany, when I should be there, and [whether] when there keep my communication with New York; that if he did not hear from me by the 12th instant he should retire.

"To which I returned the following answer by Capt. Campbell, viz. That not having received any instructions from the commander-in-chief [Howe] relative to the Northern Army, and [being] unacquainted even of his intentions concerning the operations of that army, excepting his wishes that they should get to Albany, Sir H. Clinton cannot presume to give any orders to General Burgoyne. General Burgoyne could not suppose that Sir H. Clinton had an idea of penetrating to Albany with the small force he mentioned in his last letter. What he offered in that letter he has now undertaken: cannot by any means promise himself success, but hopes it will be at any rate serviceable to General Burgoyne, as General Burgoyne says in his letter answering the offer, 'that even the menace of an attack would be of use.' "*

*For the actual reply sent to Burgoyne, which he never received, see page 193.

There is very poor comfort in this.

Clinton also sent home an account of the verbal report given him by Captain Scott, which is much the same as Campbell's, except that Scott put it in rather stronger language that "General Burgoyne begs that Sir Henry Clinton will give him an answer, conveying the plainest and most positive meaning how he should act for the good of his Majesty: whether he should proceed to Albany or make good his retreat to Canada."

The two armies were now engaged in fortifying their respective positions, but Burgoyne's army was growing smaller and smaller as the Indians responded to the "call of the wild"—farther back—and the Canadians found themselves unable to resist the temptation to go home. Gates's army was getting larger every day. The discomfort in the British camp was intense. "Many bodies not buried deep enough in the ground appeared (from the great rain) as the soil was a light sand and caused a most dreadful smell." About eight hundred sick and wounded were in tents and roughly-constructed huts, dignified with the name of hospital; it was necessary to be on the alert night and day, and supplies were running out like the sand in an hour-glass. It must have been a queer life for the ladies, the Baroness, Lady Harriet and Mrs. Commissary, for there were grave inconveniences to which the Baroness, who does not mince matters, from time to time specifically alludes. The one for whom most sympathy should be felt is Mrs. Commissary. For it is to be feared that even in all their danger, dirt and distress, the skirts of Lady Harriet and the Baroness were never so muddy and bedraggled as not to be drawn on one side, lest they should be contaminated by touching those of the General's favorite.

On the fourth of October Burgoyne held a small

council of war, Riedesel, Phillips and Fraser being present. Burgoyne proposed that two hundred men should be left in the camp to defend it and that the rest should march out and attack the enemy in the rear. Riedesel suggested a retreat to Fort Edward, which Fraser approved. Phillips would not give an opinion. As so often happens in Councils of War, there was plenty of talk, but no decision.

Meanwhile, what of Sir Harry Clinton? He had come up the Hudson with three thousand men and captured Forts Montgomery and Clinton. Here he rested on his oars and wrote Burgoyne a letter, which the latter never received. The bearer of it had it in a hollow silver bullet: blundering into the American General Clinton's camp, and perceiving his mistake, he promptly and loyally swallowed it. A "severe dose of tartar emetic" recovered it, but perhaps it was as well that it never reached Burgoyne, for it would not have brought much comfort to that distracted general. It ran as follows:

> "Fort Montgomery, October 8, 1777.
>
> "*Nous y voici,* and nothing now between us and Gates. I sincerely hope this little success of ours may facilitate your operations. In answer to your letter of the 28th September, by C. C.,* I shall only say I cannot presume to order, or even to advise, for reasons obvious. I heartily wish you success.
>
> "Faithfully yours,
> H. CLINTON."

Sir Harry reminds me of that Scandinavian young woman whom Lear has immortalized:

---

**i. e.*, Capt. Campbell. See page 190.

There was a young lady of Sweden
Who went by the slow train to Weedon,
When she reached Weedon Station
She made no observation
But returned by the next train to Sweden.

He returned with his whole force to New York. His letter to Burgoyne lacks only one thing, an appreciation of the autumn tints on the trees along the banks of the Hudson.* His defense in his letter of December sixteenth from New York to Burgoyne is not convincing. He feared that when his force was "removed out of the power of co-operating with you," Burgoyne might be overwhelmed, but he had hoped that Howe would get possession of Philadelphia and be able to send him reinforcements so that he might "try something in your favour." He goes on: "Could you with reason my dear friend expect that I should form the most distant idea of penetrating to Albany? Had I thought that with the small number I could spare from hence I should have been equal to forcing the highlands, I should not have conceived myself justified in detaching part of my garrison further, without extraordinary motives." And he ends in a somewhat Joseph Surface-like strain: "I feel for you as a friend and will not look amiss upon anything that passed when you had so much to perplex and distress you." It is really rather difficult not to agree with the opinion expressed at home that Clinton was jealous of Burgoyne.

---

*He might have written what Wilkinson actually wrote: "The weather in the autumn of 1777 on the Hudson's river was charming and the time glided away without any notable occurrence." Rather like "All quiet along the Potomac" and the *"Nichts neues vor Paris"* of the Franco-Prussian War.

On the sixth a rum ration* was served out to the British troops and on the seventh Burgoyne led out some fifteen hundred men, with ten guns, "to discover whether there were any possible means of forcing a passage should it be necessary to advance," that is to say it was a reconnaissance in force. The movement was perceived and reported to Gates, who said, "Order out Morgan to begin the game." The game began, and a bloody one it proved. "There was a very sudden and rapid attack of the enemy on our left." Arnold, who was in the American camp with no position and no authority, was here, there and everywhere. He and Gates had quarreled over the question of the command of Morgan's corps. Arnold complained bitterly that he was "huffed in such a manner as must mortify a person with less pride than I." But he forgot all his grievances in the thick of this fight. Wilkinson, not an unbiased witness where Arnold is concerned, says that he "had been drinking freely" and "behaved like a madman"; possibly, but a very heroic and courageous madman. When talebearers reported that Grant drank, did not Abraham Lincoln want to know, for the benefit of his other generals, what brand of whisky it was?

On the British side Fraser and Sir Francis Clark were mortally wounded; Acland was shot through both legs and taken prisoner; Burgoyne got one shot through his hat while another tore his waistcoat. The British were driven back into their camp, against which Arnold led a desperate attack, in the course of which he was wounded. "The intrenchments of the German reserve,

---

*Which in our time, according to a British army doctor giving evidence before a committee, had much to do with the winning of the European War.

commanded by Lieut.-Col. Breymann, who was killed, were carried and, although ordered to be recovered, they never were so, and the enemy by that misfortune gained an opening on our right and rear. The night put an end to the action." As a matter of fact, the Germans did not behave well, or rather they behaved very badly. After Breymann's death, writes Lamb, "The Germans retreated, firing until they had gained their tents in the rear of the entrenchments, but, supposing that the assault was general, they gave one discharge, after which some retreated to the British camp, but others surrendered prisoners."

In short it was a British defeat, the credit of which was entirely due to Arnold, for Gates spent the greater part of the action having what began as an academic, but ended in being a very hot, discussion on the merits of the Revolution with Sir Francis Clark, who, taken prisoner after his wound, was lying upon the American commander's bed. Sir Francis, before he died (which he did with an *insouciance* that one can not but admire) left a legacy in the shape of a written promise to Gates's servant maid,* who had treated him with the greatest care and tenderness. After the Convention she presented her claim to Captain Money, the British Deputy Quartermaster-General. Money, who should have been ashamed of so mean an act, paid it in continental bills. This came to the ears of Gentleman Johnny, and this and the Henley business are the only occasions on which it is recorded that he lost his temper, for Parliamentary tempers are generally Pickwickian. He sent for the girl and asked her to keep the paper money, and then sternly told Cap-

*Another account calls her the matron of a hospital.

tain Money to "pay the legacy in hard guineas of British coinage without reference to the sum he had already paid." Burgoyne well deserved his nickname.

Baroness Riedesel's account of this eventful day is so vivid that it is worth quoting.

> "I had just sat down with my husband in his quarters to breakfast. General Fraser and, I believe, General Burgoyne were to have lunched with me on that same day. I observed some commotion among the troops. My husband told me there was to be a reconnaissance. On my way home [*i. e.,* to the rear of the camp where all the women were collected] I met some Indians in their war-paint armed with guns. I asked where they were going and they cried out 'War, War.'* This upset me very much. When I got back I heard skirmishing and firing which grew louder and louder until there was a terrible noise. I was more dead than alive. About 3 o'clock in the afternoon instead of the guests who were to have had food with me they brought poor General Fraser upon a litter mortally wounded. The dining-table all ready prepared was taken away and a bed placed there for the General. I sat in a corner trembling. The noise got louder and louder and I feared lest they should bring in my husband also wounded. The General said to the surgeon, 'Do not hide anything from me. Am I going to die?' The ball had gone through his bowels, just as in the case of Major Harnage. Unfortunately the General had had a heavy breakfast, and his bowels were distended so that the bullet, the surgeon said, had

---

*Surely what they really did was to grunt "Waugh, Waugh," which the baroness mistranslates as *Krieg, Krieg.*

not, as with Major Harnage, gone between them but through them. I heard him often, between his groans, exclaim, 'Oh bad ambition! Poor General Burgoyne! Poor mistress Fraser.'* Prayers were read to him and he sent a message to General Burgoyne asking that he might be buried on the top of a hill which was a kind of redoubt."

Burgoyne himself has given us a fine, if in the peroration slightly stilted, account, of the funeral.

"About sun-set the corpse of General Fraser was brought up the hill, attended by the officers who had lived in his family. To arrive at the redoubt, it passed within view of the greatest part of both armies. General Phillips, General Riedesel, and myself, who were standing together, were struck with the humility of the procession; they who were ignorant that privacy had been requested might construe it neglect. We could neither endure that reflection nor indeed restrain our natural propensity to pay our last attention to his remains. The incessant cannonade† during the solemnity; the steady attitude and unaltered voice with

---

*What he probably really said was "Damned ambition! Poor Burgoyne! My poor wife!"

†Colonel Kingston said: "The enemy in this instance were I thought very defective in point of humanity: they pointed a gun or two at that very redoubt, and kept up a brisk cannonade during the whole of the funeral service, which was performed with great solemnity, and very deliberately by Mr. Brudenell, the chaplain. I never saw so affecting a sight." I have not formed a very high opinion of General Gates, so it is very pleasant to be able to add that the "brisk cannonade" was really minute guns, which the American general ordered to be fired as soon as it was perceived that it was a funeral which was taking place on the redoubt. War is hell, but it has always had its courtesies.

General Simon Fraser mortally wounded at Bemis Heights in 1777, under Burgoyne

Engraved in 1794. From a print in possession of Messrs. T. H. Parker, 12a, Berkeley Street, London, W. 1

which the chaplain* officiated, though frequently covered with dust, which the shot threw up on all sides of him, the mute but expressive mixture of sensibility and indignation upon every countenance; these objects will remain to the last of life upon the minds of every man who was present. The growing duskiness added to the scenery, and the whole marked a character of that juncture that would make one of the finest subjects for the pencil of a master that the field ever exhibited.† To the canvas and to the faithful page of a more important historian, gallant friend! I consign thy memory. There may thy talents, thy manly virtues, their progress and their period, find due distinction and long may they survive—long after the frail record of my pen shall be forgotten."

Gentleman Johnny was undoubtedly sincere in writing this tribute to General Fraser, and the allusion to the "frail record of my pen," is due, not to that pride which apes humility, but to the fact that it was impossible for him to refrain from what used to be called "fine writing."

General Gates also treated Lady Harriet Acland with the greatest courtesy. She had followed the army and her husband in "a two-wheel tumbril,‡ which had been constructed by the artificers of the artillery, something similar to the carriage used for the mail upon the great roads of England." When her husband was wounded and taken prisoner she asked Burgoyne's leave to follow him.

---

*Mr. Shaw, by the way, has included Chaplain Brudenell in *The Devil's Disciple.*

†There is, as a matter of fact, a very fine print entitled *The Burial of General Fraser.*

‡The Baroness followed the expedition in a calèche, which was rather like the Victorian dog-cart.

"I was astonished," writes the General, "at this proposal. After so long an agitation of the spirits, exhausted not only for want of rest, but absolutely want of food, drenched in rains for twelve hours together, that a woman should be capable of such an undertaking as delivering herself to the enemy, probably in the night, and uncertain of what hands she might first fall into,* appeared an effort above human nature. The assistance I was enabled to give was small indeed; I had not even a cup of wine to offer her, but I was told she had found, from some kind and fortunate hand, a little rum and dirty water. All I could furnish to her was an open boat and a few lines,† written upon dirty and wet paper, to General Gates, recommending her to his protection."

Accompanied by the chaplain, Mr. Brudenell, and her husband's servant, who had been wounded like his master, she crossed the Hudson and reached the American camp, after spending eight hours in the boat, the American sentries, not unnaturally, refusing to allow it to approach before daylight. Gates received her with

*I think he remembered that there were still a few Indians with him.

†They ran as follows:

"Sir,

"Lady Harriet Acland, a lady of the first distinction of family, rank and personal virtues, is under such concern on account of Major Acland her husband, wounded and a prisoner in your hands, that I cannot refuse her request to commit her to your protection. Whatever general impropriety there may be in persons in my situation and yours to solicit favours, I can not see the uncommon perseverance in every female grace and exaltation of character of this lady, and her very hard fortune, without testifying that your attention to her will lay me under obligations.

"I am, Sir, your obedient servant,

"John Burgoyne."

the greatest kindness, and wrote of her to his wife, "She is the most amiable, delicate piece of quality you ever beheld."*

On the eighth, leaving the so-called hospitals, full of wounded, with a letter† recommending them to Gates's sympathy, Burgoyne fell back to Schuylerville, where it was found necessary to burn General Schuyler's house, storehouses and mills.‡ It was on the evening of the ninth that, according to the Baroness, Burgoyne entertained his lady friend at supper.** Gates and his troops had come hot in pursuit and by the eleventh the British Army was completely surrounded; "their cannon and ours began to play on each other: it was impossible to sleep from the cold and rain and our only entertainment was the report of some popping shots heard now and then from the other side the great river." The British horses and live stock were living on the leaves of trees: as for the army itself, let us again quote from the Baroness: "The greatest misery and confusion prevailed;

---

*Some sentimentalist has recorded that Lady Harriet, on the death of the Major, married the Chaplain. This is not true.

†As follows:

"Sir,

"The State of my Hospital makes it more advisable to leave the Wounded and Sick Officers, whom you will find in my late Camp, than to transport them with the Army. I recommend them to the Protection which, I feel, I should show to an Enemy in the same Case.

"I am, Sir,

"Your most Humble Servant,

"J. BURGOYNE.

"Major General Gates."

(From *The Papers Respecting the Convention Troops* in *The Papers of the Continental Congress,* vol. 57.)

‡It was done in the interests of the British artillery, its line of fire being blocked by them. Schuyler, later, told Burgoyne that in his position he would have done the same himself.

**See page 143.

the Commissaries had forgotten to distribute provisions; there were plenty of cattle but none had been killed. More than thirty officers, driven by hunger, came to me. I had tea and coffee made for them and shared my food with them." She then proceeds to represent herself as a *dea ex machina;* she sent for (!) Burgoyne, talked to him like a Dutch uncle, or rather aunt, and, according to her account, he thanked her with emotion for having shown him what was his duty. The Baroness had, as her countrymen would say, too much ego in her cosmos. She remarks on another occasion that Phillips said to her he wished she was in command of the expedition instead of Burgoyne. She wrote her book some time after the war and here and there probably her memory may have misled her. On this particular occasion Burgoyne was probably excessively courteous and excessively sorry, and no doubt that was all. On the whole the Riedesels had no great cause to grumble, for the General saved quite a lot of money when in North America. The Baroness was so fond of the continent that of two daughters born there one was christened "Canada" and the other "Amerika."* How lucky that she was not more definite: just suppose one of them had been born at Oshkosh!

It was at this date that, according to a news item in a contemporary *New York Gazette and Weekly Mercury,* Burgoyne sent what few Indians were left with him, under the command of Captains McAlpine and McKay, with the military chest back to Canada. Some of the party were captured, but the money got through safely to Carleton.

On the twelfth of October a council of war was held

*One of these daughters married a numerical nobleman, Count Heinrich Reuss the 44th.

on the Heights of Saratoga, "Burgoyne, Riedesel, Phillips and Brig.-Gen. Hamilton being present." Burgoyne put the case very clearly to his council. They were practically surrounded; the provisions might hold out to the twentieth, but "there is neither rum nor spruce beer."* There were four possible courses of action, or inaction. 1. To wait the chance of favorable events. 2. To attack. 3. To retreat, repairing the bridges for the artillery. 4. To retreat by night, leaving the artillery and the baggage. The fourth was chosen, but, scouts being sent out, it was reported that it would be impossible to move without the march being immediately discovered.

And so on the thirteenth another council of war was held, all the general officers and field officers and captains commanding corps being present. Burgoyne behaved like a gentleman—and a scholar. He began by stating that he himself, and he alone, was responsible for the situation in which they found themselves, as he had asked no officer for advice, but had given instructions which were to be followed. He then, the scholar part of him coming to the surface, asked whether in military history any army in similar case had capitulated. (Here, I feel sure, some of the younger officers must heartily have wished, probably for the first time in the expedition, that they were somewhere else.) The next questions were, whether they were in such a situation that there was nothing left but to capitulate, and whether such a capitulation would be dishonorable. The answer of the council

---

*A local and indifferent brew. Young Captain Evelyn writing home from Boston in October, 1774, remarked: "Nothing would be more acceptable than a cask of porter, as our only liquor for the table here is a stuff they call spruce beer." In that comic-opera campaign, the Crimean War, the authorities insisted that the Guards should have their porter.

to the first was yes, and to the second no. While this council was sitting a cannon-ball whizzed over the table in the tent where they were collected. Burgoyne must have been reminded of La Lippe's practical exposition of gunnery in Portugal.

There is a detailed account of the negotiations in a War Office manuscript volume, *Capitulations*. On the thirteenth Burgoyne wrote to Gates that he was desirous of sending a field officer to him "upon a matter of high moment to both Armies." Gates agreed that the field officer should be received "at the advanced post of the Army of the United States" at ten o'clock the following morning, from whence he would be conducted to Headquarters. On the fourteenth Major Kingston was entrusted with the following message to General Gates; one can not but admire the bravado of its beginning:

> "After having fought you twice, Lieut.-Gen. Burgoyne has waited some days, in his present position, determined to try a third conflict against any force you could bring to attack him.
>
> "He is apprised of the superiority of your numbers, and the disposition of your troops to impede his supplies, and render his retreat a scene of carnage on both sides. In this situation he is impelled by humanity, and thinks himself justifiable by established principles and precedents of state, and of war, to spare the lives of brave men upon honourable terms. Should Maj.-Gen. Gates be inclined to treat upon that idea, General Burgoyne would propose a cessation of arms during the time necessary to communicate the preliminary terms by which, in any extremity, he and his army mean to abide."

Gates's aide-de-camp, young Captain Wilkinson, "a youth in a plain, blue frock, without other military insignia than cockade and sword" (but with, so it appears from his book, an uncommonly good opinion of himself) met Major Kingston,* "a well-formed, ruddy, handsome man *who expatiated with taste and eloquence on the beautiful scenery of the Hudson's river and the charms of the season.*" I love this meeting: it is only equaled by that historic encounter in the heart of Central Africa when Stanley, seeing a strange white man, advanced with outstretched hand and said—there being no other white man within hundreds and hundreds of miles—"Dr. Livingstone, I presume?" Good old Anglo-Saxon, poker-face phlegm! Whether in the United States, or in England, like Phyllis in the charming old ballad, it "never fails to please." Darn all foreigners with their bows, and their scrapings and their caperings and their kisses.

We now come to Gates's preliminary "Propositions." These were:

> 1. General Burgoyne's army being exceedingly reduced by repeated defeats, by desertion, sickness, etc., their provisions exhausted, their military stores, tents and baggage taken or destroyed, their retreat cut off and their camps invested, they can only be allowed to surrender as prisoners of war.

Bulldog Burgoyne replied to this: "Lieutenant-General Burgoyne's army, however reduced, will never admit that their retreat is cut off, while they have arms in their hands."

---

*Kingston, before he entered Gates's camp, was, naturally, blindfolded or as they called it then "hood-winked."

2. The officers and soldiers may keep their baggage belonging to them, the generals of the United States never permit private individuals to be pillaged.

3. The troops under his excellency, General Burgoyne, will be conducted by the most convenient route to New England, marching by easy marches and sufficiently provided for by the way.

4. The officers will be admitted on parole, may wear their side arms, and will be treated with the liberality customary in Europe, so long as they, by proper behavior, continue to deserve it; but those who are apprehended having broken their parole (as some British officers have done) must expect to be close confined.

To this Burgoyne replied—can you not hear his quill pen spluttering with indignation?—"There being no officers in this army under, or capable of being under, the description of breaking parole, this article needs no answer."

5. All public stores, artillery, arms, ammunition, carriages, horses, etc., must be delivered to commissaries appointed to receive them.

Answer: "All public stores may be delivered, arms excepted."

6. These terms being agreed to and signed, the troops under his excellency's, General Burgoyne's, command may be drawn up in their encampment, when they will be ordered to ground their arms and may there-

upon be marched to the river side to be passed over on their way toward Bennington.

The cold and severe answer to this was: "This article inadmissible in any extremity. Sooner than this army will consent to ground their arms in their encampment, they will rush on the enemy determined to take no quarter."

7. A cessation of arms to continue till sunset to receive General Burgoyne's answer.

It was the sixth article which was the crux. Kingston was instructed to give Wilkinson a verbal answer: "If General Gates does not mean to recede from the 6th Article the treaty ends at once. The Army will to a man proceed to any act of desperation rather than submit to that article." According to Wilkinson, at one moment Burgoyne said the truce must end in an hour and he says that he and the British General "set watches." Turning to Colonel Sutherland, Wilkinson said: "You will not only lose your fusee* but your whole baggage," and goes on to explain "this fusee Col. Sutherland had owned for thirty-five years and had desired me to except it from the surrendered arms and save for him as *she* was a favourite piece." Another difficulty was that Burgoyne had received intelligence that "a considerable force has been detached from the Army under the command of General Gates during the course of the negotiations": this he argued was "not only a violation of the Cessation of Arms but subversive of the principles on which the treaty originated, *viz.*, a great superiority of numbers in General Gates's Army." He even "required"

*See page 278.

that two of his officers should have ocular proof of this, to which Gates briefly replied that no violation of the treaty had taken place on his part. In addition rumors that Clinton was at hand had reached both Burgoyne and Gates.

Another British council of war was held and it was decided that "should General Clinton be where reported, yet the distance is such as to render any relief from him improbable during the time our provisions could be made to last." Gates, on his side, gave better terms than he would otherwise have done, and "after many flags passing and repassing the terms were at last mutually agreed to," though Burgoyne insisted that it was to be a convention and not a capitulation. The convention* contained thirteen articles. They were as follows:

ARTICLES OF CONVENTION between Lieut-General Burgoyne and Major-General Gates.

1.

The Troops under Lieut-Genl. Burgoyne, to march out of their Camp with the honors of War, & the Artillery of the Intrenchment to the Verge of the River where the Old Fort stood, where the arms & Artillery are to be left. The arms to be piled by word of command from their own officers.

2.

A Free Passage to be granted to the Army under Lieut. Genl. Burgoyne to Great Britain, upon condition of not serving again in North America, during the present Contest; and the Port of Boston is Assigned

*Signed by Gates on the sixteenth of October; "mutually signed and exchanged" the following day.

for the Entry of Transports to Receive the Troops whenever General Howe shall so Order.

3.

Should any Cartel take place by which the Army under Lieut. General Burgoyne, or any part of it, may be exchang'd, the foregoing Article to be void as far as such exchange shall be made.

4.

The Army under Lieut. Genl. Burgoyne to March to Massachusetts Bay by the Easiest, Most Expeditious, & Convenient Route, and to be quartered in, near, or as convenient as possible to Boston, that the march of the Troops may not be delay'd when Transports arrive to receive them.

5.

The Troops to be Supplied on the March & during their being in Quarters with Provisions by Genl. Gates's Orders, at the same rates of Rations as the Troops of his own Army, & if possible the Officers Horses, & Cattle are to be Supplied with Forage at the usual Rates.

6.

All officers to Retain their Carriages, Bat Horses, & other Cattle, and no Baggage to be molested or searched; Lieut. Genl. Burgoyne giving his honor there are no public Stores contained* therein. Major General Gates will, of course, take the necessary measures for the due performance of this Article. Should any Carriages be wanting during the March for the Transportation of officers' Baggage, they are, if possible, to be supplied by the Country at the usual Rates.

*Thus in the *London Gazette:* other versions have the word "secreted."

7.

Upon the March and during the time the Army shall remain in Quarters in the Massachusetts Bay the officers are not, as far as Circumstances will Admit, to be separated from their Men. The officers are to be Quartered according to Rank, and are not to be hindered from assembling their Men for Roll-calling & other purposes of Regularity.

8.

All Corps whatever of General Burgoyne's Army, whether compos'd of Sailors, Batteau-men, Artificers, Drivers, Independant Companies, & followers of the Army of whatever Country, shall be included in the fullest sense and utmost extent of the above Articles, and comprehended in every respect as British Subjects.

9.

All Canadians & Persons belonging to the Canadian Establishment consisting of Sailors, Batteaumen, Artificers, Drivers, Independant Companies, & many other followers of the Army who come under no particular Description are to be permitted to return there; they are to be conducted immediately, by the Shortest Route to the first British Post on Lake George, are to be supplied with Provisions in the same manner as the other Troops, and to be bound by the same condition of not serving during the present Contest in North America.

10.

Passports to be immediately granted for three officers not exceeding the Rank of Captains, who shall be appointed by Lieut. Genl. Burgoyne to carry Dispatches to Sir William Howe, Sir Guy Carleton, & to Great Britain by the way of New York; and Maj. Gen'l Gates engages the Publick Faith that these

Dispatches shall not be opened. These officers are to set out immediately after receiving their Dispatches and are to Travel by the Shortest Route & in the most expeditious manner.

11.

During the stay of the Troops in the Massachusetts Bay the officers are to be admitted on Parole, and are to be permitted to wear their side Arms.

12.

Should the Army under Lieut. General Burgoyne find it necessary to send for their Cloathing & other Baggage from Canada, they are to be permitted to do it in the most convenient manner and the necessary Passports granted for that purpose.

13.

These Articles are to be mutually Signed & Exchanged tomorrow at 9 o'clock; and the Troops under Lieut. Genl. Burgoyne are to march out of their Intrenchments at three o'clock in the afternoon.
*Camp at Saratoga, October 16, 1777.*

On the seventeenth, early in the morning, Burgoyne called all his officers together and "entered into a detail of his manner of acting since he had the honour of commanding the army; but he was too full to speak." Digby goes on in a simple and very moving strain: "About 10 o'clock we marched out, acording to treaty, with drums beating and the honours of war, but the drums seemed to have lost their former inspiriting sounds, and though we beat the Grenadiers' march, which not long before was so animating, yet then it seemed by its last feeble effort as if almost ashamed to be heard on such an occasion." He adds, and he echoed the feeling of every officer in the expedition: "Thus was Burgoyne's Army sacrificed to either the absurd opinions of a blundering ministerial power, the stupid inaction of a general* who, from his lethargic disposition, neglected every step he might have taken to assist their operations, or lastly, perhaps, his own misconduct† in penetrating so far as to be unable to return."

Burgoyne "in a rich royal uniform"‡ and Gates in a plain blue frock met at the head of Gates's camp: "when," writes Wilkinson, "they had approached nearly within swords' length they reined up and halted: I then named the gentlemen and General Burgoyne raising his hat said, 'The fortune of war, General Gates, has made me your prisoner,' to which the conqueror, returning a courtly salute, replied, 'I shall always be ready to bear testimony that it has not been through any fault of your excellency.'" Riedesel gives exactly the same words in his account of this historic scene.

An artist has pictured it. Part of it, perhaps, is not very much like what really happened, but the air of Noble Affability with which Gentleman Johnny is endowed—he looks as if he were condescendingly bestowing some order of knighthood upon Gates—is undoubtedly the real thing. Also, his position in the center of the stage in the last act of the drama, right in the limelight, is the only place for a hero.

Wilkinson, the Master of the Ceremonies, deserves a few words. His subsequent career was not a success, and he came to sad grief in the expedition against Canada

*I need not add that he means Mrs. Loring's friend.

†By which he means, of course, miscalculation.

‡One of the Brunswick officers wrote that "he wore a hat with streaming plumes and had bestowed the greatest care on his whole toilet, so that he looked like a man of fashion rather than a warrior."

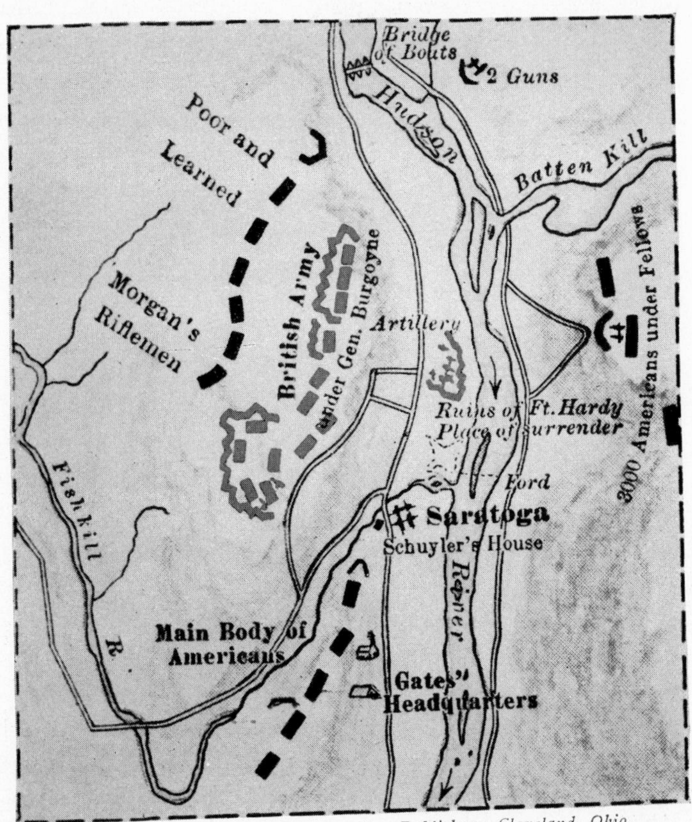


*Courtesy of The Charles Wm. Burrows Co., Publishers, Cleveland, Ohio.*

Map of Surrender of Burgoyne, October 17, 1777

From Avery's "History of the United States"

in 1813. For his conduct then he was court-martialed, one of the charges being the very singular one that "on or about 1st November 1813, in the vicinity of Ogdensburgh, he damned the army, the expedition, and himself." He had a fine and flowery style. On one occasion he wrote to Gates, "The perfidy of mankind truly disgusts me with life, and if the happiness of an amiable woman was not unfortunately too dependent on my wretched existence, I should think I had lived long enough, nor would I wish more to breathe the common air with ingrates, assassins and double-faced villains."

Gates wrote, with pardonable pride, to his wife: "The voice of fame, ere this reaches you, will tell how greatly fortunate we have been in this department. Burgoyne and his whole army have laid down their arms, and surrendered themselves to me and my Yankees. Thanks to the Giver of all victory for this triumphant success. . . . Major-General Phillips, who wrote me that saucy note last year from St. John's, is now my prisoner, with Lord Petersham, Major Acland, son of Sir Thomas, and his lady, daughter of Lord Ilchester, sister to the famous Lady Susan, and about a dozen members of Parliament, Scotch lords, etc. I wrote to T. Boone. . . . I could not help, in a modest manner, putting him in mind of the *fête champêtre* * that I, three years ago, told him General Burgoyne would meet with if he came to America. If Old England is not by this lesson taught humility, then she is an obstinate old Slut, bent upon her ruin."

Gates then branches off from the general to the particular, and, like a good husband, expresses a hope that his wife may get "ruffles to her apron."

Though he behaved with gross insolence to Washing-

*A palpable hit. See page 323.

ton,* to whom he only casually mentioned Burgoyne's surrender in a letter dated so late as November second, Gates treated Burgoyne with great dignity and magnanimity. He could afford to be generous.

Letters received in London all spoke of his courtesy and the care he took to relieve the wants of the rank and file† as well as their officers. Burgoyne, his generals and his staff were entertained by Gates at dinner, and a regular camp dinner it was. The table was formed by two planks laid across two empty beef-barrels, the menu was a ham, a goose, some beef and some boiled mutton; *vins* New England rum and cider; there were only two glasses, which were allotted to the two Generals, the rest of the company drank out of "small basons." Gates filled a bumper to His Britannic Majesty's health, Gentleman Johnny, not to be outdone, proposed that of General Washington. Phillips when called on to give a toast, thinking it well to steer clear of politics, "bluntly gave a certain toast which is often drunk in this country even before his Majesty's health and which is sure to meet with the hearty approbation and concurrence of *every good man*." You must decide for yourselves what this

*Washington administered a well-deserved snub. He wrote to Gates (October 30th) congratulating him on his "signal success" but adding "I cannot but regret that a matter of such magnitude and so interesting to our general operations, should have reached me by report only, or through the channel of letters, not bearing that authenticity, which the importance of it required, and which it would have received by a line under your signature, stating the simple fact."

†Mr. Wilson, a surgeon in Burgoyne's army, wrote home: "If our wounded live to return to England Chelsea Hospital will indeed be an Invalid-Hospital, for there never were such shocking spectacles seen as some of them represent." The Baroness gives a ghastly account of an operation on a soldier, just before the Convention. He had been laid in a gimcrack house, on a table to have a leg amputated, when a cannon-ball took off the other leg as he was lying there.

toast was. But perhaps the most kindly thing that the American general did was to allow the British troops to pile* their arms, at the word of command of a British officer, and out of sight of the American troops.† And when Burgoyne presented his sword to him, Gates returned it. On the seventeenth and eighteenth the British troops, now prisoners of war, crossed the Hudson on their way to Boston.

The Baroness draws a delightful picture of the kindness and courtesy with which the British were treated by their conquerors. She writes:

> "In the passage through the American camp, I observed with great satisfaction, that no one cast at us scornful glances. On the contrary, they all greeted me, even showing compassion on their countenances at seeing a mother with her little children in such a situation. I confess that I feared to come into the enemy's camp, as the thing was so entirely new to me. When I approached the tents, a handsome man came toward me, took the children out of the wagon, embraced and kissed them, and then with tears in his eyes helped me also to alight. 'You tremble,' said he to me, 'fear nothing.' 'No,' replied I, 'for you are so kind, and have been so tender toward my children, that it has inspired me with courage.' He then led me to the tent of General Gates, with whom I found Generals

*It is in connection with this that we get the only mention made of Burgoyne in Boswell's *Johnson*. "It was asked why piling their arms was insisted upon as a matter of such consequence when it seemed to be a circumstance so inconsiderable in itself." Johnson: "Why, sir, a French author says *Il y a beaucoup de puérilités dans la guerre.*"

†One of whom, by the way, said that Burgoyne ought to be made to stand on his head on one of his empty beef-barrels and in that position recite his Putnam Creek Proclamation.

Burgoyne and Phillips, who were on an extremely friendly footing with him. Burgoyne said to me, 'You may now dismiss all your apprehensions, for your sufferings are at an end.' I answered him that I should certainly be acting very wrongly to have any more anxiety, when our chief had none, and especially when I saw him on such a friendly footing with General Gates. All the Generals remained to dine with General Gates. The man, who had received me so kindly, came up and said to me, 'It may be embarrassing to you to dine with all these gentlemen; come now with your children into my tent, where I will give you, it is true, a frugal meal, but one that will be accompanied by the best of wishes.' 'You are certainly,' answered I, 'a husband and a father since you show me so much kindness.' I then learned that he was the American General Schuyler. He entertained me with excellent smoked tongue, beef-steaks, potatoes, good bread and butter. Never have I more enjoyed a meal. I was content. I saw that all around me were so likewise; but that which rejoiced me more than everything else was, that my husband was out of all danger. As soon as we had finished, he (Schuyler) invited me to take up my residence at his house, which was situated at Albany, and told me, that General Burgoyne would be there also. I sent and asked my husband what I should do. He sent me word to accept the invitation; and as it was two days' journey from where we were, and already five o'clock in the afternoon, he advised me to set out in advance, and to stay over night at a place distant about three hours' ride."

Here she has an adventure. In the house in which

she spent the night she found a French doctor looking after a mortally wounded Brunswick officer. The Baroness, though she may not have appealed to the Bristolians, was a very pretty woman and the doctor very quickly developed what is I believe technically called "a crush." "He made all kinds of sweet speeches and was very impertinent: he urged me to stay with him for it was better to be with the conquerors than with the conquered." He actually so far forgot himself as to press her to share his room with him, a proposal which she indignantly set aside, though perhaps in her heart of hearts she was flattered. Fortunately the Baron turns up and this chartered libertine of a Frenchman "looked very sheepish." The next day they arrived at Albany where:

> "we were received in the most friendly manner by the good General Schuyler, and by his wife and daughter, who showed us the most marked courtesy, as also, General Burgoyne, although he had—without any necessity it was said—caused their magnificently-furnished houses to be burned. But they treated us as people who knew how to forget their own losses in the misfortunes of others. Even General Burgoyne was deeply moved at their magnanimity and said to General Schuyler, 'Is it to me, who have done you so much injury, that you show so much kindness!' 'That is the fate of war,' replied the brave man, 'let us say no more about it.' We remained three days with them, and they showed us they were reluctant to let us go. Our cook had remained in the city with the baggage of my husband, but the second night after our arrival, the whole of it was stolen from us, notwithstanding an American guard of ten or twenty men who had been

deputed for its protection. Nothing remained to us except the beds of myself and children, and a few trifles that I kept by me for my own use—and this too, in a land where one could get nothing for money, and at a time when we were in want of many things; consequently my husband was obliged to board his adjutant, quartermaster, etc., and find them in everything. The English officers—our friends as I am justified in calling them, for during the whole of my sojourn in America they always acted as such—each one gave us something. One gave a pair of spoons, another some plates, all of which we were obliged to use for a long time, as it was not until three years afterwards, in New York, that we found an opportunity, although at great cost, to replace a few of the things we had lost. Fortunately I had kept by me my little carriage, which carried my baggage. As it was already very late in the season, and the weather raw, I had my calash covered with coarse linen, which in turn was varnished over with oil; and in this manner we set out on our journey to Boston, which was very tedious, besides being attended with considerable hardship."

Burgoyne, the soul of courtesy and kindness himself, appreciated these qualities in others. Later in Parliament he said that General Schuyler "was one of the first persons he met in the American camp, and when he attempted to make some explanation or excuse for his act in destroying his property, the general begged him not to think of it, as the occasion justified it, on the principles and rules of war."

"He did more," Burgoyne added, "he sent an aide-de-camp to conduct me to Albany, in order, as he expressed it, to procure better quarters than a stranger might be able to find. That gentleman conducted me to a very elegant house, and, to my great surprise, presented me to Mrs. Schuyler and her family. In that house I remained during my whole stay in Albany, with a table of more than twenty covers for me and my friends, and every other demonstration of hospitality."

De Chastellux, in his *Travels in America,* gives some interesting details of Burgoyne's sojourn at the house of General Schuyler.

"The British commander," says he, "was well received by Mrs. Schuyler, and lodged in the best apartment in the house. An excellent supper was served him in the evening, the honors of which were done with so much grace that he was affected even to tears, and said with a deep sigh, 'Indeed, this is doing too much for a man who has ravaged their lands and burned their dwellings.' The next morning, he was reminded of his misfortunes by an incident that would have amused any one else. His bed was prepared in a large room; but, as he had a numerous suite, or family, several mattresses were spread on the floor, for some officers to sleep near him. Schuyler's second son, a little fellow about seven years old, very arch and forward, but very amiable, was running all the morning, about the house. Opening the door of the saloon, he burst out a laughing on seeing all the English collected, and shut it after him, exclaiming, 'You are all my prisoners!' This innocent cruelty rendered them more melancholy than before."

Burgoyne had gaily boasted that he would eat his

Christmas dinner at Albany, as a conqueror. His fate was different.*

For the sake of convenience let us here look ahead a few weeks, and turn our attention to London. News traveled slowly in these days but toward the end of November London† was beginning to get uneasy. Walpole, writing so early as October twenty-sixth, said: "Burgoyne is said to be beaten." And on November third Horace said definitely: "Arnold has beaten the vapouring Burgoyne and destroyed his magazines. Carleton, who was set aside for General Hurlothrumbo, is gone to save him the remains of his army if he can." This of course was a baseless rumor. On the eighteenth of November Lord Shelburne, speaking in the House of Lords, said: "The issue of Mr. Burgoyne's expedition is too melancholy to be made a subject of conversation: his army, by every appearance, is destroyed," and he proceeded savagely to criticize Germain as "a man who has so great a confidence in his military talents as to think he can command an army and ensure victory in his closet‡ at three thousand miles distance from the scene of action." The Duke of Richmond was equally contemptuous of the strategy of the campaign: "Supposing, which is most improbable, that Mr. Burgoyne has got to New

*From *The Life and Times of Philip Schuyler,* Benson J. Lossing. New York, Sheldon & Company, 1873.

†One says London advisedly. The Sir Tunbelly Clumseys of this date were so busy chasing village maidens round haycocks and drinking port that they took little interest in public affairs outside their own parish and its pump. It is amazing to read that the town of Frome, concluding from his name that Burgoyne was a Frenchman, "made great rejoicings on his being taken prisoner."

‡*i. e.,* his study or library. In the eighteenth century a dull play would be dismissed with the words "more suitable for the closet than the stage."

York, what has he effected? He has lost several thousand men and he might have arrived at New York two years ago by sea from England without any loss at all." The Duke, though he did not say so in so many words, knew the value of sea power. Definite news of the surrender reached London, by way of Quebec, on December second.*

On the third Colonel Barré in the House of Commons "called upon Lord George Germain to declare upon his honour what was become of General Burgoyne and his brave troops and whether or not he had not received expresses from Quebec informing him of his having surrendered himself with his whole army prisoners of war?" Germain shuffled. The news certainly had arrived, by deserters *via* Ticonderoga to Quebec. It was not authenticated. He hoped the House would suspend judgment, both on the General and on ministers. Barré rose again and said he was "shocked at the cool easy manner in which the noble Lord related the fate of the brave Burgoyne. Nobody could say that Burgoyne had failed through his own misconduct. The minister who had planned the expedition was to blame, it was "an inconsistent scheme, an impracticable one, unworthy of a British minister, and rather too absurd for an Indian chief." Edmund Burke followed: "Ignorance had stamped every step taken during the course of the expedition, but it was the ignorance of the Minister for the American department, not to be imputed to General Burgoyne of whose good conduct, bravery and skill he did not entertain the shadow of a doubt." He then put his finger on the weak point in any defense that Germain

*Burgoyne's despatch did not reach Whitehall until December 15th.

might concoct. "The intended measure was a conjunction between Howe and Burgoyne, it was to be produced in the strangest way he had ever heard of: the armies were to meet—yes: Howe was travelling southward, and Burgoyne in the same direction!" Fox was even stronger in his attack: "An army of 10,000 men destroyed through the ignorance, the obstinate, wilful ignorance and incapacity of the noble Lord, called loudly for vengeance. . . . A gallant general sent like a victim to be slaughtered, where his own skill and personal bravery would have earned him laurels, if he had not been under the direction of a blunderer, which circumstance alone was the cause of his disgrace, was too shocking a sight for humanity to bear unmoved. The General and the House had been imposed on and deceived: Burgoyne's orders were to make his way to Albany, there to wait the orders of Sir William Howe and to co-operate with him; but General Howe knew nothing of the matter, for he was gone to a different country, and left the unhappy Burgoyne and his troops to make the best terms for themselves."

The House of Lords was equally emphatic. On December fifth Chatham paid high compliments to the courage, zeal and abilities of Burgoyne. The plan of campaign he condemned as a "most wild, uncombined and mad project." And on the same date the Earl of Shelburne denounced "the Pall Mall planners of the expedition," and prophesied that if Burgoyne's instructions were laid before the House they would display the incapacity of ministers in the most glaring colors. He returned to the charge on December eleventh: "Mr. Burgoyne is directed to march to New York or to effect a junction with Mr. Howe. Mr. Howe goes aboard his ships and,

General Schuyler
Painted by Alonso Chappel

after beating to the southward, gets on the other side of Philadelphia. If I do not hear full and sufficient reasons for this extraordinary conduct I protest I think Mr. Howe would deserve to be brought home in chains." Instead of which, when he did go home, he had his Mischianza first.

And all this time Germain must have felt as uncomfortable as he did upon that heath near Minden, with honest old Colonel Sloper exclaiming contemptuously, "You see that man."

# CHAPTER X

## BURGOYNE'S APOLOGIA

DESPATCHES and gazettes, especially those which report disasters and mishaps,* are inevitably very carefully written and as carefully edited before they appear in print. It is always pleasant to read the news contained in them as it struck the man in the street, or rather the soldier in the ranks. Elijah Fisher in his *Journal While in the War for Independence* (Badger and Manley, Augusta, Maine, 1880) handling his pen as bravely as though it were a bayonet, gives the following delightful account of the surrender.

> "October the 17th. Gen. Burgoin and his howl army surrendered themselves Prisoners of Ware and Come to Captelate with our army and Gen. Gates (five thousand seven hundred Prisoners besides the seven hundred toreys that Gen. Gates would not take as Prisoners of Ware that the Ingens garded to Canady) surrendered themselves prisoners of war. Then at one of the Clock five Brigades was sent for Albeny (for there come nuse that Gen. Clinton was a comin up the North river to Albeny) and all the stores belonging to the army was there and crossed the river at the New City we Come to Greenbush of agnst (over

*At the time of the Boer War the official designation of such was "regrettable incidents."

against) Albeny at Brake of Day in which time we march'd forty miles. Gen. Clinton having nuse that Gen. Birgoyne had capetlated and had surrendered his army prisoners of war he Returned back to New York. By reason of the hardships heat and cold and hard marches broght that Pain on in my side again."

Let us now consider the question, why did Burgoyne fail and "Come to Captelate" as Mr. Fisher so pleasantly puts it? Well, in the first place, the whole plan of campaign was crazy. A lover in an old play made a modest request of the gods: he asked them to "annihilate but space and time." Could that have been done Burgoyne, Howe and St. Leger might have met at the same date at Albany. But as things are in this world, British ministers were banking on the impossible. The reason for the descent from Canada was that in the old French and Indian Wars that had been the recognized route. But, Britain having command of the sea, it is ridiculous that Burgoyne should have been sent by a long and extraordinarily difficult land route with the ultimate object of reaching New York, when he and his troops could have been transported thither with no difficulty by sea. The scheme adopted gave the Americans the advantage of "interior lines," though the phrase had not then been invented. Insane strategy apart, the reasons for Burgoyne's failure have been indicated in previous chapters. And they come out pretty clearly in his apologia, which he called *A State of the Expedition from Canada as Laid before the House of Commons by Lieutenant-General Burgoyne and Verified by Evidence*. This was published in 1780, and it is typical of Gentleman Johnny that it is a fine quarto and that he chose a publisher whose office was "Opposite Burlington House, Piccadilly"—no Grub Street for him, but the heart of the West End. To this book he prefixed a narrative which he divided into three "periods"; he really meant Acts, for the sense of the drama was always strong in his mind.

Act I covers the period from his appointment to the pursuit immediately after the capture of Ticonderoga; Act II deals with the events from that date to the crossing of the Hudson; and Act III takes the drama up to the signing of the Convention. The tragic hero (with a touch of comedy) is John Burgoyne himself; the villain of the piece, who is indicated early, is the Minister who would not allow him any "latitude." Burgoyne begins by paying a handsome compliment to Sir Guy Carleton, who did everything he could to "expedite his requisitions and desires." Difficulties arose even before he left Montreal. The Canadians did not come up to expectations in numbers, whether as fighting men or as laborers (corvées), and the contractor who had undertaken to supply drivers for the transport proved a broken reed. He gives his effective strength on the day he encamped before Ticonderoga, 3,724 British and 3,016 Germans rank and file, that is 6,740 regulars (exclusive of artillery men, 473 in all), about 250 Canadians and Provincials and about 400 Indians. The estimate for the Canadian troops had been 2,000, so there was a serious deficiency here. He met the charge that he had been "over-artilleried" by explaining that many of his guns, particularly the heavy ordnance, were left at Ticonderoga, and some at Fort George. Moreover artillery was particularly necessary for "the attack of block-houses, a species of fortification peculiar to Americans," and also to defend Albany—if he got there.

The chief scene in Act II is Bennington. Burgoyne mentions no names but he says that those who knew the country best were most sanguine of success (which means the incompetent idiot Skene), and he felt himself compelled to add that "my cautions were not observed nor the reinforcement advanced with the alacrity I had the right to expect," which is, and not unfairly, to the address of Baume and Breymann.

Act III begins with the crossing of the Hudson. Why did he cross it? Well, Why not? "My army was conscious of having the superiority and was eager to advance; I expected co-operation; no letters from Sir William Howe removed that expectation. . . . I read again my orders—I believe for an hundredth time—and I was decided." And further, had he retreated he would, he says, have been universally blamed. He also says definitely that it was not true, as asserted by some, that Fraser and Phillips were opposed to the crossing of the Hudson. The action of September nineteenth he claims as a victory without "any immediate advantages," due, he admits, to the valor of the army of the enemy. Why did he not retreat? Because he expected at any moment the cooperation of Sir Henry Clinton, because his sick and wounded were recovering fast and "the more I delayed the stronger I grew,"* and also because he hoped that Colonel St. Leger and his troops would come by way of Ticonderoga to his assistance. His defeat on the seventh of October was entirely due to Arnold, not to Gates. If Arnold had not been there he, Burgoyne, was confident that he would have defeated the unenterprising Gates, in spite of the vigor and the obstinacy of the American troops.

---

*A very weak argument.

The witnesses were then called, the first of them being Sir Guy Carleton. Sir Guy is extraordinarily cautious. Like the Italian witness in the Enquiry into the Conduct of Queen Caroline* he often falls back on *"non mi ricordo"*—"I don't precisely recollect." He is always begging the Committee to judge for themselves from the printed papers before them; indeed, he said in so many words, "I have an objection to give an opinion on almost all points." It is, as a minor point, interesting that he continually uses the picturesque word "fall" where most English would say "autumn." When asked what he would have done in Burgoyne's position, he replies: "Every man must decide for himself. What I would have done I really don't know." When questioned about Howe he drew even further into his shell: the most he would say was: "I took it for granted that Sir William Howe knew what he was about and would do what he thought best for the public service." On the whole it may be said that Carleton's evidence was for Burgoyne about as helpful as Sam Weller's was for Mrs. Bardell.

The evidence of the Earl of Balcarres is chiefly interesting for his opinion of the fighting quality of "the rebels"; at Hubbardton they behaved with great gallantry; on the nineteenth of September, and indeed whenever he fought them, he was much struck with their obstinacy and courage, and he pays a fine tribute to Burgoyne, who "at all times shared the dangers and afflictions of the army in common with every soldier; as such they looked on him as their friend." Questioned as to Sir William Howe's proceedings, he declined to commit himself, saying that he was a soldier and not a politician.

---

*George IV's consort, charged, I think unjustly, with being a Royal Vamp.

Captain Money, the Deputy Quartermaster-General, testified chiefly as to transport difficulties, and the shortcomings of the Canadian contractors, but he gave very damning evidence about the Brunswickers on October seventh. They quitted their position* as soon as the firing began, and did not leave a man behind them. After some difficulty they were "brought to make a stand in the rear of the artillery, but in no order." Two German officers, with drawn swords, "kept them up." He also spoke highly of Burgoyne and of the trust the army had in him; had he retreated when it was reported that Sir Henry Clinton was coming up the river, "the army would never have forgiven him nor would he ever have forgiven himself." The Earl of Harrington's evidence relates chiefly to the misconduct of the Indians, but he also said that there never was an army "more deservedly pleased with the conduct of their general" than Burgoyne's.

The most interesting point in the evidence of Major Forbes of the 9th Regiment is that the whole army expected that Sir William Howe was going to cooperate up the North River (the Hudson), and, had he done so instead of going to Philadelphia, Burgoyne's army would never have been taken prisoners; this was in fact the opinion of the army generally. Captain Bloomfield of the Artillery was called and examined by Burgoyne to prove that the expedition was not "over-artilleried." He had "lived in the family" (*i. e.*, been on the staff) of General Phillips and his opinions might be taken as representing those of his chief. He gave full details as to the number and caliber of the guns and as to the number left at Ticonderoga, Fort George and St. John's.

---

*Anburey also says definitely that they bolted and that Breymann was killed while trying to rally them. See also page 196.

The last witness was Lieutenant-Colonel Kingston, and his evidence is important. He elucidates the baggage question. On May thirtieth Burgoyne had issued an order that officers were not to take more baggage* than was absolutely necessary: small notice was taken of this, so another order was issued on July twelfth and it was pointed out that in the last war in America "the officers took up with soldiers' tents and often confined their baggage to a knapsack for months together." The Germans seem to have been special offenders and Burgoyne wrote personally to Riedesel upon the matter. Questioned about another kind of baggage, the number of women† with the army, Colonel Kingston made the pleasant reply: "I had really so much to do that I had not much leisure to pay much attention to the ladies, and I know very little of their beauty or their numbers." And when asked if the women were "more of impediment or of comfort to the King's troops," he made the gallant reply that he had never heard anybody describe them as an impediment. He throws a light on the medical arrangements; the biers and hand-barrows were so primitive that many wounded preferred to lie where they fell rather than be carried on them. It also appears from his evidence that Fraser had been opposed to the Germans being sent on the Bennington business, as "they are not a very active people," but he had not expressed this objection to Burgoyne. Kingston also put in a return, a copy of Gates's, showing the strength of the American troops at Saratoga. Asked definitely what, in his opinion, were the causes of the

*Ewald, a Brunswick officer, wrote that the British officers took with them "portmanteaux full of bags of hair-powder, pomatum, cards, novels and plays." Including, one may safely say, one or two by their General.

†It was said at the time that they came to about two thousand.

failure of the expedition, he said in so many words: "I looked upon our force not to be equal to the forcing our way to Albany without some co-operation," and, further questioned, replied that he expected such cooperation from New York up the Hudson River. Congress made a fuss about the cartouch-boxes and the last question put to Kingston and his reply throw light upon this matter.

> "Q. Was it by consent of General Gates that the soldiers after the convention retained their cartouch-boxes?
>
> "A. They retained their belts, and I really don't recollect whether their cartouch-boxes were in general retained or not: but talking with Mr. Gates when the King's troops marched by with the accoutrements on, Mr. Gates asked me (we had been old acquaintances formerly) whether it was not customary on field days for arms and accoutrements to go together? I told him, there was nothing said in the convention that I had agreed to with him relating to the accoutrements, and that he could have no right to anything but what was stipulated in that treaty. He replied, 'You are perfectly right,' and turned to some of the officers on their service by, and said, 'If we meant to have had them, we ought to have inserted them in the convention.'"

Burgoyne in reviewing the evidence expressed his regret that Sir Guy Carleton had not said more than he did, but he quoted, with the latter's consent, his letter from Quebec of November 12, 1777, in reply to Burgoyne's, announcing his failure. This letter of Sir Guy's contains a very significant passage which is as true now as when it was written: "This unfortunate event, it is to be hoped, will in future prevent ministers from pretending to direct operations of war in a country at three thousand miles distance, of which they have so little knowledge as not to be able to distinguish between good, bad, or interested advices, or to give positive orders in matters which, from their nature, are ever upon the change, so that the expedience or propriety of a measure at one moment, may be totally inexpedient or improper in the next."

Burgoyne then points out what we have already seen, that the Indians were of very little use indeed, and he very properly castigates St. Luc,* who had described him (Burgoyne) to Germain in a phrase which the latter quoted in the House, as being "brave, *mais lourd comme un Allemand.*" St. Luc is dismissed as a "wily partizan" who had sought to curry favor with Germain by depreciating the General under whom he had served. He pays Riedesel a high compliment as being a "frank, spirited and honourable character," but of the troops Riedesel commanded he says: "The mode of war in which they were engaged was entirely new to them; temptations to desert were in themselves great and had been enhanced and circulated among them by emissaries of the enemy with much art and industry." The Canadians were not to be depended upon; they were all the time longing to go home, and as rangers (*i.e.,* skirmishers) they compared very poorly with the enemy; perhaps there are few better Rangers in the world than the corps of Virginia Riflemen which acted under Colonel Morgan." The Provincials, consisting of professed Loyalists, had

*Called by a contemporary "that arch devil incarnate."

gone on the expedition, some for what they could get out of it, others for revenge against their personal enemies, and all were totally undisciplined or, as our dear old Pomposity must put it, "repugnant even to an idea of subordination."

It is obvious that Burgoyne was aware that Bennington required some explaining away, for in this review of the evidence he devotes nearly six pages to it. Here he is, naturally, a very special pleader. He had been assured by persons of long experience and residence in America who had been present there when the rebellion broke out (again he means Skene) that the friends of the British cause were as five to one. The original suggestion was Riedesel's, who wanted to get horses for his dragoons, and the idea was approved by Phillips; if Fraser had been opposed to Germans being sent (see Colonel Kingston's evidence), it was because he "grudged a danger or care in other hands than his own." Riedesel spoke the English language well;* Baume did not follow his instructions; Breymann was slower than would have been thought possible; the arrival of General Starks *(sic)* and Colonel Warner was purely accidental, and was admitted by the Americans themselves to be "a providential circumstance."

To the argument that he (Burgoyne) might have made a forced march, the men carrying their rations, he replies: "He must be a patient veteran and of much experience in scarcity who is not tempted to throw the whole contents of his haversack into the mire: he feels the present incumbrance grievous, want is a day remote: 'let the General find a supply: it is the King's cause and

*This may be, but he could not write it. He called Skenesborough "Skinsbury."

the General's interest, he will never let the soldier be starved.'" It is curious that Anburey uses almost the same words: the men would throw away their rations, exclaiming, "Damn the provisions; we shall get more at the next encampment, the General won't let his soldiers starve."*

Burgoyne had admitted that he had acted on his own judgment, and not consulted any officer, in the matter of crossing the Hudson, and Germain had publicly blamed him for this; his reply to Germain proves that he was a more formidable opponent on paper than in the field: it is worth quoting in full:

> "That a man, chief in authority, should take entirely upon himself a measure of doubtful consequence, and upon mere principle preclude himself from any future means of shifting or dividing the blame that might ensue, appeared incredible at Whitehall: the greater part of that political school concluded the profession of such candour must be a finesse, and that, in fact, the General had not communicated with his officers, because he knew opinions would have been against him. When little minds think they have got a clue of littleness, with what zeal and dexterity they pursue and improve it. Correspondence and intelligence were not wanting; disappointed jobbers, discarded servants, dissatisfied fugitives of every sort, spies, tale-bearers, and sycophants, whom it is the honour of a General to have his enemies, and a disgrace to Office to encourage, abounded in town."

*Anburey also wrote, and wisely, "For one hour General Burgoyne can devote in contemplating how to fight his army, he must allot twenty to contrive how to feed it." Throughout the expedition the men baked their own bread. The meat until it ran out was salted pork, hot or cold.

This is plain speaking, and one hopes that Germain felt uncomfortable; that brazen face was long past blushing.

Burgoyne pays a high tribute to the courage of the Americans and also to their tactics, particularly to their use of "great numbers of marksmen armed with rifle-barrel pieces" who from the tops of trees picked off the British officers. In one instance Captain Green, aide-de-camp to Phillips, "happening to have a laced furniture to his saddle," was shot as he was giving a message to Burgoyne; the rifleman had thought that it was Burgoyne himself at whom he had aimed and it was believed for some time in the American camp that the British general had been killed. Another of his difficulties was that he could get no information: "the deserters were often suspicious, the prisoners very few," and they would give nothing away. Finally he pleaded that the terms he obtained were better than could have been expected in view of the desperate state of the army.

In his "Conclusion" Burgoyne brings a damning charge against Germain which, as we have already seen, is entirely justified, and that is that Howe had been given no instructions to cooperate with the expedition from Canada, until "it was physically impossible that it should have any effect," that is to say Germain's letter of May eighteenth wherein he casually expressed the hope that "whatever Sir William Howe may meditate it will be executed in time to co-operate with the army ordered to proceed from Canada" was not received by Howe until August sixteenth, when he was so far south from the Hudson River, that any cooperation was impossible. This of course is the crux of the whole matter: the detailed instructions to Howe were never sent. Germain got his week-end in the country, his horses were not kept waiting in the cold, and the American Colonies were lost. For Saratoga was the beginning of the end.

In the debate in the House of Commons in May, 1779, the scoundrelly thief Rigby, one of Germain's creatures, whose acquaintance we have already made, denounced Burgoyne as having no *locus standi:* he (Burgoyne) "sat in that house under the authority of a rebel Congress"; he was, in fact, there on sufferance, and had no rights. "Mr. Fox now rose" and tore Mr. Rigby to bits. He quoted a precedent, very much to the point. A noble Lord, Lord Frederick Cavendish, had been (like Gentleman Johnny) at the Misfortune of St. Cas. Less fortunate than Burgoyne, he had been taken prisoner and appealed to the Court of France to know what exactly, being a prisoner on parole, his position was as regarded his duty in Parliament. Fox went on: "The answer he received was that sitting and voting in Parliament would be no more a breach of his parole than getting his wife with child." Charles James Fox also argued that "no blame was imputable to the honourable General and that the miscarriage of the expedition from Canada was owing to the ignorance and incapacity of the Ministers who planned it and not to the General intrusted with its execution." Governor Johnstone took much the same line: the failure of the expedition was due to lack of cooperation on the part of Howe, a cooperation which Burgoyne had been led to expect. The propriety of Sir William Howe going to the southward, instead of going up the North River must be demonstrated. This, of course, Howe was most reluctant to demonstrate: he could not be brought to confess that he had been misled by the advice of the traitor Charles Lee.

It is a great point in Burgoyne's favor that Major-General Robertson, Germain's only witness, that is to say, the only witness for the prosecution against Burgoyne, when asked what was the opinion of the army in general as to Howe's movement south, replied: "I conversed with many officers on the subject; many of them feared that General Burgoyne's army would be lost, if not supported. I wrote myself, on being informed of the situation of the different armies, to a gentleman in this House, telling him that if General Burgoyne extricated himself from the difficulties he was surrounded with, that I thought future ages would have little occasion to talk of Hannibal and his escape." And he stuck to his guns. Howe tried to pin him down by asking whether, after the capture of Ticonderoga, when there did not appear to be any considerable army likely to oppose Burgoyne's advance to Albany, he (Howe) should have gone up the Hudson, Robertson replied: "That depends on Sir William Howe's intelligence, and if that led him to believe that General Burgoyne was not to be opposed by a considerable army, I am sorry his intelligence was not verified." By intelligence he, of course, means information. Of real intelligence, that is to say, common sense, there was very little on the British side during this war.

In apportioning the personal blame for the failure of the expedition from Canada Germain is, *facile princeps,* the real offender; next, although a minor character, comes Skene, with his ridiculous optimism and foolish advice; third is Gentleman Johnny himself. And his share of the blame is, in my opinion, entirely due to his obstinacy and in a minor degree to his love of the dramatic. He saw the whole affair as a stage play to end with a triumphant third act in which he would take the center of the stage, with George III and North in the background, bowing their acknowledgments to the general who had suppressed the rebellion and brought the colonists to their knees and their senses.

Minor causes undoubtedly were the totally wrong view taken as to the possible value of the Canadians, the Indians and the Brunswick troops. The Canadians and the Indians were, as we have seen, of no use whatever: the Germans, no doubt, did their best, but the best of hirelings is never very good.*

I once saw a bumblebee, a gorgeous reddish-brown fellow, indignantly struggling in a spider's web. Burgoyne, in his fine uniform, plunging through the woods of North America, reminds me very much of him. Gates may stand for the spider. But the web was woven, not by Gates, but by Germain, Schuyler and Arnold. And perhaps if Gentleman Johnny had been less of a bulldog, less of a fine man about town with a passion for gambling and taking chances, and a keen sense of the dramatic, he would have made his way back to Canada. It requires great moral courage for a general to retreat. Wellington said that it was the mark of a great general to know when to retreat and, knowing this, to have the courage to do so. No general in military history had greater physical courage than Burgoyne. He enjoyed fighting and, therefore, naturally he would not go back. And of course, had he done so, "that Man" would have let him have the court-martial which was, most unjustly, denied him. Indeed Germain, an authority on courts-martial, would have insisted upon it.

---

*Haldimand wrote home from Canada in May, 1778, that the German troops then with him were quite unfitted for an American war and deserted in shoals.

## CHAPTER XI

### CAMBRIDGE AND THE CONVENTION TROOPS

LET us now return to North America. Howe received Burgoyne's despatch announcing his failure at the beginning of November and put it in his General Orders for the third, with the appropriate "Parole Burgoyne: Counter Sign Phillips." It ran as follows:

"Sir,

"In Conformity to my Orders to proceed by the most Vigorous Exertions to Albany I passed the Hudson River at Saratoga on the 13th September. No exertions have been left untried.

"The Army under my Command has fought twice against a Superiority of Numbers; the first Action was on the 19th September when after four Hours Sharp Conflict we remained Masters of the Field of Battle; the second Action (on the 7th October) was not so successful, and ended with a Storm on two Parts of our Intrenchments: the One defended by Lieut. Colonel Breymann who was killed upon the Spot and the Post Lost, the other defended by Lord Balcarras at the Head of the British Light Infantry who repulsed the Enemy with great Loss. The Army afterwards made good their retreat to the Heights of Saratoga unable to proceed further, the enemy having Possession of all the Fords and the Passes on the East side Hudson's River.

"The Army then waited the Chance of Events, and offered themselves to the attack of the Enemy till the 13th Inst, when only three days Provisions at short allowance remained: at that Time the Last Hope of Timely assistance being exhausted; my Numbers being reduced by past Actions to three Thousand five Hundred fighting Men, of which about thirteen Hundred were British, invested by the Enemy's Troops to the amount of sixteen Thousand Men; I was induced by the General Concurrence and Advice of the Generals, Field Officers and Captains Commanding Corps to open a Treaty with Major General Gates: Your Excellency will observe by the papers transmitted herewith, the disagreeable Prospect that attended the first Overtures. The Army determined to die to a Man rather than submit to Terms Repugnant to National and Personal Honour.

"I trust you will think the Treaty inclosed consistent with both."

On October twentieth, at Albany,* which, as we have seen, he had expected to reach under very different conditions, Burgoyne wrote two letters—as usual long letters—which are of great interest. The first was to his friend, Colonel Philippson, of the 3rd Dragoon Guards. In it he says that he has sent a copy of his despatch to Lord George Germain to Lord Derby, "in order that it may be published by him in case that the Ministry should curtail or mangle any part of it in their Gazette."†

---

*Where he was entertained by Mr. Philip Van Rensselaer at a large dinner-party at 13 North Pearl Street.

†Unworthy thought!

General Benedict Arnold

Drawn from life at Philadelphia by Du Simitier

From a print in possession of Messrs. T. H. Parker,
12a, Berkeley Street, London, W. 1

It is very interesting to find (in the Marquis of Lothian's Manuscripts) Sir John Irwine writing to the Earl of Buckinghamshire:

> "General Burgoyne's letter [to Germain] does him harm in the publick. His charge against ministers, with regard to his orders, is thought unfair, and those who are in the secret of them say it is unjust; however, the ministers are determined to let the blame lie at their door till his return, before they expose his orders* to the public view. You will I presume be astonished to know that General Burgoyne sent a duplicate of his letter to Lord George to Lord Derby, and that his Lordship was actually reading to the company at Almack's that letter much about the time Lord George sent the original to the King at the Queen's house.† This makes much conversation."

Burgoyne goes on that he expects "Ministerial ingratitude will be displayed, as in all countries and at all times is usual to remove the blame from the orders to the execution." He argues that in view of his orders had he retreated to Canada he would have been as guilty as a sergeant in charge of a forlorn hope who should retire because his destruction was probable. "Mine was a forlorn hope, with this difference, that it was not supported." He continues: "This army has been diminished by scandalous desertions in the collateral parts,‡ by the heavy drain of the garrison of Ticonderoga, and by great loss of blood. It has been totally unsupported by Sir William Howe. When my conduct, in advancing so far

---

*And Sir William Howe's?

†Where Buckingham Palace now stands.

‡*i. e.*, the Canadians, the so-called Loyalists, and the Noble Red Men.

as to leave my communication with Canada, is arraigned, face the accusation with the wording of my instructions, and ask the accusers what they would have said had I remained supine in a camp at Fort Edward." He again refers to the fact that his instructions left him neither "latitude" nor alternative, and mentions that the Germans "were dispirited and ready to club their arms at the first fire." And he points out: "I dictated terms of convention which save the army to the State for the next campaign." This phrase got him into trouble: Clinton's friends protested against the word "dictated" and argued that but for Clinton's "brilliant enterprize," as they called it, up the Hudson, Gates would have granted less favorable terms. In other words, even Gates thought that Clinton would not be content to rest on his oars on the Hudson River and gently to drift back with the stream to New York. This is evident from a letter from Wilkinson to Congress in the *Papers Respecting the Convention Troops,* Vol. 57. Wilkinson writes:

> "I have it in charge from Major General Gates to represent to The Honourable, The Congress
>
> "That
>
> "Lieutenant General Burgoyne, at the time he capitulated, was strongly entrenched on a Formidable Post, with Twelve* Days' Provisions: That the reduction of Fort Montgomery & the Enemies consequent Progress up the Hudson's River, endangered our Arsenal at Albany: a reflection which left Him no Time to contest the

*Burgoyne says three days (see page 240).

Capitulation with Lt. General Burgoyne, but induced the necessity of immediately closing with his Proposals, hazarding a disadvantageous Attack, on retiring from his Position for the security of our Magazine; this delicate situation abridged our Conquest & procured Lt. General Burgoyne the Terms he enjoys . . . had an attack been carried against Lt. General Burgoyne; the dismemberment of our Army must necessarily have been such as would have incapacitated it for further Action this Campaign.

"With an Army in Health, Vigour & Spirits, Major General Gates now waits the commands of the Honourable Congress.

"James Wilkinson,
"A. General, N. Army.

"York Town
"October 30th, 1777."

Abigail Adams, writing from Boston October twenty-fifth to her husband John Adams, very sensibly points out: "General Gates by delaying and exacting more might have lost all." In the same letter she pleasantly suggests that the "vaporing Burgoyne" had better set to and write another play, *The Blockade of Saratoga.*

The final paragraph in Burgoyne's letter is very interesting: "I have understated Gates's numbers in calling them 16,000; and sorry am I to add that a better armed, a better bodied, a more alert or better prepared army in all essential points of military institution I am afraid is not to be found on our side." Here of course Burgoyne was trying to "save face" as the Chinese say. He had been beaten, but would not anybody have been beaten by the magnificent troops he encountered? The champion face-saver in military history is, probably, the most incompetent general who ever blundered through a campaign, the Austrian Mack. After the capitulation at Ulm, Mack actually presented in his defense to an astonished court-martial a certificate signed by Napoleon "testifying to General Mack's military talent and his admirable dispositions at Ulm." Napoleon's tongue must have been very far in his cheek when he signed this amazing document.

In the American Manuscripts in the Royal Institution is the second letter, dated Albany, October twentieth, by Burgoyne. This is to Sir William Howe. He again says he had no "latitude" and, for Howe's private information, adds: "Circumstances of a very melancholy nature, viz. a scandelous *(sic)* defection of the Indians, a desertion or timidity worse than desertion of provincials and Canadians, a very few individuals excepted, and a strong disposition in the Germans to be prisoners rather than endure hard blows . . . it was notorious that they meant to have given one fire and then have clubbed their arms." And then he has a dig at Germain and Co. "I think it not impossible that the persons who are most bound to vindicate me will be the first to attack my reputation; those for whom I cheerfully undertook a forlorn hope, and who would have crushed me had I remained inactive, I expect to find my accusers for rashness. These men* know I have it in my power to justify my conduct and it is a duty to myself and my profession not to be absent when occasion calls upon me to produce that justification."

In a later paragraph he says: "The treatment of the

---

*A curious parallel to Colonel Sloper's "That Man."

officers and troops in general is of so extraordinary a nature in point of generosity that I must suppose it proceeds from some other motive than mere kindness of disposition." These last few words are rather ungenerous. The British soldiers were, indeed, very kindly treated by the soldiers who had defeated them. Congress, as we shall see later, was not quite so generous. But then politicians are not, as a rule, soldiers.

Although Gentleman Johnny was, as he says himself, "exhausted to that degree with business that I can really scarce hold my pen," he found time, on this day, to write a little note to "My dearest Nieces"; he sums up his troubles in a few words:

> "I have been surrounded with enemies, ill-treated by pretended friends, abandoned by a considerable part of my own army, totally unassisted by Sir William Howe. I have been obliged to deliberate upon the most nice negotiations and political arrangements that required the most undisturbed reflection, and exhausted with laborious days and sixteen almost sleepless nights, without change of clothes or other covering than the sky. I have been with my army within the jaws of famine; shot through my hat and waistcoat; my nearest friends killed round me; and after these combined misfortunes and escapes I imagine I am reserved to stand a war with ministers who will always lay the blame upon the employed who miscarries."

And he adds in a simple, unaffected style which one wishes he used more often in his correspondence: "In all these complicated anxieties, believe me, my dear girls, my heart has a large space filled with you; and I will bring it home, when God shall so permit, as replete with affection as when I left you."

On October twenty-fifth, still at Albany, he wrote another letter to Howe, repeating his uneasiness as to what "those men" were likely to do, and expressing a hope that he may be allowed to return home as soon as possible in order to defend himself. He also puts in a word for Major Acland, hoping that he may be exchanged, and says: "Mr. Gates has got Ethan Allen* in his head and will exchange no field officer unless he is given up."

Anburey gives a lively picture of the march of the British troops to "Cambridge in New England." The Americans are delighted to give nine paper dollars for a guinea; a young officer goes ahead and, pretending to be General Burgoyne, gets the best quarters in a small village; they took two days to cross the Green mountains; a baby is born in a baggage-cart during a heavy snowstorm; at Williamstown they get from eighteen to twenty paper dollars for a guinea; he delicately refuses to "bundle" with "our Jemima," a very pretty black-eyed girl of seventeen, on which her astonished parents say, "Oh la! Mr. Ensign, you won't be the first man our Jemima has bundled with, will it, Jemima?" to which Jemima archly replies, "Not by many, but it will be with the first Britainer"; Lieutenant McNeil of the 9th Regiment, "thought to be a little witty," says to an old woman in a crowd of sight-seers, "So, you old fool, you must come and see the lions," to which the old fool aptly replies, "Lions! lions! I declare now I think you look more like lambs"; another old lady, anxious to see a

---

*See page 104.

Lord, having pointed out to her Lord Napier, soaked with rain and covered with mud, lifting up her hands in astonishment, exclaims, "Well, for my part, if that be a Lord, I never desire to see any other Lord than the Lord Jehovah"; and if "bundling" astonished Anburey, he is even more astounded by "tarrying,"* for an account of which interesting and very sensible ceremony I must refer you to pages 87-88 of the second volume of Anburey's entertaining *Travels,* a book which would well be worth while reprinting.

The British officers and men were treated with great kindness on their way to Cambridge. At Great Barrington in October, Burgoyne, who was "indisposed and depressed in spirits," remained for several days the guest of Colonel Elijah Dwight in the Henderson House. "Many of the prisoners were sick, suffering from camp fever, and it is related that Captain Truman Wheeler collected roots, boiled them down and personally distributed the concoction among the invalids with good effect, and that one of the British officers presented Captain Wheeler with a substantial token of his own appreciation of the kindness shown the prisoners."† And in *Historic Hadley,* by Alice M. Walker (New York, 1906), there is a most interesting note of the kindness of Colonel Elisha Porter, who had made Burgoyne's ac-

*My friend Mr. C. L. Bayne of the War Office has brought to my notice that most interesting work *Folkways,* by W. G. Sumner (Ginn & Co., Boston, 1906). The Rise, Decline and Fall of "bundling" and "tarrying" are here set out at length. It appears that they lingered on in Scotland up to so recent a date as 1868. Mr. Bayne is, like myself, a Civil Servant and I hasten to say that there is very little tarrying for the Civil Servants of the modern day. I rather think that Mr. Pownall (see page 45) was an expert at it.

†*The History of the Town of Great Barrington.* By C. J. Taylor, Great Barrington, 1882.

quaintance at the surrender. Colonel Porter was High Sheriff:

"Moved by sympathy for the defeated general, well-nigh helpless with illness, he extended to him the hospitality of his house and allowed his bodyguard to encamp within the deer yard. The round eyes of the six Porter children stared with astonishment at the gay uniforms and gorgeous trappings brought so suddenly to their very door, and Puritanical ears were horrified at the careless speech of these disgusted British soldiers.

"The English general found the quiet Hadley home a very haven of rest, and his natural foes converted into kindly hosts, by whose ministrations his health was restored, and he was able to resume his journey. In taking leave, Burgoyne presented to Colonel Porter the dress sword which he had surrendered and received again at Saratoga. This invaluable relic was left by its owner to his son Samuel, and from him descended to his daughter Pamela, who married Dudley Smith. Their son Samuel Smith and daughter, Miss Lucy Smith, now own the sword of Burgoyne, a three-edged rapier, with embossed silver handle and filigreed guard. The visitor examining the sword is interested to decipher on the blade, near the handle, the monogram G. R., while on the other side appears the coat of arms, with the motto 'Honi soit qui mal y pense.' "

But the most pleasing episode took place at Kinderhoek, as related in *A History of Old Kinderhoek,* by E. A. Collier (New York, 1914).

"Burgoyne himself and his American escort, General Phillips, were entertained at the elegant home of Mr. David Van Schaack. In the family was an adopted daughter, Lydia Van Vleck Van Schaack, a charming young girl, who became the wife of Francis Silvester, whose daughter, Margaret, told us the following incident: After the dinner given Generals Phillips and Burgoyne, several toasts to hosts, guests, and others were offered, in a kindly spirit, with careful avoidance of names and subjects forbidden by courtesy. At last, however, one turned to Lydia and asked her for a toast, whereupon she replied, 'To the King and Queen and all the Royal Family.' That there was a moment of embarrassment if not consternation we may well believe, but General Phillips was so charmed by the grace and artlessness of the girl that he smiled and laughed the embarrassment away."

This was a very graceful compliment on the part of Miss Lydia and surely Handsome Jack was immensely pleased: she may have made a *faux pas* so far as etiquette goes, but it was a very kind heart that prompted it. For Phillips, by the way, one should read Glover, that is to say General John Glover, who had been appointed by Gates to conduct Burgoyne and his troops from Saratoga to Cambridge. In Jared Spark's *Correspondence of the American Revolution* (Boston, 1853) there is an interesting letter from Glover to Washington. He writes:

"I was honored with the command of conducting him [Burgoyne] and his troops from Saratoga to Cambridge, for the better supplying of whom, and the convenience of the inhabitants of the country through which they marched, I divided them into two Divisions:

the British by Williamstown and Northampton; the Germans by Kinderhoek and Springfield; with Commissaries, Quarter-masters, and Wagon-masters for each, with particular directions to take bills for what supplies they received, and give orders on me for payment. This order not being fully attended to, I was obliged to send Quarter-master Story back to Albany to collect the outstanding accounts. When that is done I shall charge General Burgoyne with the whole, in one general account; and as many of the charges in my opinion are unjust, and others extravagantly high, large sums being charged by the inhabitants for damages in burning fences, destroying hay, grain, flax, &c., also for clothing, furniture, &c., stolen out of their houses (these charges I know General Burgoyne will object to), the inhabitants look to me, and expect I shall see them paid.

"To acquit myself of censure, I am determined to lay them before the General Court, and desire that a Committee may be appointed to examine them, and make what deductions shall appear to them just, which I hope will give satisfaction to both parties. When this is done, I have to present it to him for payment, and then advertise the inhabitants to come and receive their moneys. I shall lose no time in bringing the whole to a close as soon as possible.

"Thus, Sir, I have given account of what I have been doing, and still have to do, which I hope will meet your Excellency's approbation."

"The town of Cambridge," says Anburey, "is about six miles from Boston and was the country residence of the gentry of that city; there are a number of fine houses in it going to decay, belonging to the Loyalists." And here, on November sixth, arrived the remnants of that fine force which set forth to quell "that unnatural rebellion"; the appearance of many of the rank and file was such, poor souls! that it would have been more appropriate had they arrived on the previous day.* Cambridge did not exactly receive them with open arms. General Heath foresaw that he would have no easy task, and in his letter of October twenty-fifth to John Hancock pointed out "the importance of replenishing our stores with provisions" and mentioned in particular that "wood is now at the price of twelve or thirteen dollars per cord," and, to take the evidence of a lady who kept house in Cambridge, Mrs. Winthrop, "two hundred and fifty cords of wood will not serve them a week." And indeed the Convention Troops, as one should call them in future, wanted wood. "As bare as a barrack" is proverbial: those on Winter Hill and Prospect Hill, where the prisoners were lodged, could not well have been more bare: according to a German prisoner, "wind, rain and snow swept through them; they had no windows, only holes."

Heath, most amiable of generals, foresaw other difficulties. He writes in his *Memoirs:* "The capture of Gen. Burgoyne and his whole army, who were now on their way to Boston, opened a new, important and delicate field for our General.† This army, in which there were

---

*Still celebrated in England and very much so in Boston in 1767, when a Mr. Henry Hulton wrote home: "It is the most riotous day in the year: the mob carried twenty Devils, Popes and Pretenders through the streets with labels on their breasts, Liberty and Property and No Commissioners." Hulton was a commissioner but, as Mr. Pickwick would have done, he "laughed at 'em with the rest."

†This is his pleasant way of alluding to himself. The word "I" does not occur in his *Memoirs.*

many officers of military condition, and some of refined and courtly manners, who had a high opinion of national honour and prowess, and who, in consequence of the Convention which they had formed, had their spirits by no means depressed as those who are compelled to surrender at discretion—were sure to lay a heavy task on his shoulders." But the first thing this genial old gentleman did was to invite Generals Burgoyne, Phillips, Riedesel, Glover (of Massuchusetts) and Whipple (of New Hampshire) to "an elegant dinner." This took place in Boston. Before dinner Phillips tried to "put one over" Heath. He said, "Sir, you well know the disposition of soldiers, and that they will more or less in all armies commit some disorders: suppose you should delegate to General Burgoyne the power of seeing your orders executed."

But Our General was not so simple as he may have looked. He said that while he hoped General Burgoyne and the other British officers would do all they could to maintain discipline, he (Heath) would exercise his own command and enforce his own orders. "Gen. Burgoyne smiled and Gen. Phillips turned it off by saying, 'I only meant it for your easement, Sir.' "

It was a great day in Boston. The streets were filled, the doors, windows, tops of the houses and fences all thick with men, women and children anxious to see the British General. After dinner Burgoyne asked leave to go out by way of Charlestown, and Heath went with him to the ferry: "The streets were so crowded that it was difficult getting along, but not a word or a gesture that was disrespectful." Burgoyne was impressed and said, rightly, (remember poor Baroness Riedesel at Bristol), "Sir, I am astonished at the civility of your people: for, were you walking the streets of London, in my situation, you would not escape insult" (or even in those rough days, half-a-brick). Our General's note on this occasion is very pleasant. "O my dear countryman! how did this your dignified conduct at that moment charm my very soul! Such conduct flows from a greatness of mind that goes to conquer a world."

In ancient Rome the lives of prisoners of war were spared, but they were made slaves; the word *servus* derives from *servare,* to preserve. In medieval times they were not made slaves, but their lives were preserved in order that they might be ransomed; that is to say a prisoner of war had a cash value. And then the Law of Nations, later to be known as International Law, enlarging on the text *parcere subjectis,* laid it down—on paper—that the victor should "remember that prisoners of war are men and unfortunate."* Cambridge, at this time, and perhaps now, the most learned town in the United States, must have known this perfectly well, but it did not act on it. Which is remarkable, for it was the United States, and Prussia, who were the first, in an article of a treaty signed in 1785, to lay down and agree to definite rules as to the kindly treatment of prisoners of war. But Cambridge proved inhospitable. "It was not infrequent," writes Lamb, "for thirty, or forty persons, men, women, and children, to be indiscriminately crowded together in a small, miserable, open hut; their provisions and fire-wood on short allowance, and a scanty portion of straw their bed, their own blankets their only covering. In the night-time, those that could lie down, and the many

*But never, in the whole course of military history, so unfortunate as some of those who suffered in certain Internment Camps in Germany during the European War.

who sat up from the cold, were obliged frequently to rise and shake from them the snow which the wind drifted in at the openings." It is interesting that it is a citizen of Cambridge, Mr. Samuel F. Batchelder, who has described in an extremely interesting brochure, *Burgoyne and His Officers in Cambridge, 1777-1778,** the cold welcome which the Convention Troops received in this center of culture. The citizens passed a resolution that the prisoner officers of the British Army "may not be permitted to have the range of the town of Cambridge." A Committee of both Houses of Assembly suggested to Heath that the British officers should be accommodated in Charlestown in certain houses, including "the Widow Prentice's, except the West chamber": for what, one wonders, can that chamber have been reserved?

Burgoyne was in very poor health,† and the quarters allotted to him were not calculated to improve it. He wrote on November fourteenth to Gates a letter dated (by one used to date his letters from White's and Almack's!) "Public House in Cambridge:

"Sir,

"I transmit to you by Captain Seymour, a correct return of the forces under my command the day of signing the Convention, the Provincials and Canadians Companies excepted, which could not be ascertained but which taken together certainly did not exceed two hundred bearing arms. I should have acquitted myself of this engagement sooner had I been able to find a proper conveyance.

---

*Reprinted from the *Proceedings of the Cambridge Historical Society.*

†Glover wrote to Gates, November 16th, "The Badness of the Roads was almost too much for General Burgoyne's shattered constitution."

"I have the satisfaction to inform you, Sir, that the British Troops accomplished the march without any complaint either on their part or against them. There were some differences between Major General Riedesel and the officer of your troops who accompanied his division, but no disagreeable consequences ensued. I understand there has been a refusal of quarters and refreshment to the Hospital by a Committee upon the road, but having no regular report I will not trouble you with complaint.

"I am sorry I cannot speak with satisfaction upon what happened and still passes here. The officers are crowded into the barracks, six and seven in a room of about ten feet square & without distinction of rank. The General Officers are not better provided for. I & Genl. Phillips after being amused with promises of quarters for eight days together, are still in a dirty miserable tavern* lodging in a bed room together, & all the gentlemen of our suite lodge upon the floor in a chamber adjacent a good deal worse than their servants have been used to. The only prospect that remains to me personally, is, that I shall be permitted to occupy a house without a table, chair, or any one article of furniture, for the price of an hundred and fifty pounds sterling 'till the first of April, but the same sum is to be paid tho' I should embark in ten days.

"While I state to you, Sir, this very unexpected treatment, I entirely acquit M. Genl. Heath & every gentleman of the military department of any inatten-

*But a tavern which has its place in history. The Blue Anchor saw Percy and his men jingle past on their way to Lexington, was the headquarters of Rufus Putnam's Regiment and must have witnessed many brave doings on Commencement Days.

tion to the publick faith engaged in the Convention. They do what they can; but while the supreme powers of the state are unable or unwilling to enforce their authority, & the inhabitants want the hospitality or indeed the common civilisation to assist us, without it the publick faith is broke, & we are the immediate sufferers.

"I cannot close my letter without expressing the sense I entertain of the honor, the candour & the politeness of your proceedings in every respect, towards the army & myself, and I am, with sincere regard,

"Sir,

"Your most obedient

"Humble servant,

J. BURGOYNE.

"P. S. M. Genl. Phillips who is now with me desires you to accept his compliments.

"M. Genl. Gates."

(From *Papers Respecting the Convention Troops,* in *The Papers of the Continental Congress,* vol. 57, folios 31-5.) Congress attached such importance to this document that it resolved "that Major General Gates be requested to lodge among the papers of Congress, in the secretary's office, the original letter" in question. *(Journal of Congress,* March, 1778.)

This letter was to cause Burgoyne sad trouble: the unfortunate phrase "the public faith is broke"* was made by Congress the miserable excuse for detaining the Convention Troops in North America.

---

*He had, a few days before (November 10th), in writing to Heath on this same question of quarters, used a similar phrase: "The Convention is infringed in several circumstances."

Heath, whom Mr. Batchelder describes as "a Roxbury farmer, but also an officer and a gentleman to the tips of his work-hardened fingers," wrote a very warm letter to the Council of Massachusetts about the "unhappy and disgraceful situation of General Burgoyne and his officers" and said plainly, "The honour of the state is in danger, the public faith responsible."

But if Cambridge behaved shabbily Congress was worse. Article II, the "free passage" to England of Burgoyne's army, stuck in their gizzard. Burgoyne had prided himself upon this article. In his letter of October twentieth from Albany to Germain he says:

> "Had the force been all British perhaps the perseverance had been longer; but, as it was, will it be said, my Lord, that in the exhausted situation described, and in the jaws of famine, and invested by quadruple numbers, a treaty which saves the army to the state, for the next campaign, was not more than could have been expected? I call it saving the army because, if sent home, the state is thereby enabled to send forth the troops now destined for her internal defence; if exchanged, they become a force to Sir William Howe, as effectually, as if any other junction had been made."

Some historians have attacked Burgoyne for this, but surely it is a General's duty, firstly to be, if possible, victorious, secondly, if defeated, to make the best terms he can. One might just as well criticize Washington, who put his finger on this weak point of the Convention immediately. Writing on November fifth to Mr. Powell, he said: "As soon as they [the prisoners] arrive [in

England] they will enable the ministry to send an equal number of other troops from their different garrisons to join General Howe here, or upon any other service against the American states. . . . If they can be accommodated, I think, in point of policy, we should not be anxious for their early departure." And on the same day he wrote to Heath: "I do not think it to our interest to expedite the passage of the prisoners to England; for you may depend upon it that they will immediately upon their arrival there throw them into different garrisons and bring out an equal number." He repeated this in a second letter to Heath dated November thirteenth. "Policy and a regard to our own interests are strongly opposed to our adopting or pursuing any measures to facilitate their embarkation and passage home which are not required of us by the Capitulation." Washington also suggested that it should be insisted that Boston must be the port of embarkation and not Rhode Island or "some port of the Sound." He says, "I know he [Burgoyne] has received a hint upon the subject from General Howe."

Writing on November twenty-sixth to Laurens, Washington said: "If the embarkation is confined to Boston it is likely that it will not take place before some time in the spring or at least towards the end of February; whereas if it were allowed at either of the other places it might be made this month or at the beginning of next, and the troops arrive in Britain by the month of January: a circumstance of great importance to us, as the moment they get there the most scrupulous and virtuous observance of the Convention will justify the Ministry in placing them in garrison and sending others out to reinforce General Howe or upon any other expedition that they may think proper to undertake against us." So Congress resolved on the first of December that the port stipulated by the Convention must be the port employed.

To return to the discomforts of Cambridge, the unfortunate Von Riedesel, with his wife, three small girls and a maid, had to live in one room and a garret until a house could be provided for them. In the barracks there would be six officers living in a room not twelve feet square, and so scarce was fuel that the men would cut down the rafters of the rooms for firewood.

"Our General" had a very hard row to hoe. The Heath Papers in the *Papers of the Continental Congress* bring this out very clearly. He had very little in the way of supplies for the six to seven thousand men he had to feed; for, in addition to the Convention troops and other prisoners of war there was the guard. In addition there was little money in the Pay Office. Congress tells him not to issue any more salt provisions to the prisoners; whereupon the Commissary remarks, in a kind of despair, that if the salt beef is not issued, it will soon go bad; "some of it already begins to smell." The Convention Troops cost only twenty thousand dollars per week for food and fuel, but there were huge expenses for unloading and transporting the stores lately arrived from France. The citizens too were grumbling about the damage done by the English soldiers. A Mr. Blodget* had built "a Bake House and a small Dwelling House contiguous to the Barracks." In Mr. Blodget's absence the Convention Troops seized all the boarding in these houses for fuel.

*I can not refrain from wondering if this was an ancestor of the "Reverend Elexander Blodgett, one o' the Lord's poor servants."

Mr. Blodget was naturally annoyed—who would not be?—and Heath had to promise him reparation. Heath had, also, many political worries. For he was the mouthpiece of Congress.

But worse things were in store for Burgoyne than discomfort. Writing to Howe on November twenty-sixth, he mentioned that he had applied to General Washington for consent to some other port than Boston being used for the embarkation. This same letter* contains a very remarkable instance of Burgoyne's interest in his troops. Certain sergeant-majors were recommended for ensigncies "upon my personal observation of distinguished conduct before the enemy." This promotion was most unusual at this day when the British Army fought under the "cold shade of aristocracy"; even in the Peninsula period promotion from the ranks was very rare.

The reply of Congress to Burgoyne's application for a change of port was a resolution on the seventeenth of December that it would not entertain any suggestion for altering the terms of the Convention. Congress did not behave well in another matter, that is to say over the question of the payment for the upkeep and support of the Convention Troops. For this Congress paid in paper: from Burgoyne they demanded reimbursement in "hard dollars." As the hard dollar was worth about three times the paper one, Burgoyne was called upon to pay three times what he should have done. This, to put it mildly, was rather sharp practise. Heath protested, but on delightfully ingenuous grounds: "General Burgoyne supposes his solid coin to be worth three times as much as our currency. But what an opinion must he have

*American Manuscripts in the Royal Institution.

of the authority of these States to suppose that his money would be received at any higher rate than our own in public payment. Such payment would be at once depreciating our currency with a witness." Heath was in a very awkward position. With the kindest heart in the world he was the channel between Congress and Burgoyne. In other words, a simple, benevolent old soldier had to speak as though he were a crafty and pettifogging attorney.

On November eighth Congress resolved:

> "That Major-General Heath be directed forthwith to cause to be taken down the name and rank of every commissioned officer, and the name, former place of abode and occupation, size, age and description of every non-commissioned officer and private soldier, and all other persons comprehended in the Convention made between Lieut. Gen. Burgoyne and Maj. Gen. Gates, on the 16th day of October, 1777, and transmit an authentic copy thereof to the Board of War, in order that if any officer or soldier, or other person as above mentioned, of the said army, shall hereafter be found in arms against these States in North America, during the present contest, he may be convicted of the offense, and suffer the punishment in such cases inflicted by the law of nations."

On this Heath issued a General Order, dated November twentieth, giving briefly the terms of the resolution and adding:

> "Lieutenant General Burgoyne will please immediately to order his Deputy Adjutant General to prepare

the lists accordingly; and Major Andrew Brown is directed to receive lists, and to pass the non-commissioned officers and soldiers, strictly observing that the descriptions are rightly noted, and correct them where there are any mistakes.

"This business is immediately to be attended to."

This was transmitted to Burgoyne, and now we come to the "Descriptive Lists" trouble. On the same day, November twentieth, Burgoyne wrote to Heath:

"Sir,

"I have received a paper, dated Head Quarters, Boston, Nov. 20th., purporting to be founded upon express orders from the honourable Continental Congress, which paper I return as inadmissible, because extending to matters in which the Congress have no right of interference.

"A list of the names and ranks of every commissioned officer, and the numbers of the non-commissioned officers and soldiers may be necessary to you, Sir, for the purpose of fulfilling the Convention in the quartering officers, and the regular delivery of provisions, fuel, etc. Such lists shall be prepared at your request; but before any other lists can be granted, I must be assured of the purposes for which they are intended, and the word *Order* must neither be mentioned nor implied."

Heath's reply was very tactful; parts of it sound sarcastic, but he was so simple and kindly a soul that I do not think he meant to be so. He wrote on November twenty-first:

"Sir,

"Yours of yesterday is before me; and although you might at first imagine that the Hon. Continental Congress have no right of interference in matters of the Convention, yet I conclude upon further reflection you must be convinced, that as that body are the Representatives of that people who are to reap the advantages or disadvantages of the Convention, and as all Continental officers are acting by virtue of their authority, and under their direction, they assuredly have a right of interference, and to give such orders to their officers as they may think proper, for the full completion of the Convention, and for the safety and good of the people. The paragraph of my orders of the 20th inst. respecting the troops of the Convention is founded on reason and justice, being designed only to ascertain the officers and soldiers who were comprehended in the Convention, that in case of any of them (contrary to their faith and honour) should hereafter be found in arms against these States, in North America, during the present contest, they may be convicted of the offence, and suffer the punishment in such cases inflicted by the Law of Nations. I must therefore insist that you furnish me with proper lists of names, and descriptions, for the purpose before mentioned, as soon as may be.

"The other lists of the names and rank of the commissioned officers, and number of non-commissioned officers and soldiers, so essentially necessary for the several purposes of regularity with quartermasters and commissaries (and which should be frequently renewed, as circumstances may vary) should long ere this have been exhibited. Some days since, I directed my

Deputy-Adjutant General to call for them; and I expect they will be sent in without delay, for the purposes above mentioned.

"I shall at all times endeavour to found my orders on the principles of honour, reason and justice, and not to infringe those delicate principles in others; but my orders for the purposes of order and regularity must be obeyed by every man and all bodies of men placed under my direction; and fully determined I am, that offenders shall not pass with impunity."

And Heath ends with a delightful mixture of friendliness and formality, "I am, with great personal regard, Your Excellency's most obedient servant."

The whole of this letter was so simple, straightforward and yet dignified in tone that no one, least of all Gentleman Johnny, could take offense at it. But he postponed furnishing the "descriptive lists."

As mentioned above, Burgoyne in a letter to Gates used the unhappy phrase "the public faith is broke."* Gates, "who was at heart a sneak,"† communicated this letter to Congress. Congress jumped at it. They argued that this meant that Burgoyne did not mean to stand by the Convention; in short they tore the phrase from its context and twisted it to suit their own convenience. Further, they questioned Gates as to the British standards, the military chests, the cartouch-boxes, the cartridges, the muskets, bayonets, scabbards and belts, where were some of these, why were the others so few in quantity?

Gates replied:

---

*Common in these days for "broken." Germain, for instance, was "broke" for his cowardice at Minden.

†Mr. S. F. Batchelder.

"Albany, December 3rd, 1777.

"Sir.

"I had the Honor to receive Your Excellency's Letter of the 23rd Ulto. by Mr. Pierce, and immediately proceed to dispatch to Congress the required answers. Respecting the Standards,* General Burgoyne declared upon his Honor, that the Colours of the Regiments were left in Canada. As to the Military Chest,† its Contents might be so easily disposed of, that, to have sought for it, would have been superfluous. The British Army, all last War, left the Pay Master General and the Military Chest in some secure Town; and Warrants were granted upon the Pay Master General there. From the best accounts the Enemy's Army had been lately cleared off; so that it is not probable there was any Military Chest. The Medicines were left with the General Hospital, which General Burgoyne left behind him at Freeman's Farm. Many of the Cartouch Boxes were left, and some were carried away. The mentioning of the accoutrements was forgotten in the Convention. These that were carried off have been sold upon the road to Boston for Drams. The Quantity of fixed ammunition, of Musket

*The Colors question is difficult of solution. The Baroness definitely says that the colors of the German regiments were hidden in her bed and subsequently sent surreptitiously to Halifax. A somewhat similar fate was that of the colors of the 9th Foot. Lieutenant Colonel Hill of that regiment ripped them from their poles, placed them in his personal baggage and took them home with him to England in 1781. He presented them to George III, who appointed him aide-de-camp, and promoted him to the rank of Colonel in the Army. There was similar trouble at Metz in 1870. Bazaine ordered that the French colors should be sent to the Arsenal and burned. But at the same time the officer in charge of the Arsenal was instructed to preserve them so that, on the capitulation they might be handed over to the Germans. At Bazaine's trial he first denied having given any such instructions, and when confronted with them, said he had forgotten them!

†See page 202 for what happened to the military chest.

Cartridges taken are by no means inconsiderable. The rest was used and destroyed before the Treaty Commenced. The Muskets will ever be less in number than the Prisoners, as the Drummers and Staff Officers do not carry Firelocks. Many Arms were lost in the Two Hundred Batteaux that were taken from the Enemy upon their Retreat from Freeman's Farm. These, and many others were plundered by the Militia on the East side of the River. The Bayonets were also pilfered by our own people; the very Guards themselves, supplied their wants from the piles. Many of the Scabbards for the Bayonets were disposed of in the like manner. I believe there was no Destruction of Military Stores after the Convention, by, or with the privity of, General Burgoyne, or his officers. It is so extraordinary for a British Army to Surrender their Arms, that we ought not to wonder at the Violent and Disappointed, for Committing some Irregularities; but I do not conceive that anything of sufficient Consequence was done to justify our Charge of their having violated the Convention.

"On the day General Burgoyne surrendered, I received repeated Expresses to inform me that the Enemy's Fleet had advanced up to within a few hours sailing of Albany. The removal of the Army was immediately necessary, to cover that City, and secure our Magazines, my principal attention seems, therefore, directed towards that object. Generals Glover and Whipple gave me their assistance and entire approbation in the settlement of the Convention. When Things of such importance must be done in a Hurry, some Articles of seeming Importance never fail to be omitted. The Arms were piled up agreeable to the Letter of the Convention; and their condition as good as can be expected upon such Occasions. Their being wholly returned unfit for Service is partly owing to the Land and Water Carriages, but chiefly to the want of proper carriages to secure them. Our own Men must have changed them; but here, I think, we should not imprudently expose the infant State of our Military Discipline. Inclosed I send your Excellency, General Burgoyne's Return of the Troops, included in the Convention, with a Copy of his letter to me of the 14th Instant. General Glover in his letter to me of the 16th following says: 'After a Troublesome Journey of thirteen days, we arrived Safe in Cambridge, where we have been put to the greatest difficulty to obtain Quarters for the General and Field Officers; Hope we shall be able to effect it in a day or two to their Satisfaction.'

"The German Interpreter whom I sent with the British Army to Boston, is just returned. He says that when he left Cambridge the 16th Ulto., upwards of eighteen hundred Germans and English had deserted; I am persuaded very few will Embark for Europe. Had it been wise to attempt to force General Burgoyne's Army to have surrendered prisoners of War, those who engaged with us might have done it by permission, and continued in their allegiance; but now they have taken a side.

"I am, Sir,
"Your Excellency's
"Most Obed. Humble Serv't.
"HORATIO GATES.

"His Excellency
"Henry Laurens, Esq're."*

*(From *The Papers of the Continental Congress, the Papers Respecting the Convention Troops,* vol. 57.)

Congress would not accept this or any other explanation.

John Witherspoon, one of the signers of the Declaration of Independence, who as a youngster had fought in Scotland for Prince Charlie, made a speech in Congress on January second which puts the official view: "We have reason to conclude that if Mr. Burgoyne is of opinion that the Convention is broken on our part, he will not hold to it on his own. He would act the part of a fool if he did." But Mr. Witherspoon did not strengthen his case by adding that Burgoyne had used the word "broke" in a passion, he was a fool to have used it but "his folly is our good fortune."

Henry Laurens went into more detail. After Burgoyne's return to England he said that he was convinced that Howe had instructed Burgoyne, directly his troops were on the transports, to take them to New York or Delaware. Burgoyne, staggered by so dishonorable a suggestion, had used the phrase "the public faith is broke" to justify himself, if occasion should arise. Furthermore, argued Laurens, the resentment of the British court against Burgoyne after his return was due to the fact that his "marplot delicacy" had spoiled the whole conspiracy. This of course is all conjecture. It is making mountains out of molehills. The weak point in the argument is that it credits Howe with a Machiavellian cunning, and it is difficult to find anything in Sir William's lethargic career and pleasure-loving nature to justify this. Congress acted, not only with caution, but also, to use Witherspoon's own words, "with jealousy and suspicion."*

---

*See Vol. 3. of Burnett's *Letters of Members of the Continental Congress* (Washington, 1926).

It has not very much reason to be proud of the resolution of January 8, 1778: "That the embarkation of Lieut.-Gen. Burgoyne and the troops under his command be suspended till a distinct and explicit ratification of the Convention of Saratoga shall be properly notified by the Court of Great Britain to Congress."* The Convention of Saratoga was a scrap of paper. Congress tore it up, for they knew that it would never be ratified. As Phillips said to Heath: "It was made between General Gates and General Burgoyne, and neither the United States nor Great Britain mentioned: the Ministry would have nothing to do with it." Most Legislative Assemblies in every country in the world have resolutions on their record that can only be described as blots. This is one of them. Congress made no attempt to justify itself. When, later on, in September, 1778, Clinton wrote, by command, to request that the Convention be fulfilled, he received a letter signed Charles Thompson, Sec.

"Sir—Your letter of the 19th was laid before Congress, and I am directed to inform you that the Congress make no answer to insolent letters." Which the Earl of Carlisle, one of the commissioners then in the United States, called "an uncouth and profligate reply." "Honors easy" as they used to say at whist.

---

*With, in some printed versions, a small "c" for "court" and a large "C" for "Congress." A small but interesting point.

## CHAPTER XII

### THE PRISONERS' FRIEND

ANGLO-SAXONS do not make good prisoners of war. They have too much *sacro egoismo*. They do not take captivity easily, and they do their best to make it as unpleasant as they possibly can for those who have taken them captive. Burgoyne's men tried to get even with their American guardians by showing their contempt for them. It is only human nature to do so. There were constant rows between the Convention Troops and the townsfolk at Cambridge. The British laughed and jeered at the Americans: it was complained against them that they "constantly buzzed." One of the English soldiers, "being at Medford in the shop of a mechanick," when addressed as "one of Burgoyne's lobster-backs,"* resented it and struck the speaker. Another, Sergeant Reeves, loudly remarked *coram populo*, "King Hancock is come to town: don't you think him a saucy fellow for coming so near General Burgoyne?" On being reprimanded by a provincial American officer for this, Reeves referred him to a portion of his anatomy not usually mentioned in polite circles. Another prisoner addressed an American officer with "You God damn clown with a sword under your arm." "God damn the Yankees" was also often in their mouths. These men, and others, were not

*Thomas Lobster was the nickname of the British soldier at this date. The more aristocratic Atkins came later on.

unnaturally punished by confinement to barracks for their insubordination. Colonel Henley, who was in command at Cambridge, was not the best-tempered of men. He said to Reeves, "I believe you to be a great rascal." "I am no rascal," replied the English sergeant, "but a good soldier, and my officers know it," and he added that he hoped soon to carry arms under General Howe; which, by the way, rather throws a light upon what the rank and file thought of the Convention. Colonel Henley lost his temper and exclaimed, "Damn your king and your country, when you had arms you was willing enough to lay them down." With this he seized a firelock, with a fixed bayonet and "made a lounge" at Reeves, inflicting a slight wound. He also, so it was alleged, "pushed his sword" into the side of Corporal Hadley, who was slow to leave parade. This of course was unpardonable.

Burgoyne naturally fired up. He wrote on January ninth to Heath:

> "A report has been made to me of a disturbance that happened at the barracks on Wednesday afternoon, for which I am much concerned; and though the provocations from your people, which originally occasioned it, were of the most atrocious nature, I was willing the offender on our part should be properly punished. But Col. Henley, not content with that, made prisoners of eighteen innocent men and sent them on board a guardship, as alleged, by your order. It is not only a duty to my situation to demand the immediate discharge of these men, together with a satisfactory apology; but I also mean it as an attention to you, Sir, that I give you an immediate opportunity to disavow so unjustifiable a proceeding, as committing

men to the worst of prisons upon vague report, caprice and passion.

"Insults and provocation, at which the most placid dispositions would revolt, are daily given to the officers and soldiers of this army. Regular, decent complaints are received by your officers, sometimes with haughtiness, sometimes with derision, but always without redress. These evils flow, Sir, from the general tenour of language and conduct held by Col. Henley, which encourages his inferiors, and seems calculated to excite the most bloody purposes.

"For want of sufficient information, and not bringing myself to believe it possible that facts as related by common report could be true, I have hitherto declined taking public notice of this man; but upon positive grounds, I now and hereby formally accuse Col. Henley of behaviour heinously criminal as an officer, and unbecoming a man; of the most indecent, violent, vindictive severity against unarmed men; and of intentional murder. I demand prompt and satisfactory justice, and will not doubt your readiness to give it. Whenever you will inform me that a proper tribunal is appointed, I will take care that undeniable evidence shall be produced to support these charges."

Heath in his reply pointed out that the Convention Troops had been insolent and abusive; that he intended the orders he gave to be obeyed; and that it was he and not Burgoyne who would punish those who disobeyed his orders. But he added that he had ordered Colonel Henley under arrest and appointed a Court of Inquiry. He said further that he had received many complaints about the Convention Troops, including a number of officers who on December twenty-fifth—the date seems to excuse it—had made themselves conspicuous at Bradish's Tavern: moreover passes had been counterfeited and "filled up in the most affrontive manner," which presumably means that the counterfeiters had allowed their sense of humor to overcome their sense of fitness.

Burgoyne protested against a Court of Inquiry and demanded a court-martial on Colonel Henley. The Court of Inquiry agreed that for the honor of Colonel Henley and for the satisfaction of all concerned a court-martial would be more fitting, so a court-martial there was, with Brigadier-General Glover as president. It began at the end of January (1778) and by adjournments ran well into February. Gentleman Johnny was in his element: he was stage-manager, gave stage directions and set the Court right as to procedure. As usual he was terribly pompous, but his sincerity is very evident. He said he had three motives (of course he must call them "impulsions") for appearing in person, the chief being "gratitude, esteem and affection to that meritorious, respectable part of my country, the brave and honest British soldier, a private man, defenceless, because unarmed, ignorant of your laws, unqualified to make good his cause in a Court of Justice. . . . I confess I am too selfish to resign to any brother officer the pride and gratification of standing in the front for the defence of men, faithful comrades of honour and misfortune, who have fought bravely under my orders, who have bled in my presence, and who are now exposed to oppression and persecution by the abuse of a treaty signed by my hand." Not forgetting that he was a Member of the Mother of Parliaments, he reminded the Court that they were "trustees for the honour of an infant state, and therefore evasion, subterfuge and law-craft, were any man hardy enough to offer such at your tribunal, would be of no avail." When he said "law-craft" he probably looked hard at the Judge-Advocate, Lieutenant-Colonel Tudor, who was a Boston lawyer.

There is one really eloquent passage in his address: "We arrived at Cambridge passengers through your country, under the sanction of a truce, relying confidently on the hearts of a generous people, honour, respect for the brave, the hospitable wishes that usually press to the relief of the unfortunate, the stranger and the defenceless." He gives short shrift to Colonel Henley, who was guilty of "independency, scurrility and impiety," all indicative of "most horrid passions boiling in the breast." Colonel Henley had drawn his sword against an unarmed prisoner; such a sword, said Burgoyne, "is no longer the badge or distinction of a gentleman; it is degraded with the implements of the assassin and hangman and contracts a stain that can never be wiped away." Anburey, who was present at the court-martial, noted that here "Colonel Henley changed colour and appeared bursting with rage."

After witnesses for Colonel Henley had been called, examined and cross-examined, the Colonel read a very brief and rather remarkable apologia; he declined to say a single word in answer to the illiberal abuse thrown upon him, he was perfectly willing to accept the decision of the Court, so conscious was he of having always behaved with humanity. Gentleman Johnny then replied. Colonel Henley had made use of terms to which his [Burgoyne's] ears had not been accustomed, but this would not draw from him an intemperate reply; the Colonel had by his address been a most valuable witness as it had proved the heat of his temper. He then went through the evidence, and ended with a peroration in his best House of Commons manner:

> "I stand in this circle, at best an unpopular, with the sanguine enemies of Britain perhaps an obnoxious character. This situation, though disagreeable, does not make me miserable. I wrap myself in the integrity of my intention, and can look round me with a smile. Implacable hatred is a scarce weed in every soil, and soon is overcome and lost, under the fairer and more abundant growth of cultivated humanity. To the multitude who only regard me with the transient anger that political opinions and the occurrences of the time occasion, I retain not a thought of resentment, because I know the disposition and hour will come, when steadiness of principle, that favourite characteristic in America, will recommend me amongst my worst enemies: as Christian I trust they will forgive me; in spite of prejudice I know they will respect me."

He then thanked the Court (and they deserved it) for the patience with which they had heard him.

Then Lieutenant-Colonel Tudor, the Judge-Advocate, "a little vain, conceited fellow," according to a British eye-witness, addressed the Court "in a pert and flippant manner." He began with a phrase which to modern ears sounds strange: "The Court sits upon truth and honour"; he then proceeded: "To state the facts as they rise from the evidence stripped of all that meretricious colouring which uncommon ingenuity and refined eloquence have thrown upon it: it is not my intention to catch the crowd by well-turned periods." He, after this back-hander, complimented Burgoyne on his "Attic language." He got in one very shrewd hit. Burgoyne had argued *qui facit per alium facit per se, i. e.*, that a superior in command was responsible for the action of his inferiors. The Judge-Advocate slyly retorted, was not then General Burgoyne responsible for, or a party to, the murder of Miss McCrae? He then frankly avowed himself "the Prisoner's Friend." "My friend Col. Henley is known to be of a warm temper: it must be allowed that warmth carried him too far; but a more generous, honourable or humane man does not live in the American or any other Army: the behaviour of the British troops in general, who, notwithstanding their situation, treated ours upon every occasion with pride, contempt and outrage, is notorious." This is the language not of a judge-advocate nor of a judge, but of an advocate. It got Colonel Henley off. Heath's General Order promulgating the acquittal ended with:

> "The General thinks it his duty on this occasion to observe that, although the conduct of Lieut.-Gen. Burgoyne (as prosecutor against Col. Henley) in the course of the foregoing trial, in his several speeches and pleas, may be warranted by some like precedents in British courts martial, yet as it is altogether novel in the proceedings of any general court martial in the army of the United States of America, whose rules and articles of war direct that the Judge-Advocate-General shall prosecute in the name of the United States; and as a different practice tends to render courts martial tedious and expensive—he does protest against this instance being drawn into precedent in future."

One can not but smile at Burgoyne's grandiloquence, which has more than a smack of Mr. Serjeant Buzfuz. But on the other hand one can not but admire his boiling indignation, however pompous its expression, on behalf of the rank and file who had fought so gallantly by his side on the banks of the Hudson. Consideration for one's inferiors in rank has always been reckoned one of the marks of a gentleman; it was certainly always one of the marked characteristics of John Burgoyne. I think his soldiers must have loved him more than ever for the way in which he stood up for them. Would Wellington, in the inconceivable hypothesis that he and his army had ever been taken prisoners, have acted as Burgoyne did?

John Burgoyne lost his case, but do you not think that he comes out of the affair with far more credit than Colonel Henley? There is only one touch of comic relief in this sad business, and that is that a colonel serving on the court-martial bore the pleasing name of Popkin, a name otherwise not known to history, but worthy to appear in any *dramatis personæ,* that is to say in a not too serious drama.

A Britisher can not but think that the finding of the court was wrong and unjust. The best that can be said for it is the old tag, *inter arma silent leges.* Against the Henley court-martial it is pleasant to set the trial of Captain Preston, which arose out of the Boston Massacre of 1770. Captain Preston could find no counsel to defend him. One of his friends waited upon a young Boston lawyer, a certain John Adams. There was probably no more zealous patriot than he then in North America. But he accepted the brief for one whom he must have regarded as an enemy of his country and won a verdict of Not Guilty. He risked a career (which, I may remind

English readers, brought him to the White House) for the sake of Justice.

Less important, but equally irritating to everybody, was the fuss over the fusees. The "minds of the populace" were uneasy about these "fusees"* which, under the Convention, were the British officers' property. Heath admitted this, but, to placate the citizens, proposed to Burgoyne that these should be given up and he would be responsible for their safety. Burgoyne objected. Then the rumor spread that all sorts of arms were secreted in the barracks. A search was made and, to quote Our General, "a wag, coming from the barracks, was asked if anything was found: he answered, 'Yes—in one of the rooms a large brass mortar.' The fact was that in one of the rooms was a large bell-metal pestle and mortar, for family use." And so, this particular trouble ended happily, with loud laughter.

All this time Burgoyne was chafing to go home. One can understand his feelings. Every day that he remained in America gave Germain, "willing to wound and yet afraid to strike," more time to make out a case on paper against the soldier whom his blundering incapacity had sent on a mission doomed to failure. The American Colonies might be lost, but Germain must keep his position. In the brave old days incapable Ministers lost their heads on the scaffold. The Minden man did not fear that, he was anxious about a much more important part of his anatomy—his seat.

Burgoyne had written to Gates on February eleventh on the subject of his return. He had just heard of the

---

*Or fusils: *i. e.*, a light musket carried by officers of flank companies. In 1792 these were abolished, and swords were carried instead.

After these explanations & answers to the several charges contained in the report &c. I trust no words of so harsh a nature as to imply a distrust of my personal honour will be suffered to remain upon the Journals of Congress. but shou'd any doubt still subsist that the idea of being released from the engagements of the Convention has been adopted by any part of these Troops, I am confident there is not an Officer who will not join his signature to mine for a further pledge of faith provided the suspension is immediately taken off: and animated by the most substantial principle of Truth & Honour, I propose to the Congress this last expedient within my power to restore the mutual confidence of the contracting parties in the Convention of Saratoga; & to save at once Great Britain, and America, from yet more serious evils than we already reciprocally endure in the prosecution of our unhappy Contest.

I have the honour to be with due respect Sr. Your most Humble Servant

J: Burgoyne Lt. Genl.

The Honble: Henry Laurens President of the Congress.

Last page of Burgoyne's Letter of February 11, 1778, to the Hon. Henry Laurens, President of the Congress

resolution of Congress of the eighth of January, mentioned above, and said that it caused him "an astonishment that no occurrence ever before occasioned."* He appeals to Gates to use his influence; it is essential that he should go home to defend himself. As he puts it: "To die in this country is nothing; but to leave my honour unvindicated in my own is more than philosophy or fortitude can be expected to bear." At the same time he wrote to Laurens, asking for a passport to England, "as matter of indulgence." His health is very indifferent, he has a complaint (his old enemy, gout) that only the Bath waters can alleviate, he has complicated accounts to settle with the Treasury of Great Britain and above all, "by my detention in this Country I am deprived of every possible means to give an account of my actions; and my character stands exposed after an intricate and unsuccessful Campaign to all the aspersions and erroneous interpretations that the malevolent, the prejudiced, or the misinformed may chuse to cast upon it." John Burgoyne never forgot his manners, and his mode of address at the end is interesting; it runs:

"with due respect, Sir, Your
"Most Humble Servant
"J. BURGOYNE,
"Lt. Genl.

"Hon. H'y Laurens, President of the Congress."

In addition to this letter, Burgoyne sent Laurens a paper, with the request that it should be laid before Congress. This is a very important paper: it was laid

*Washington thought, writing to Heath on January 22nd, that Burgoyne when he heard of the resolution would regard himself as "at liberty to make use of any means to effect an escape."

not only before Congress but also, later on, before Parliament. It is, in effect, a review of the Report of the Committee of Congress dated January 8, 1778. This report ended with the resolution (mentioned in the previous chapter) which was, to all intents and purposes, a tearing up of the Convention. The Committee argued that the cartouch-boxes and other articles of accouterments (or equipment, as one says nowadays) had not been delivered up; it alluded to "many instances of former fraud in the conduct of our enemies"; it made great play with the "descriptive lists" question; pounced (as we have already seen) like a terrier upon a rat, on Burgoyne's unfortunate phrase "the public faith is broke," which, and which alone, they found "a strong indication of his intentions, and affords just grounds of fear that he will avail himself of such pretended breach of the convention in order to disengage himself and the army under him of the obligation they are under to these United States."

Burgoyne took up the cudgels in defense of his "private honour and personal conduct." As regards the cartouch-boxes, most of them had been left in Canada, as pouches were found more convenient, and as to the accouterments, they were the private property of the colonels of the regiments and Gates had said in the presence of Lieutenant Noble, acting aide-de-camp to Phillips, that "he did not mean to injure private property, and as the colonels would suffer by the loss of their accouterments, the soldiers might take them."* As to the charge of "former frauds in the conduct of our enemies," Burgoyne practically remarked (as a modern Cockney

*See also Gates's letter of December third, page 265.

would say), "there ain't no words for it," only, of course, he puts it in much more dignified language. "My consternation in finding the British honour in treaties impeached is the only sentiment I can express upon the subject." (Cf., as commentators say, the historic "My amazement, my surprise" rebuke of Sir Joseph Porter, K. C. B.) The demand for "descriptive lists" he regarded as "dishonourable and unprecedented," but when Heath had pointed out to him that there *was* a precedent, that of the American officers and men captured by Burgoyne himself and sent to Canada, he would have yielded the point had not his time been taken up by "an unhappy affair" *(i. e.,* the Henley court-martial). This excuse is perhaps thin, but I think he has a strong case in dealing with "the public faith is broke" point. What he meant was that "the treaty was not complied with in respect to the stipulation of quartering officers." We have already seen what discomfort officers and men suffered. Burgoyne points out that there were empty houses more than sufficient for the purpose, that there were other houses possessed by people who would have been willing to receive officers had they not been prevented by the Committee of Cambridge; that he, Phillips and their aides-de-camp had been quartered "in a miserable public-house"; and that the men had been lodged "twenty and twenty-four in a room, three in a berth, without candle and scarce wood enough to cook their victuals, much less to warm their rooms." Finally he trusted "no words of so harsh a nature as to imply a distrust of my personal honour will be suffered to remain in the journals of Congress," and suggested that he and his officers should sign a "further pledge of faith" so that Great Britain and England might be saved "from yet more serious evils than we reciprocally endure in the prosecution of our unhappy contest."

So far as Gentleman Johnny himself was concerned, all's well than ends well. In due course he got permission to go home. Gates wrote a kindly letter to him, from which it appears that he had at Albany, on his own responsibility, offered that he should "go to England in a Vessel that the State of Massachusetts Bay would at my request have provided." One can understand that Burgoyne could not have accepted this and have left his troops in the lurch. Gates goes on:

> "Your Case I feel as I ever shall that of the unfortunate Brave: if Courage, Perseverance and a Faithful attachment to your Prince could have Prevailed, I might have been your prisoner. The Chance of War has determined otherwise. The Congress now send the passports you desire, and I am happy to acquaint you that the Major and Lady Harriot Acland are in New York, and may possibly be in England as soon as, or very soon after, You."

An equally kind and courteous letter came from Washington (to whom Burgoyne had written) from Headquarters, Pennsylvania; he is, he writes,

> "ever ready to do justice to the gentleman and the soldier, and to esteem, where esteem is due, however the idea of a public enemy may interpose. You will not think it the language of unmeaning ceremony if I add that sentiments of personal respect, in the present instance, are reciprocal. Viewing you in the light of an officer contending against what I conceive to be the

rights of my country, the reverses of fortune you experienced in the field cannot be unacceptable to me; but abstracted from consideration of national advantage, I can sincerely sympathise with your feelings as a soldier—the unavoidable difficulties of whose situation forbid his success; and as a man, whose lot combines the calamity of ill-health, the anxieties of captivity, and the painful sensibility for a reputation exposed, where he most values it, to the assaults of malice and detraction."

Not only is this the letter of a soldier and a gentleman, but it shows that the writer, with the sagacity that was natural to him, clearly foresaw what kind of reception Burgoyne was likely to get from that Personification of Malice and Detraction, my Lord George Germain.

Although Congress had decided that the Convention Troops were not to return to England, transports arrived to take them there. This led to a kind of *pas de trois* correspondence* between Captain Hugh Dalrymple, R. N., of the *Juno,* Burgoyne and Heath. Heath, with that artlessness which makes him so charming a personality, notes on February twenty-third that General Lincoln had arrived from Albany at Boston "still very lame, on a moveable bed with handles, with a canopy and curtains: in this was blended ingenuity and convenience." His next entry, February twenty-eighth is "Intelligence was received that the British transports destined to take away the troops of the Convention had arrived at Holmes's Hole." A spot with so homely a name as this was evidently no place for a vessel with so stately a name as the *Juno,* so she proceeded to Cape Cod Harbor,

*In the Library of Congress, Manuscripts Division.

whence on March fourth Dalrymple sent by a cartel a letter to Burgoyne. He informed the General that he had been appointed to convey him and the troops home, enclosed a list of the transports, with their tonnage, and added that he had a number of private letters for various officers and "a large box of letters for the army." Burgoyne immediately wrote to Heath notifying him that Dalrymple had arrived with 8930 tonnage to convey the Convention Troops to England, and adding (in italics) *"I request to be informed what part you mean to take in regard to the embarkation."* I think Gentleman Johnny thought that here he was going to score off Heath, but Heath declined to be scored off and replied to Burgoyne's request for information: "As the Hon. Congress were pleased by their resolutions of the 8th January last (Copy of which I did myself the Honor to transmit to your Excellency) fully to determine the matter,—as their Servant I can take no other part than such as they are pleased to point out as my duty, to which I shall strictly conform." Next Burgoyne wrote to Heath, noting that he (Heath) was bound by the resolution of Congress and requesting that the letters in Dalrymple's charge should be delivered unopened: "I admit that there would be an impropriety in making the same request for letters to pass from here, but as no intelligence we can receive can, in our present position, possibly affect the interest of America, you have it in your power to lay this Army under obligation for one of the greatest pleasures in life—that of hearing from friends." Burgoyne also wrote (through Heath) to Dalrymple, telling him that in view of the resolution of Congress of January eighth, there was no occasion for the transports. He softened this unpleasant news by begging "your acceptance of a turkey which shall be delivered you herewith." The turkey went with Burgoyne's letter to Heath, who immediately wrote to Dalrymple: "I do myself the pleasure to send down to the Flag a Turkey sent here by General Burgoyne." He also said: "Although I wish on every occasion to extend the utmost generosity to the Gentlemen of the Convention, yet to allow letters to pass unopened would be betraying the trust reposed in me, therefore any Idea of granting such an indulgence can not be admitted." And he wrote to Burgoyne on this point: "As to allowing the private letters on board the Fleet being sent to the Officers unopened, although I wish on every occasion to treat the Officers with generosity, in this Instance Duty to my Country and Station forbid a gratification and, I think, no Officer can say that a Denial is a want of Generosity, as you must be sensible, Sir, it is too much to be expected, and I assure myself you will excuse me." Heath of course was perfectly right: Burgoyne was "trying it on," as the saying is, and found, as he had found before, that Heath, for all his simplicity and kindliness, was not to be bamboozled. I think on the whole this correspondence does credit to everybody, the turkey included, and one hopes Captain Dalrymple did justice to this bird, served, no doubt, "with the usual trimmings" of cranberry sauce and, perhaps, sausages?

Heath also notified Burgoyne that Congress had decided to let him go home, which, he quaintly says, "was joyous to the General." "Our" two Generals had a little business discussion on money matters. Burgoyne asked Heath if Congress seriously desired that he should pay in specie what they had expended in paper money. "Our General" replied that he " supposed that honourable body were serious in all their resolutions." Burgoyne retorted that this was not just, as the odds were double, and did Heath really think it just himself? Heath replied that it was not for him to judge or determine whether the orders of his superiors were just or not. Gentleman Johnny saw the force of this, and they came to an agreement. Burgoyne was to pay partly in specie and partly in kind, and would leave a "box of gold" as a pledge for any deficiencies in the provisions supplied. So every thing ended happily, and on April second he dined at headquarters in Boston with Heath. After dinner, Burgoyne, on saying good-by to Heath, said, with his usual courtesy, "I know your situation, Sir, and the difficulty of obtaining many foreign necessaries you may want or wish. If you will give me a memorandum, on my arrival in England, I will with great pleasure forward them to you." "Our General" thanked him for his politeness, but was careful not to mention any, "choosing rather to suffer with his fellow-countrymen the necessities of the times than to avail himself of so exclusive a favour." One does not know whether to admire more the kindness of heart which prompted the offer, or the sense of duty which prevented the acceptance of it. On this same day Burgoyne signed his parole. It ran as follows:

> "I, John Burgoyne, Lieutenant General and Commander in Chief of the British Troops under the restrictions of the Convention of Saratoga, do pledge my faith and sacred honor that I will go from here to Rhode Island where I am to embark for Great Britain; that I will not during my continuance at Rhode Island, or in any other part of America, directly or indirectly, hold any communication with, or give intelligence to, any person or persons that may be injurious

General William Heath
Painted by H. Williams

to the Interest of the United States of America or either of them; and I do further pledge my faith and sacred honor that should the embarkation of the Troops of the Convention of Saratoga be by any means prolonged beyond the time apprehended I will return to America upon demand and due notice given by Congress and will re-deliver myself into the power of The Congress of the United States of America, unless regularly exchanged.

"Given under my hand this 2d day of April, 1778.

"J. BURGOYNE.*

"Lt. Genl."

Before taking leave of "Our General," for whom I have formed a real affection, I should like to quote the letter which Major Harnage wrote him, June 10, 1779:

> "I must beg leave, previous to our departure, to trouble you with these our acknowledgments for the civility and attention you have been pleased to show us, and to assure you that Mrs. Harnage, Capt. Houston and myself shall ever retain a due sense of all favours by which you have kindly endeavoured to alleviate, and make easy, the restraints and disagreeable circumstances that unavoidably attend our present situation."

There is a portrait of Heath which has a distinct resemblance to Lord Hill, one of Wellington's most trusted Peninsula Generals. To his troops Hill was always "Daddy"; and no wonder, for in kindness of heart, and also in appearance, he was a military Samuel Pickwick. Major-General William Heath, although

*From *The Papers of the Continental Congress*, vol. 57, *The Papers Respecting the Convention Troops*. (Library of Congress, Manuscripts Division.)

nicknamed by the French officers serving in North America "The Marquis of Granby," may have cut no great figure in the field. But if there was a courteous and kind-hearted gentleman on either side in this war, it was this Roxbury farmer. He describes himself in his *Memoirs* as "very corpulent and bald-headed"—hence his nickname. I hope that somewhere in Massachusetts there is a very corpulent and bald-headed statue. If there is, any Englishman visiting Boston should make a point of paying a pilgrimage to it. Among those generals who have done whatever they could to preserve what used to be called "the Amenities of War" William Heath takes a very high place.

One last word regarding the Convention Troops. It is pleasant to be able to say that, like all prisoners of war, they managed to amuse themselves. It is true that the first attempt at an entertainment was a sad fiasco. Burgoyne and Phillips decided to give a ball, and invitations were issued to the ladies of Cambridge and Boston. "Whereupon all the Committees issued a prohibition order to the effect that no one was to be bold enough to appear there." A ball without ladies is like beef without mustard, or oysters without red pepper and vinegar, or, to put it more pleasantly, a flower-garden without roses, or a hothouse without peaches, not to mention peacherinos. In spite of the presence of General Schuyler's two daughters, whose address the General himself had given to Burgoyne (whose host, it will be remembered, he had been after Saratoga), this ball of Gentleman Johnny's must have fallen rather flat. Indeed, I think it must have borne a certain resemblance to the party got up by another Great Man, the hero of *The Gold Rush,* that most pathetic party to which the ladies concerned forgot that they had been invited. Still, there were other amusements in Cambridge. There was a race-course, of sorts; there was fowling, cock-fighting, tenpins, beer and billiards. The billiards, as a matter of fact, led to a General Order. "Complaint has been made* to the General, that some of the officers of the Convention have set up a billiard-table in a house near the centre of the town of Cambridge, and that company is frequently there at very unseasonable hours, to the disquietude and uneasiness of the inhabitants. The General means not to prohibit innocent diversions to those officers, but forbids the exercise of them at those hours that discompose others." Not an unreasonable General Order, for billiards can be a very noisy game, especially when punctuated, as it sometimes is, by the constant and pathetic parrot-cry "The marker's dry."

Burgoyne sailed for home in, appropriately enough, the *Grampus,* for like that marine monster, he was, and justly, puffing and blowing with indignation. He arrived in the middle of May, 1778, and at once demanded a court-martial. Germain received him with much appar-

*Was it, I wonder, made by Mrs. Warren, who said that the Convention Troops were "an idle and dissipated army and corrupted the students of Harvard College"? Or perhaps by Mrs. Winthrop, who said, of the Hessians, "Such effluvia filled the air while they were passing that had they not been smoking all the time I should have been apprehensive of being contaminated." Which reminds me of a character in *The Belle of New York* who demanded the instant removal of another character (Mr. Kenneth Mug, I think) on the grounds that "he contaminates the air." As one who has seen this classic drama at least a score of times I realized with extraordinary interest that Burgoyne on his way as a prisoner from Saratoga to Albany must have passed over the site of what was later the home-town of Mr. Bronson, the famous

> "Far Cohoes
> Where the hopvine grows
> And the youth
> Of the town
> Are prone to dissipation."

ent kindness and proceeded to pump him. He then produced an order that he should prepare for an inquiry, which Burgoyne welcomed, and then the astute Minister casually mentioned that pending such an inquiry, etiquette demanded that he should not appear at Court and see the King. It was a carefully devised plot, and everything was done by the unscrupulous and wily Germain to make it appear that Gentleman Johnny was given a square deal. On May twenty-first Charles Gould, the Judge-Advocate General, wrote from the House Guards to Burgoyne:*

"Sir,

"Having received a Warrant under the King's Royal Signature reciting that in March 1777 His Majesty was pleased to send directions to the Commander in Chief of His Majesty's Forces in Canada to detach you [Lieutenant General Burgoyne] with a number of the said Troops and to give you Orders to pass Lake Champlain and from thence by the most vigorous exertion of the Force under your Command to proceed with all expedition to Albany and put yourself under the command of Sir William Howe, and until you should have received Orders from Sir William Howe to act as exigencies might require, and in such manner as you should judge most proper† for making an impression on the Rebels and bringing them to Obedience, and further reciting that the Troops sent for these purposes have failed of Success, and

*J. A. G.'s Letter Book,* 1773-78.

†This, of course, is quite untrue. It implies that Burgoyne had the "latitude" which he so bitterly, and so often, complained was not given him.

commanding me to convene five General Officers in the said Warrant named, viz. General John Earl of Loudoun, Lieutenants General the Honorable Robert Monckton, the Honorable Thomas Gage, Majors General William Amherst and Staats Long Morris, to examine and inquire into the Causes of such failure, I give you this early intimation thereof, as a matter wherein you may be materially interested."

The General Officers met the next day, May twenty-second, with Gould as president. They reported: "Notice being taken of an opinion which universally prevails, that Lieutenant General Burgoyne is returned to Great Britain by permission from the Congress under a parole or engagement to return to North America when required by them to do so," it was resolved that General Burgoyne "should be desired to explain with precision" the nature of his parole. Burgoyne replied on the same day: "I have never been considered a Prisoner of War and I hold myself a free man in every circumstance except that I am restricted not to Serve in America during the War, with this further Parole on my leaving America that should the embarkation of the Convention troops be by any means prolonged beyond the time apprehended I will return to America upon demand and due notice given by Congress and will redeliver myself into the power of the Congress unless regularly exchanged."

This was made an excuse. So long as Congress had a *lien,* as it were, upon Burgoyne, English authorities could not begin any inquiry "which may in any wise tend, however remotely, to restrain or affect his person." The above is the gist of a very long Report which the Board of General Officers made on May twenty-third, and on the twenty-fifth George III issued a warrant that he "did approve* their caution observed in not summoning the said Lieutenant General Burgoyne." Although an inquiry would have "produced many lights,"† the difficulties and inconveniences arising from Burgoyne's peculiar situation made it expedient to defer the contemplated inquiry. The Board was discharged and Burgoyne was notified. There was to be no inquiry, therefore he could not see the King. Germain had a respite, for George III was a just man and did not forget old friends. It was fresh in Germain's memory that His Majesty had treated him with some asperity when he had tried to do Carleton an ill turn. Encouraged by his success, Germain pulled further strings and put the Law Officers of the Crown on the job of proving that Burgoyne did not, as it were, exist and could not therefore appear in Parliament.‡ This failed, so recourse was had to Barrington, the Secretary at War. He wrote on June fifth to Burgoyne that His Majesty, judging his presence material to the troops detained as prisoners in New England, was pleased to order that he should repair to Boston as soon as his health allowed. On the twenty-second Burgoyne replied that his doctor had ordered him "repose, regimen of diet and repeated visits to Bath"; he pointed out that if he were sent back to North America the troops would conclude that the British Government thought it inexpedient to ratify the Convention, or despaired of a ratification resulting in the army being allowed to sail for home. Barrington replied on the twenty-seventh that

*So no doubt did Germain, who of course drafted the warrant.

†Somewhat lurid, so far as Germain's conduct of the war was concerned.

‡See page 236.

the King attached such importance to Burgoyne's presence with the prisoners that it was his pleasure that he should return to them so soon as he felt well enough to do so; in fact he repeated his letter of the fifth. Nothing happened until September 24, 1779, when Charles Jenkinson, who had succeeded Barrington as Secretary at War, wrote: "I am commanded* by the King to acquaint you that your not returning to America, and joining the troops prisoners under the Convention of Saratoga is considered as a neglect of duty and disobedience of orders transmitted to you by the Secretary at War in his letter of 5th June, 1778."

Burgoyne wrote back in indignation: "The time in which I am charged with neglect of duty has been employed to vindicate my own honour, the honour of the British troops and of those of his Majesty's allies, under my late command, from the most base and barbarous aspersions that ever were forged against innocent men by malignity supported by power." He makes one very good point. He had been deprived of a court-martial because he was not amenable to the law, but in the same breath he *is* found amenable to the law when it is a question of ordering him to return to North America. In short his enemies (Germain and Co.) are "systematically desirous of burying my innocence and their guilt in the prisons of the enemy and of removing in my person to the other side of the Atlantic Ocean the means of renewing parliamentary proceedings which they have reason to dread." He ended his letter by saying that if he were not allowed a court-martial he felt himself compelled to

*The original draft has "directed," but some zealous clerk in the War Office, remembering that Kings do not direct, but command, altered it.

resign his appointment on the American staff, his colonelcy of the Queen's Regiment of Light Dragoons and the governorship of Fort William: he wished to keep his rank as lieutenant-general in the army so that he might be amenable to a possible court-martial later on and "to fulfil my personal faith,* should I be required by the enemy to do so."

Jenkinson replied on October fifteenth that His Majesty was pleased to accept the resignation of the appointments specified in the previous letter, and reiterated that a court-martial was out of the question. Burgoyne replied on the seventeenth that he did not admit that he could not legally have a court-martial and ended his letter: "I request you to assure his Majesty, with all humility on my part, that though I have reason to complain heavily of his Majesty's Ministers, my mind is deeply impressed, as it ever has been, with a sense of duty, respect, and affection to his royal person." With this the correspondence closed.

Burgoyne then wrote an open letter to his constituents, that is to say, "To the Gentlemen, Clergy, and other Voters of the Town of Preston," and a fine slashing letter it is. He reviews his political career; he had been a constitutional supporter of the Crown, but had always regarded himself as having a free hand. For example, he had been "agin the Government" in the Falkland Islands debate,† and in the matter of the East India Company had acted on his own initiative and taken his own line. He then adverts to his military career from 1775 onward. He had, when chosen to go to North America, tried to put himself upon as good terms as possible with the First

---

**i. e.*, to return to North America.

†See page 32.

Lord of the Treasury, or, to give him the designation by which he (Lord North) was always known in Parliament, "the Gentleman with the Blue Ribbon." It is to be feared that this is true. Burgoyne, like all politicians, was always trying to get into the good graces of those in power. He mentions his service at Boston as "the humblest upon the list of Major-Generals," touches lightly on his return to England and his share in the campaign in Canada in 1776; and says that when he was "pitched upon" for the command of the troops destined to make a junction with Sir William Howe, he was delighted to accept it, owing to "severe private misfortune," by which he means the death of his wife, Lady Charlotte. He then explains how, when he came home after the Convention, an "etiquette" was invented to prevent his access to the King's "closet," *i. e.,* to a personal interview with the King. Not only this, but lies were spread abroad as to the strength of his army and of the enemy's at the date of the surrender and he himself was charged in the same breath with being dilatory and precipitant. His friends in the army had been passed over for promotion, and he himself had been personally insulted by being given a "sentence of banishment" when it had been publicly announced that "not a soldier could be spared from our internal defence."

It is impossible not to come to the conclusion that, just as Byng was shot "because Newcastle deserved to be hanged,"* so Burgoyne was sacrificed because the Minden Man was an unscrupulous scoundrel, as well as a convicted coward.

---

*Sir John Fortescue.

## CHAPTER XIII

### ENGLAND, HOME AND BEAUTY

WE HAVE already seen what scurvy treatment Burgoyne received from Ministers and officials on his return to England where he arrived in May, 1778. And after such treatment it is not surprising that he should have thrown himself into the arms of the Opposition. Fox met his old friend at Hounslow on his way from Portsmouth to London. He had little difficulty in persuading him that Germain would accuse the soldier in order to save the ministerial skin, and that the King's mind had been poisoned against him. Fox was knocking at an open door, for Burgoyne had realized that he was to be "devoted," that is to say sacrificed as a scapegoat by ministers. Temple Luttrell's championship of Burgoyne led to a scene in the House of Commons. He roundly said that had the General "receded from his colours, disobeyed the commands of his superiors and hid himself from danger, such conduct would have given him pretensions to the honours and emoluments of the American Secretaryship." Even Germain could not swallow this without comment. He challenged Luttrell to a duel. But nothing came of it. In the words of Horace Walpole "Lord George Germain grasped his sword—and then asked pardon for having been grossly affronted." Burgoyne himself appeared in the House on this occasion—May twenty-sixth—(see also page 236) when Mr. Vyner moved that "this House will now resolve itself into a Committee of the whole House" to consider the state of the army which had surrendered and also how it was that Burgoyne had been released and had returned to England. Wilkes seconded the motion. He wanted to go further and to get information as to the conduct of the campaign which had been withheld by Ministers. And then, as was his wont, he waxed warm. "Unhallowed feet" had been set in America; there had been a disgraceful capitulation; savages had been employed; houses had been burned. Burgoyne had shown great personal bravery, but why had he issued that unhappy proclamation?

Burgoyne replied, as he would have said himself *ore rotundo*. He had always regarded the Indians as a necessary evil. He pointed out that in 1776, when in Canada, he had at a great meeting of the Indians, refused the pipe of war when he might "by a single whiff of tobacco have given flame and explosion to a dozen nations!" And during his past campaign the case of Miss "Mecree" was pure accident.

He then delivered a slashing attack on St. Luc who had formerly been "instrumental in scalping many hundred British soldiers upon the very ground where he was this year employed." St. Luc, he added, had been closeted with Lord George and had complained that he (Burgoyne) had discharged the Indians. This was not quite right. He had not discharged them—they had deserted, St. Luc at their head. Regarding the charge of burning houses, the only instance was that of General Schuyler's property. This had been a military necessity and General Schuyler had said that he would have done the same thing in Burgoyne's place. (See page 218.)

He then touched upon the condition of the army at

Cambridge where they had undergone hardships as severe, though of a different nature, as any they had experienced while in the field. He explained his personal position, his return on parole, and read to the House Washington's letter which has already been quoted. He gives one interesting piece of information, that between five or six hundred of the Convention Troops* had deserted, and he called this an "honourable desertion," that is to say that most of them had tried to make their way through the woods in order to join the armies under Sir William Howe and Sir Henry Clinton. Then he tackled Germain. Germain had laid papers before the House, including a private letter from Burgoyne written in 1776 which had been used to endeavor to prove that the writer had intrigued against Sir Guy Carleton regarding the command of the expedition. Germain might have produced other private letters showing that there was not a word of truth in this charge, but had not done so. Burgoyne admitted that the plan of campaign was largely based upon his *Thoughts*. But, and it was an important but, his *Thoughts* had been changed and garbled. The "latitude" that he should act, if he thought fit, against New England had been struck out, nor was his proposal that, if necessary, the junction with the southern army should be made by sea,† allowed to stand. Much had been made of the phrase at the end of his Instructions,

---

*In the Amherst Papers at the Public Record Office there is a "General Return of the Troops of the Convention of Saratoga as they left the Province of Massachusetts Bay 15th November 1778" signed by Phillips: The totals (all ranks) are 2,340 British and 1,949 Germans. At the surrender at Saratoga they numbered British, 2,442; German, 2,198. A certain number, of course, had been taken prisoners before the surrender.

†But we must remember that he had only put this forward as a *pis aller*. See page 112.

"You are to act as exigencies may require." That is to say it was argued from this that he should not have crossed the Hudson. Burgoyne reasoned, and rightly, that this saving clause referred to exigencies that might arise upon his arrival at Albany. Regarding the passage of the Hudson, Germain had spread the report that both Phillips and Fraser had remonstrated against it. "That is a direct and abominable falsehood." Here he received unexpected corroboration. Lieutenant-General Fraser, a relation of Burgoyne's Fraser and a Member of the House, said that he had received confidential letters from his relative written at the time of the crossing of the Hudson, and there was no word in them of disapprobation but "on the contrary Brigadier General Fraser spoke his opinion in the strongest terms in favour of General Burgoyne and his measures." Gentleman Johnny ended his speech with elegant extracts from Roman history which appear to have made Wilkes yawn prodigiously. Germain then rose and explained the presence of Burgoyne's private and confidential documents among the official papers. It was an accident. And a very convenient accident for Germain. The rest of the debate is as dull as most debates except for a speech by Lord George Gordon (of the Riots) who, his usual bee buzzing loudly in his Scotch bonnet, attributed the disaster at Saratoga to the fact that the Government had, by the Quebec Act, countenanced Popery in Canada. Saratoga was not so much a disaster as a "heavenly interposition of the Divine Providence."

Burgoyne was not, as already stated, allowed to see the King, was not allowed a court-martial, and when he got his Committee (see page 228, etc.) Parliament was suddenly prorogued and the Committee was thus prevented from reporting, and, on the evidence, there can be little doubt that Germain would have got his deserts. But he did not—instead, he got a peerage. And there was an interesting debate upon the question whether an officer who had been cashiered for cowardice was fit to be a member of the House of Lords. The moral of the whole story of course is that, in the eighteenth century at all events, if a soldier fell foul of a minister he was doomed. The soldier fought with his bare hands, the hand of the minister grasped a knuckle-duster.

One is rather glad that Gentleman Johnny's wife did not live to see this dismal eclipse of a military career which had begun with such a blaze of splendor in Portugal. Lady Charlotte must have been a delightful creature. In the Duke of Argyll's *Intimate Society Letters of the Eighteenth Century* (1910) there are two letters written by her to the Duchess of Argyll which are as gossipy, and therefore as interesting, as anything in Horace Walpole. She writes from Kensington Palace of the recent fray at Vauxhall, of her saunterings in the Gardens (where, it will be remembered, Mr. Hutchinson met her), of Mrs. L.'s adventures with the gentlemen of the road at Kensington Gore, of her Loo parties, of the wintry August weather, of Miss P. who lost two thousand pounds at cards in two successive nights, of the *most passionate* letters written by the Duke of Devonshire (who must have forgotten the family motto *cavendo tutus)* to Lady Charlotte Spencer, and finally of that never-failing source of gossip, the Duchess of Kingston, that remarkable lady who from the date of her first love-affair at the age of fifteen to her death in 1788 entertained the town with one mad escapade after the other. Lady Charlotte notes the odd fact that the

Duchess figures in the Duke's will as "my dearest wife Elizabeth Duchess of Kingston *alias* Elizabeth Chudleigh *alias* Elizabeth Hervey." Horace Walpole also noted this and, writing about the same date as Lady Charlotte, adds, "Did you ever hear of a Duchess described in a will as a street-walker is indicted at the Old Bailey?"

It is a very pleasant picture that Lady Charlotte sketches in these letters of the life in Kensington Palace then both in spirit and in atmosphere as remote from St. James's and Westminster as Hampton Court Palace now is. But one can not help thinking that Gentleman Johnny must have found Loo with ladies just a little bit lacking in that excitement which was no doubt necessary for a politician spending daily many dreary hours in a dreary House of Commons.

The banks of the Hudson are more picturesque and more romantic than those of the Thames at Westminster, or of the Liffey, and the rest of Burgoyne's public career is, to tell the truth, not so interesting as the years he spent in North America.

But he had not entirely done with the United States. He had, as it were, in his pocket a return ticket to Boston, and he was not sure when he might not be called upon to use it. Congress had not forgotten him. On April 3, 1781, on the motion of Mr. Thomas Bee, seconded by Mr. Thomas McKean, it passed a resolution recalling him, and on the sixteenth Washington wrote to Clinton pointing out that late exchanges had released all officers absent on parole except Burgoyne, whose return was required.

This led to the very interesting letter from the famous

Edmund Burke to the equally famous Benjamin Franklin. He writes from Charles Street, August 15, 1781, on a matter in which he has "no small concern." He has learned with astonishment that Congress has made an application for the return of his friend General Burgoyne, "the most opposite interests conspiring in the persecution of a man formed by the unparalled Candour and Moderation of his Mind to unite the most discordant parties in his favour." He attributes this to "some unusually artful management" by which, of course, he means some intrigue of Germain's. He gives Gentleman Johnny a fine testimonial, and that coming from Burke was worth having. He has always "behaved with the Temper which becomes a great Military Character that loves nothing so much in the profession as the means it so frequently permits of generosity and humanity." He has made great sacrifices "piqued to the resignation of so much rank and emoluments both so justly earned." His native land in fact had treated him hardly, as we have seen. "Shall America too," asks Burke, "call for sacrifices which are still more severe?" And he appeals "not to the Ambassador of America but to Doctor Franklin the Philosopher, my friend and the lover of his species."

Burke's eloquence and Franklin's benevolence had the desired effect and in due course Clinton suggested to Washington that the American and British Commissaries General of Prisoners should meet and "adjust the exchange" of Burgoyne. These two gentlemen, Major Abraham Skinner on the one side and the Sultana's complaisant husband, Joshua Loring, on the other, threshed the matter out. The question was ultimately settled February 9, 1782, Burgoyne being exchanged for one thousand and forty-seven officers and rank and file.

General Burgoyne

Engraved in 1801

Early in November, 1781, North had the King's speech ready for the opening of Parliament, promising a successful and speedy end to the war. He was anticipated. On November twenty-fifth came news of the surrender at Yorktown. "O God! it is all over," exclaimed the Prime Minister and in due course retired, with a pension of four thousand pounds a year. He was succeeded by Rockingham and there was the usual General Post (Noodle replacing Foodle) and scramble for places. Burgoyne was rewarded with the Commander-in-Chiefship in Ireland, and was made a Privy Councilor. He was also Muster Master General for the Foreign Forces in Canada. In the Haldimand Papers in the Manuscripts Department at the British Museum there are letters from him on the question of cutting down his deputy's allowance, from twenty shillings to five shillings per day. Though he was in close touch with the Castle he did not like Dublin. There are occasional allusions to him in the Dropmore Manuscripts where we find Earl Temple, the Lord Lieutenant, writing of the Commander-in-Chief's anxiety to get back to England, either on leave or permanently, and his hope to be made Lieutenant-General of the Ordnance. In which hope he was disappointed, as this was given to our old acquaintance Sir William Howe—not the first time that Howe had stood between Burgoyne and the realization of his ambitions.

The Board of Ordnance was of great antiquity, claiming indeed to trace back to an official once responsible for the supply of arrows for crossbows. It had a standing feud with the Secretary at War who finally defeated it after very many years, during the Crimean War when it was abolished. This was, from a Whitehall point of view, the most important victory gained during that campaign.

While Commander-in-Chief in Ireland Burgoyne paid one important visit to London, and that was in 1783. Fox had brought in his celebrated East India Bill the object of which was, practically, to abolish John Company. Burke backed him and told the East India Company what he thought of them, and those of the directors who were present at the bar of the House of Commons must have felt very uncomfortable. Gentleman Johnny came rushing across the Irish Channel: in his own words he "came over directly from a country in which he had the honour to hold a high post, crossed the sea and travelled 300 miles post" in order to support the bill. He was very stern. The reports on the table "exhibited the face of Tartarus itself." The nabobs who amassed fortunes in "Indostan" could only be compared with some scoundrels whom Æneas met when he went down to Hell, and here the General quoted half a dozen lines from Virgil which he had first learned in his old school a few hundred yards away (not from Hell, but from the House of Commons). It is curious that although other speakers in this debate drew on Shakespeare and Milton for images, Gentleman Johnny was the only one to go to the classics for an illustration. On his visits to London he kept the Lord Lieutenant, Lord Northington (who had succeeded Temple) posted up as to politics at Westminster. These letters are in the British Museum (Add. MSS. 33,100) and some of them are interesting. Thus on November 28, 1783, he writes to the Lord Lieutenant praising "Charles" *(i. e.,* Fox) who in attacking the East India Company dealt so convincingly with figures and accounts that "it would have made strangers believe he had been educated in the Bank."* But on

*If "Charles" ever added up his debts he must have been a pretty useful arithmetician.

December fifteenth he writes of "a juncture of imminent confusion and pregnant with consequences that every Lover of his Country must shudder to look to." All this because George III had said to Lord Temple that Fox's East India Bill was unprecedented, unparliamentary and subversive of the Constitution, adding that if it were to pass, "I am no more a King." Though the bill got through the Commons, Temple in the Lords hinted that it was most distasteful to the King, and it was thrown out. The East India Company continued to misgovern (and incidentally to add largely to the Empire) and the pagoda tree went on shaking like an aspen in a gale.

But the most interesting letter of Burgoyne's to Lord Northington is that dated "December 22nd 1783, 9 at night." The subject-matter is not important, dealing with his possible resignation. But the handwriting is most significant. He mentions casually that he has been "in our friend Charles's company" and it is very evident from the blots and erasures what Charles and Gentleman Johnny had been doing. It seems to me that they must have spent the whole day "setting them up" and keeping the "drawer," or as we should say wine-steward, very busy. Just as, on an historic occasion Mr. Pecksniff was unaware that he had "muffin on his knee" so our old friend can not have realized that his signature looked not so much like J. Burgoyne as J. Gargoyle. (As a rule his handwriting is very free, flowing and legible: he was evidently never at a loss for a word—a long word for choice.)

In 1782 he was given the colonelcy of the 4th Foot. One reads with horror in Wraxall's *Memoirs* that there had been previously some question of Eliott being recalled from Gibraltar and Burgoyne sent out in his place.

Fortunately, this was not done. Burgoyne was evidently not happy in Ireland, and all the time was longing to get back to England, Bath and Beauty as represented by Miss Susan Caulfield,* an opera singer of some gifts with whom he had, in the phraseology of the day, "formed a connection" a few years previously. Such alliances were not rare at this—or any other—date between the Army and the Stage. There was such an one, for instance, between Tarleton, who had also fought in North America and "Perdita," Mrs. Robinson, the first of George IV's many fancies. This Tarleton liaison lasted for sixteen years and a contemporary gossip says, in a very tantalizing way, "on the circumstances which occasioned its dissolution it is neither necessary, nor would it be proper to dwell."

An additional reason for Gentleman Johnny's anxiety to get home was that Susan presented him with a son. He was baptized in August, 1782, at St. Anne's Soho; Charles James Fox was his godfather, and the little boy was christened John Fox. On Burgoyne's death in 1792, Lord Derby, with the best of intentions and the kindest of hearts, took him (and the later arrivals) from the custody of poor Susan, and saw to their education. Lord Derby had been for some years separated from his first wife,† and little John Fox Burgoyne seems to have

*She was always "his dearest Sue." There is a pleasant letter in which he tells her he is sending her a pheasant and a brace of partridges (to be kept for a week) and he adds a delightful P. S. "Fie! Fie! to get such colds and pains in the stomach by feasting. If you did but take such care as I do!" Susan was a friend of the talented and famous Miss Farren, the actress whom Lord Derby married on the death of his first wife.

†Mrs. Montagu, the Queen of the Blues, writing in December, 1779, of three ladies of illustrious rank against whom divers suits were pending, says of their husbands, Lord Percy was "a nobleman of a most

passed an Esmondish sort of life at the Oaks and at the great mansion in Grosvenor Square. He went to Eton, was fag to Hallam the historian, entered the Royal Engineers and after a distinguished career became Field-Marshal Sir John Burgoyne and a baronet, thus winning laurels which Fate, aided by the Minden Man, had withheld from his father. There is a statue of the Field-Marshall near the Duke of York Steps: the careless often take it to represent Gentleman Johnny himself.

Burgoyne's "humble request" to resign the command in Ireland, which the King sanctioned in 1784, was couched in his usual Micawberish and flowery style. Witness this passage:

> "At my age, and with a temper that finds no terror in the loss of income, there may be little merit, but there will be solid comfort, in laying up for the close of life this reflection, that at a juncture which I thought a crisis in the fate of my country I took a decided part, and voluntarily, without a complaint of hardship or anger against any man or power, relinquished a splendid, a profitable, and in many respects a pleasing professional station, to pursue my parliamentary duty in connection with those men, and in support of those principles, by which alone I believed my country would be redeemed."

Gentleman Johnny, for all his pomposity, was such a good fellow that one hates to laugh at him, but, in order

---

distinguished merit, Lord Carmarthen is the prettiest man in his person, Lord Derby, to be sure, has nothing on his side but the seventh commandment." But you can not expect a blue-stocking to have much in common with a patron of the turf: to Mrs. Montagu a betting-book would most emphatically have been a *biblion abiblion.*

to justify the epithet "Micawberish" I must quote a passage from a letter written by him just after this date. He had, as Mr. Micawber so often had, occasion for a sum of money, five hundred pounds to be exact. He wrote to a friend, Mr. Nathaniel Day* and, granted the inconceivable impossibility that Mr. Wilkins Micawber could ever have possessed a valuable diamond, would he not have written in much the same strain as this?

> "I seek not to borrow it, even from a friend, without positive security, but this is of a nature that, however irreproachable to borrower or lender, I would not willingly offer to a stranger. I would take the money for six months certain, or optionally for twelve, and I purpose, besides the common security of a bond, to lodge in your hands my diamond, the gift of the King of Portugal, valued upon occasions when large jewels are in demand at about £1,000, but certainly marketable at any time for much more than the sum proposed—more valuable infinitely to me as a pledge of honour to be transmitted to those who would preserve my memory, and therefore sure to be redeemed, and not to be trusted in any hands where the deposit could not be sanctioned by integrity and confidence."

It is melancholy to think that John Burgoyne should have had to contemplate giving as security that jewel which must have been, from the gallantry which won it, the pride of Lady Charlotte's life. And therefore it is very pleasant to be able to add that Mr. Day was "truly happy" to accommodate his old friend with the sum in

*Day was Commissary General in Canada when Burgoyne started on his expedition. Earlier he had been a cornet in Burgoyne's Light Horse.

question, but expressly stipulated that "it must be accepted *without* that which you have mentioned."

Burgoyne had had, it will be remembered, a little trouble at a previous election, and that of 1784, when he was again elected for Preston, did not pass without incident, in which pistols again figured. A political opponent, a Mr. Elton, handed a valuable watch to Burgoyne's servant and told him to take it to his master and ask him "if he could tell them the time of day." Mr. Elton was playing with fire. Burgoyne put the watch and a couple of pistols on a tray, bade his servant carry it to the tap-room and followed him there. He asked the company present to whom did the watch belong, and Mr. Elton, his beer having suddenly turned more sour than vinegar, remained silent. Upon which Burgoyne pleasantly observed, "Since the watch belongs to none of you gentlemen it remains my property," and he handed it to his man with the words, "Take this watch and fob it in remembrance of the Swan Inn at Bolton." A crushing, and well-deserved snub.

In 1785 King George appointed a board, or as it would be called nowadays a Royal Commission, to consider the Defenses of the Country against a possible foreign invasion. The Duke of Richmond, Master General of the Ordnance, was President and Burgoyne was one of the twenty-three members. It was an industrious and a hungry board. When it visited Portsmouth it sat from six A. M. to four P. M., had a three-hours dinner, and then sat again from seven to ten. Probably it did better work at its morning than at its evening session. These hours did not evidently suit Lord Cornwallis, who was also a member of the board, for he writes of Burgoyne as being the biggest blockhead and sycophant he had ever seen. It was all for fortresses and fortification and proposed to spend enormous sums on the defense of the dockyards. Only three members, John Burgoyne, Earl Percy (whom we last met at Boston) and Sir D. Lindsay were strongly opposed to any such scheme. Burgoyne was in fact many years in advance of his time. He was a member of the Blue Water School long before such a school had come into existence. He said practically:

> Britannia needs no bulwarks,
>   No towers along the steep,
> Her march is o'er the mountain waves,
>   Her home is on the deep.

In other words he looked to the Navy to defend England from invasion, as it had done in the days of the Spanish Armada, rather than to fortresses which would cost vast sums* to build and which would lock up men to defend them who could ill be spared. In fact he anticipated not only the Blue Water School but what was to be known in recent years as the Fortress Incubus. As usual he was, so far as paper is concerned, perfectly right.

There was published in 1785 *A Short Essay on the Modes of Defence Best Adapted to the Situation and Circumstances of this Island* "by an Officer" which puts Gentleman Johnny's view so forcibly that I can not help thinking he must have had if not a hand, at least a finger in it. "When the rage of innovation and novelty seizes on the imagination of a projector, reason is sacrificed to fancy, love of country to vanity, and utility to whim." Except perhaps for the short last word, is not this exactly

*Coming to, it was reckoned, about £2,370,000, which if spent on ships would have doubled the strength of the Navy.

in the manner of our highfalutin old friend? The Board's proposals were brought before the House in 1786 and rejected by the casting vote of the Speaker. When Napoleon formed his great camp at Boulogne and when England really was in danger of invasion we took a wiser and cheaper course than that recommended by the Duke of Richmond. Martello Towers sprang up like mushrooms all along the South Coast, where many of them still exist and furnish agreeable summer lodgings for young couples. And Volunteers poured in, although it was unkindly said at the time that they expressly stipulated that they should not be sent out of the country—save in the case of invasion.

In 1786 when the question of a pension for the wife and sons of Sir Guy Carleton* came before the House of Commons, Burgoyne warmly supported it, and, as he had done before, spoke with great appreciation of the way in which Sir Guy had done everything he could to help in the preparations for the Expedition from Canada in 1777, in spite of the fact that he felt that he had been unjustly passed over by Germain for the command of it.

When Warren Hastings, like Clive before him, got into trouble for his doings in India, Burgoyne with some of the most famous statesmen of the day, Fox, Burke, Sheridan and Johnson's great friend Windham, was one of the "Managers" set up to conduct the prosecution. How very seriously he took this will be seen in the anecdote told by Miss Burney, quoted later on. In 1788 when tea nearly caused another war, this time with Spain which seemed to think that trade with China was her prerogative, Burgoyne offered his services as a soldier

*Created Baron Dorchester in this year.

to Pitt in a letter almost as lengthy but not quite so pompous, as his famous Putnam Creek Proclamation. But in spite of the long words and resounding phrases it is obvious that, keen soldier that he was and always had been, his one wish was that if there was any fighting in prospect, he wanted to be in the thick of it. But of course he must express it thus: "I hope it will not be construed a professional rant, or appear in any degree a forced sentiment in an old soldier to say that should his period in the destination of Providence be near, he would rather meet it in the duties of the field than amidst the sorrows and afflictions of a sick bed."

From time to time he spoke in the House, and spoke most sensibly, on Army questions, notably in 1789 when he supported the proposal that there should be a Commander-in-Chief, one of whose duties would be to "bring military merit to the foot of the throne and to draw it forth from the places where ministers now never looked for it—the field of actual service." His last speech in the House of Commons was one of the most sensible he ever made and, once again, he was far in advance of his time. It was proposed to increase the private soldier's pay, a proposal which John Burgoyne, ever the Soldier's Friend, heartily approved. And he added, "I only wish that the situation of the subaltern officers had been considered at the same time: they are still obliged to subsist on their scanty pittance, although every article of subsistence is at least 30 per cent. dearer than when their pay was originally settled." It took the European War to bring about a real reform in this.

In December, 1790, Boswell put him up for "The Club" but, much to Bozzy's disgust, he was blackballed, a distinction bestowed at the same time upon the Bishop of

Carlisle and Sir Charles Blagden. "The ballot is secret," but trust Boswell for finding out, and telling us, that the members who objected to Burgoyne were Sir Joseph Banks the scientist and George Steevens the Shakespeare commentator: the latter may have objected to Gentleman Johnny's mauling of *As You Like It,* to which we shall come in Appendix I.

On the third of August, 1792, John Burgoyne who had always been "enamoured of the stage" as that ornament of it, Mrs. Inchbald, puts it, was at a play in the Little Theatre in the Haymarket.* He died the following day in his house in Hertford Street,† Mayfair. In his will, which had been drawn up while he was Commander-in-Chief in Ireland he begins, as was sometimes the testamentary custom in those days, by analyzing his own character: "During a life too frequently blemished by the indulgence of one predominant passion, it has been a comfort to me to hope that my sensualities have never injured, nor interrupted the peace of others." On the other hand he pleads Not Guilty to any possible charge of injustice or malevolence.

He left the famous diamond to Lord Derby: the bulk of his property he bequeathed to Miss Susan Caulfield, with reversion to her (and his) son John Fox and three more of their children. But alas! his old habit of getting into debt had clung to him: what little property he left went to satisfy his creditors, and it was Lord

---

*Where the present Haymarket Theater stands.

†Which leads from Park Lane (in Burgoyne's day called Tyburn Lane) to that delightful spot Shepherd Market. This, though only a mashie shot from Piccadilly, is unknown to most people. It is one of the quaintest corners in London, chiefly inhabited by gentlemen's gentlemen, with very rosy faces and gaily striped waistcoats. An agreeable air of beer pervades the atmosphere.

Derby who took upon himself the charge of looking after the children. Burgoyne may have made enemies among the Rigbys and the Germains whose names are now completely forgotten, or only remembered with contempt and derision: the names of his friends, Reynolds, Sheridan, Fox, Burke, Windham and Lord Derby belong to history, in the case of Lord Derby, it is true, to the annals of the turf. But in English history there have not from time to time been lacking Prime Ministers, let us hope there never will be, who would far rather win the "Blue Ribbon of the Turf" than any other distinction.

John Burgoyne was buried in the cloisters of Westminster Abbey, near Lady Charlotte. At his own request the funeral was private: he who all his life had been for pomp and circumstance was for simplicity at the last. In the words of the *Gentleman's Magazine* of the day "one coach only attended with four gentlemen: a lady was likewise present whose convulsive agitation showed her to have that within which passeth show."

One can not but feel very sorry for "My dearest Sue."

## CHAPTER XIV

### THE MAN

YOU can not spend five or six evenings a week for the best part of a year in the company of a man—or woman—without forming a pretty definite opinion about him, or her. Well, I have spent many evenings, not in Gentleman Johnny's company, but surrounded by all the books and material I could lay hold of about him and I have grown to like him tremendously, and even to respect him. I hope I have clearly indicated, or rather let him indicate himself, his weak points. He was pompous, he was a gambler, in morals a latitudinarian—his outspoken age would have used a blunter word—and, I have naturally left the worst for the last, he was a politician. He was both a tragic and a comic figure. As a soldier, though of unimpeached courage—even the Minden Man and the Grub Street guttersnipes whom he subsidized did not dare to impugn that—he was not a success in the field.

That sour, old, dyspeptic Carlyle grudgingly admits the "pretty way" in which he began at Valencia and says that he might have become "a kind of General." To this it might be retorted that at all events Lady Charlotte, and Susan too for that matter, each had with Gentleman Johnny a much happier life than Jenny had with her Thomas. John Burgoyne was not a great dramatist, nor was he a great general. He was a courteous and polished man about town; he loved his profession, and his soldiers loved him. He always gave his men the credit due to them, a little formality which some great generals of the past have neglected. He never called his soldiers "scum." There has never been in British military history a soldier so shockingly let down by the minister at home, because there has never been in military history a war minister so casual, so incompetent, so mean, so contemptible, so cowardly* as "that man."

Regarding his morals it must be remembered that the eighteenth century was an immoral age, or perhaps one should say that it was a less hypocritical age than others have been. Burgoyne owned up to his weakness for womankind like a man, as we have seen in the extract from his will. With his Westminster fondness for Latin tags he must often have said of himself:

*Video meliora, proboque,*
*Deteriora sequor.*

A far worse charge than immorality can be brought against him and that is that he had, so it seems to me, no sense of humor though he was certainly witty; many lines

*I have already mentioned—once or twice—his cowardice at Minden. He showed a similar lack of enterprise, to put it mildly, in the First Expedition to St. Malo in 1758. A wit of the day wrote of him:

"All pale and trembling on the Gallic shore
His Lordship gave the word, but could no more.
Too small the corps, too few the numbers were,
Of such a general to demand the care.
To some mean chief, some Major or a Brig.
He left his charge that night, nor cared a fig;
'Twixt life and scandal, honour and the grave,
Quickly deciding which was best to save,
Back to the ships he ploughed the swelling wave."

(The "Brig." was Brigadier-General Mostyn.)

in his plays can be brought as evidence for this. As to his pomposity, many men of his day, when they had pen in hand, took for their model the Great Cham of Literature, Samuel Johnson, whose written style is not remarkable for its ease and elegance. Like all pompous people Burgoyne was apt to take himself too seriously. This is well brought out by a little anecdote told about him by Miss Fanny Burney, who was present with her brother in 1788 at the trial of Warren Hastings at which Burgoyne was, as it were, one of the stage-managers. She writes:

> "When the Managers were all arranged, one from among them whom I knew not came up into the seats of the House of Commons and said 'Captain Burney,* I am very glad to see you.'
>
> " 'How do you do, Sir,' answered James, 'here I am come to see the fine show.'
>
> "Upon this the attacker turned short upon his heel and abruptly walked away. I inquired who he was:
>
> " 'General Burgoyne,' James told me.
>
> " 'A Manager!' cried I, 'and one of the chargers! and you treat the business of the Hall† with such contempt to his face!'
>
> "James laughed heartily at his own uncourtly address but would not repent, though he acknowledged he saw the offence his slight, and slighting speech, had given."

---

*Later Admiral Burney and a friend of Charles Lamb. The Admiral was the husband of that Whist-disciplinarian, Lamb's Sarah Battle. It will be remembered that Jem Burney and Burgoyne had gone out to North America in the same ship.

†*i. e.*, Westminster Hall.

A less pompous man would, of course, have laughed it off.

Gentleman Johnny was in conversation not so witty as he is represented by Mr. Shaw in *The Devil's Disciple.* Still if any dramatist were to make any historical character talk in the way in which he probably really did talk when alive, why, the audience would walk out. Shakespeare makes Duncan when first he appears before Macbeth's Castle at Inverness exclaim:

> "This castle has a pleasant seat; the air
> Nimbly and sweetly recommends itself
> Unto our gentle senses."

There is a story told of an actor of the old school who had been promoted, in an emergency, from a very insignificant part to that of Duncan. He could not refrain from celebrating his advancement. He entertained his friends; his friends entertained him. They "set them up" again, and again, and again. And when the play began, though he may have forgotten his words, he remembered the gist of them. He made a magnificent entry, accompanied by hautboys and torches, looked round him, and with a kind of affable condescension pleasantly remarked to his astonished host, "Nice little place you've got here." And probably the real Duncan said something very much to this effect.

The best things about John Burgoyne were his courage, his courtesy, his kindness to, and consideration for, his men, who, as we have seen, had a real affection for him, and his John Bullish obstinacy. Though a politician his hands were clean: he certainly owed much to family connections, but in fashionable London of his day, who did not? He was essentially a gentleman, and, if he had lived longer, he would have made an admirable mentor for "Prinney," later George IV, many of whose intimates were of a raffishness that would have disgusted John Burgoyne.

It is evident that he was devoted to his wife Lady Charlotte, and she to him. Miss Caulfield also was obviously very fond of him. Perhaps some may ask why, as he was a widower, did he not marry his dearest Sue and, as the odd old-fashioned phrase has it, "make an honest woman of her"? I do not know, and in any case it is none of our business.

I like to think of Handsome Jack being driven post-haste in a post-chaise kissing Lady Charlotte's "sweet little Twiddle-diddles"* with (probably) the lady's father shaking a gouty fist, tearing his wig, and zoundsing in the background—it would make a fine picture. I like to think of him riding gaily at the head of his own Regiment of Light Dragoons into Valencia d'Alcantara—the very name sounds like a gallop; I like to think of Gentleman Johnny putting on his very best uniform and, with an air of noble condescension, receiving his sword back from Horatio Gates; and I like to think of him offering to send "Our General," our delightful and Pickwickian General, a few delicacies (no *tea,* I hope) from England.

On the other hand I do not like to think of poor Susan Caulfield all alone in the cold Abbey with the tears streaming down her pretty face at the loss of her old friend; still less do I like to think of her being deprived by the great nobleman, no doubt with the very best intentions in the world, of her children.

John Burgoyne died in 1792 but, like the soul of another J. B. he "goes marching on."

Before the Great War you could see him any day in Hyde Park near The Ladies Mile taking his ease and appraising "Fillies," in Pall Mall going into his Club, at Ascot (gamblin'), in Leicestershire (huntin'), and at first

*To quote Mr. Alscrip (page 334).

nights, especially at the Gaiety Theater, applauding Letty Lind's dancing and Florence St. John's singing. And after the show it was his pleasant habit to take a pretty chorus girl or two to supper at Romanos. The modern John Burgoyne, it is true, did not write for the stage, but he was a devoted admirer of it, especially when the *Corps de Ballet* was kicking its twinkling toes in the air. You will find him, magnificently flamboyant, in the pages of Ouida, where he sometimes so far forgot himself as to shoot grouse with a rifle. He sometimes, like his spiritual ancestor, even sat in Parliament, always ready, when told to do so by his leader, to "right about turn." He was with the Duke all through the Peninsula, riding to hounds between battles and flirting with senoritas. His "phlegm," as jealous, excitable, and gesticulating foreigners put it, had a great deal to do with the winning of Waterloo. Wherever he served his men were always ready to follow him hell-for-leather through hell. He has won V. C.'s innumerable. He gallantly blundered, with the most amazing whiskers, through that burlesque campaign, the Crimean War; he muddled through the Boer War; he helped to win the last war. And, as the years went by, though he may never have had the facile pen of Gentleman Johnny, he became more intelligent, and acquired, what is quite as important, a sense of humor.

In short, John Burgoyne with his gallantry, his philanderings, his gambling, his keen enjoyment of life, his tinge of pomposity, which has now nearly disappeared, is a very British type. And may it be long before the type is worn out.

On the other hand—God save us from Germains!

THE END

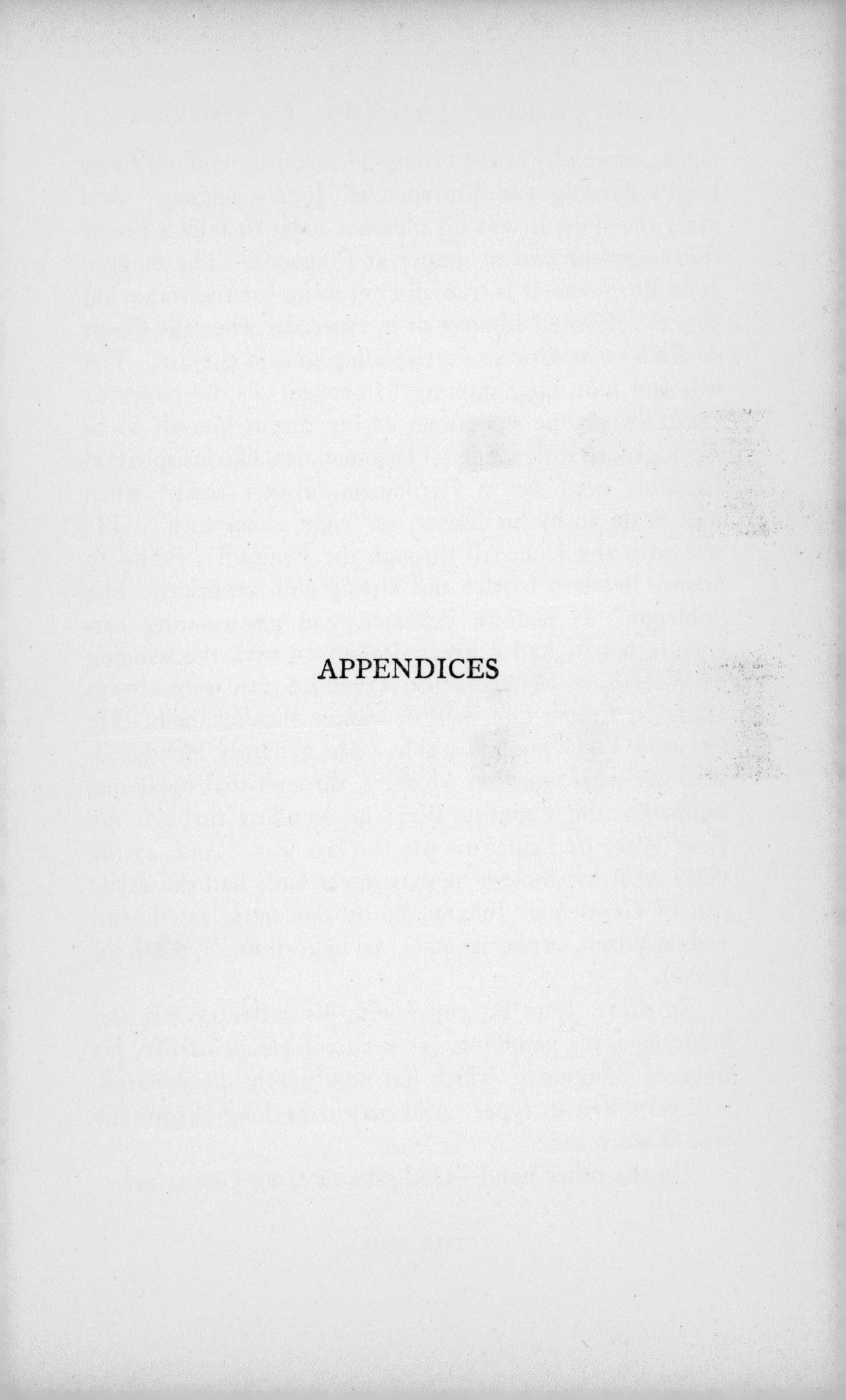

# APPENDICES

## I

### GENTLEMAN JOHNNY AS DRAMATIST

GENTLEMAN JOHNNY as a dramatist deserves a separate chapter, for soldiers, though they have often played the chief part in tragedies, and sometimes in comedies, have rarely written for the stage. John Burgoyne wrote *The Maid of the Oaks, The Lord of the Manor, The Heiress,* and he translated and adapted Sedaine's *Richard Cœur de Lion.* In June, 1774, Lord Stanley, the nephew of Lady Charlotte and later on Lord Derby, celebrated his "nuptials" as they used to call a wedding in those days, with Lady Betty Hamilton, daughter of the Duke of Hamilton. On this "auspicious occasion" a *fête champêtre* (which one may translate lawn party, though it originally meant a picnic) was given at "The Oaks," a country seat near Epsom which has lent its name to a very celebrated race, dating from 1779, just as an even more celebrated race, first run in 1780, derived its name from the noble owner of "The Oaks."* It owed its origin to an after-dinner chat at "The Oaks" between Lord Derby and his friend Sir Charles Bunbury. A spin of a coin decided that the new stakes should be known as "The Derby" and not as "The Bunbury." And yet there are people who do not believe in Providence!

Burgoyne, the wit and good-looking man about town

*It is stated in Manning and Bray's *History of Surrey* that Burgoyne once owned "The Oaks," or "Lambert's Oaks" as it used to be called. This is not correct. In 1788 under a private Act of Parliament William Lambert an infant, sold the estate for £4,550 to Lord Derby. (I am indebted for this information to Sir Henry Lambert, K. C. M. G.)

was naturally made Master of the Ceremonies or "principal manager and conductor"; he greeted the assembled company and "conducted the nobility and other visitors through the house to the voluptuous scene on"—O dreadful anti-climax!—"the Back Lawn." Here there was an orangerie, a concealed band of music, swains in fancy dress playing nine pins, shepherdesses swinging, with shrieks of apprehension and tempestuous petticoats, in swings, archery, dancing, and nymphs kicking at a *tambour de basque* suspended from a tree. The branches of the trees in the background bent under the weight of the Surrey yokels whose heads appeared among their leaves "as thick as codlings in a plentiful season." Then followed a supper "on the most costly dishes all hot and tempting," and on the top of that came minuets and country dances until three o'clock in the morning. This went on for five days; can you beat it in the records of Long Island? As a contemporary reporter remarked, "the greatest compliments are due to the skill and abilities of General Burgoyne on this occasion." It was, in fact, quite as splendid and as ludicrous an entertainment as the Mischianza with which Sir Billy was entertained just before he left Philadelphia.

Early in 1774 the greatest actor, not even excepting that fine mummer Sir Gorgeous Greasepaint, that England has ever produced, had put on what a contemporary critic called "a chaos of absurdities" called *Sethona* at Drury Lane. David Garrick was looking about him for something to succeed this when Burgoyne approached him with a dramatic entertainment which he had written round the *fête champêtre,* and which he called *The Maid of the Oaks.* Garrick was delighted to make the acquaintance of so fashionable an author; he took his *Maid,* touched her up here and there, overhauled the dialogue, and staged it at Drury Lane. It ran for several nights and so, for those days, may be deemed a success. Horace Walpole who, as we have seen, never lost an opportunity of sneering at Burgoyne, ran it down. He writes, "12th November 1774. There is a new puppet-show at Drury Lane, as fine as scenes can make it, called 'The Maid of the Oaks' and as dull as the author could not help making it." Horace is wrong, there are some good things in the play; though, it must be admitted, the less said about the plot the better, but this applies to so many plays. Sir Harry Groveby is on the point of marrying Maria, the ward of Mr. Oldworth. Sir Harry has an uncle, "Old Groveby," briefly described as "an old crab"* who, like all stage uncles, does not approve of the match. But, again like most stage uncles, he meets Maria, not knowing who she is, and falls a victim to her charming disposition. (Cf. old Mr. Winkle and young Mrs. Winkle, née Arabella Allen.) Mr. Oldworth overcome by "Bells ringing, Music playing, huzzas at a distance, and a chorus of merry, merry villagers singing ''Tis Maria's bridal day'" breaks down completely, and discloses the fact that he is really not Maria's guardian, but her father. "O Sir," says Maria, not unnaturally, "explain this mystery." Mr. Oldworth does so. And it is a pretty lame, bald and impotent explanation. It appears that when Maria was born "the hour of your birth made me a widower, and you a splendid heiress. I trembled at the dangers of that situation, to be the object of flattery in the very cradle and made a prey to interest, is the common lot attending

*Or as one would say nowadays "grouch."

it." This unnatural parent, therefore, levanted—he did not want to be bothered with a baby—and concealed Maria's birth, "being abroad at the time the plan was easily executed." He reminds one very much of that mid-Victorian lover, the hero of that pathetic, yet cynical song so dear to one's grandparents, *In the Gloaming*. ("Gloaming" was that period of the day when the Victorians first gloamed at each other, and then exchanged "chaste salutes.") This selfish fellow after starting with:

> In the Gloaming,
> O my Darling,
> Think not bitterly of me—

and after a lot of specious flattery explains his faithlessness with the terribly cynical words:

> It was best to leave you, Darling,
> Best for you and—*best for me.*

However, Maria's father did the best he could for her by announcing that she should inherit Oldsworth's Oaks, which so moved the old crab that *he* announced that if Maria, in the natural course of events, has a son, he shall inherit Gloomstock Hall. Which is all very like amateur theatricals. But there are two delightful characters in the play, Mr. Dupely and Lady Bab Lardoon. Mr. Dupely is very much a man of the world, and as for Lady Bab, "Oh she's a superior! a phœnix! an epitome, or rather a caricature of what is called very fine life, and the first female gamester of the time." This does not impress that rascally rogue Mr. Dupely. He knows all about women. "Maria, Lady Bab, Pamela Andrews,

Clarissa Harlowe, the girl that steals a heart in a country church, or she that picks your pocket in Covent Garden, are one and the same creature for all that—I am always too quick for them and make fools of them first, they are as transparent as glass," or as he would have said nowadays, easy fruit.

Lady Bab is much in advance of her day; she evidently possessed if not a latch-key, a large front door-key. She and her friends understand liberty as well as men. "We drop in at all hours, play at all parties, pay our own reckonings and in every circumstance (petticoats excepted) are true, lively, jolly fellows." She lived by her wits. "Jack Saunter of the Guards lost a hundred and thirty to me upon score at one time; I have not eat him half out yet—he will keep me best part of next Winter." Naturally she can not keep out of the papers (at the present day she would have had a press agent:) "We hear a certain lady, not a hundred miles from Hanover Square, lost at one sitting, some nights ago, two thousand guineas." And then they dot the *i*'s. "Lady Bab Lardoon has tumbled down [*i. e.,* at gambling] three nights successively, a certain Colonel has done the same; and we hear that both parties keep house with sprained ankles." Upon which honest Mr. Oldworth comments "That last paragraph sounds a little enigmatical." She has a pleasant scene with Dupely the skilled lady-killer. Disguised as a shepherdess, Philly Nettletop of the Vale—everybody was in fancy dress at the *fête champêtre*—she unpins her nosegay and "with the air of the most perfect naivete," proffers it to Mr. Dupely. He accepts it and, while thanking her, remarks—the libertine!—that his wishes extended a little further. For a country maiden, or rustic lass, Philly for all her "Lack-a-dazy heart's" and "bless me's" is somewhat cynical. She describes fine gentlemen as those who "take wives for fortunes and mistresses for show;* squander their money among tailors, barbers, cooks and fiddlers; pawn their honour to sharpers and their estates to Jews, and at last run to foreign countries to repair a pale face, a flimsy carcase and an empty pocket." No wonder Dupely exclaims, "Hey-day! where has my Arcadian picked up this jumble?" The dreadful dog then struggles to kiss her, and urges her to "fly with him to the true region of pleasure in his chaise and four"; but of course her identity comes out, he is forgiven and Lady Bab accepts him, in the delightful slang of the day, as her "Cavalier Servante and Cicisbeo."

When *The Maid* was produced at Drury Lane, Lady Bab was played by Frances Abington, the original Lady Teazle.† In the books on the eighteenth-century stage, there is no more charming portrait than that of Mrs. Abington. She was, for her looks and talent, the Marie Tempest of her day. Starting life as a cobbler's daughter, rising to be a flower-girl known as "Nosegay Fan," she ended by setting the fashion. She was the first to wear her own hair unpowdered, and knew the charm of a *négligée*.‡ She was very proud of her hands, and had a delightful little trick of "turning her wrist and seeming to stick a pin in the side of her waist." Altogether evidently a most enchanting little rogue.

---

*John Gay was more to the point when he wrote the line: "A Miss for Pleasure, and a Wife for Breed."

†Horace Walpole who saw the first night of *The School for Scandal* May 8, 1777, wrote: "Mrs. Abington was equal to the first of her profession." Garrick did not like her. He called her "the worst of bad women."

‡I understand, from what I have seen at the Cinema that the Vamp's motto is "Give me a *négligée* and twenty minutes."

Broad comic relief in *The Maid of the Oaks* is provided by an old retainer, Hurry, and the best that can be said for him is that he is not more tedious than many of Shakespeare's clowns. However, he throws an interesting light on Drink below Stairs in those days. He complains, "I have not touched a drop of liquor to-day—but two glasses of punch, a pint of hot negus to warm me, a bottle of cyder to cool me again, and a dram of cherry-bounce to keep all quiet." Does not this, barring the "cyder," make your mouth water?

*The Lord of the Manor* is another comedy—a musical comedy*—of artless subterfuge. It was produced anonymously and the *quidnuncs* put it down to Sheridan,—high praise indeed. When it was published with the author's name, Burgoyne wrote in the preface of Sheridan: "As an author he is above my encomium; as a friend it is my pride to think we are exactly upon a level": rather a compliment this as Sheridan was not so well-born as Burgoyne. He certainly was a real friend to the General, for he helped him when he was writing *The Heiress,* which explains why this is the best of Burgoyne's plays. Indeed they might not unfairly be described as "Sherry and water." The best characters in *The Lord of the Manor* are a French valet, a recruiting officer, Captain Trepan (probably the reason for the anonymity), and an old Mother Slapcabbage of a soldier's wife, Moll Flagon, a part played by a well-known comedian of the day with the very appropriate name, for a comedian, of Mr. Suett. It contains what is I think the best verse that Burgoyne ever wrote in the song:

---

*William Jackson known as "Jackson of Exeter" was responsible for the airs.

Encompassed in an angel's frame
An angel's virtues lay;
Too soon did Heaven assert the claim
And call its own away.

My Anna's worth, my Anna's charms
Must never more return!
What now shall fill these widow'd arms?
Ah me! my Anna's urn!

Very artificial of course and very like a translation from Latin verse by some scholar. But it is a good effort for a soldier, certainly better than that of the widowed stockbroker in a poem by Doss Chiderdoss, that remarkable bard of the 'nineties. This gentleman, according to Doss, made up his mind to write some lines upon his loss. He set out the lady's portrait, with such stock-brokerish accompaniments as a decanter full of whisky and a syphon much less full of sodawater; the touching result was:

He gazed on the sad reminder
Of the form that had made him weep
Then swallowed a stiffish binder*
And suddenly fell asleep.

To return to Anna, there is poor comfort in an urn. This reminds me of a story told, I think, by Gronow of the Prince Regent and his friend Mr. R. B. Sheridan. The Regent being in speculative and meditative mood had been discussing what the delicate Victorians used to call *embonpoint*. The Regent suggested that mankind admired it owing to some faint recollection of having in early infancy derived nutriment from what Mr. Micawber termed "nature's fount." Sherry turned this down. He remarked coldly that he had been brought up on a pap-bottle and he had no inclination whatever to fondle

*I hope it is not necessary for me to explain that a "binder" means a final drink.

pap-bottles. I can see George's fat sides shaking with laughter and hear him choking over his arrack-punch.

The French valet gives a good description of what he calls "the macaroni's knapsack." "It contains a fresh perfumed fillet for the hair, a pot of cold cream for the face, a calico under-waist coat compressed between two sachets *à l'odorat de Narcisse;* with a dressing of Maréchale powder, court plaister and *eau de luce.*" Captain Trepan, who reminds one rather of Farquhar's Sergeant Kite, throws a lurid light on the recruiting methods of the day. He has a number of bills (what theatrical folk call "throwaways") showing the advantages of the army, which are posted up in the village. One represents "a London tailor with his boots upon the neck of the French King"; and another is an East Indian scene depicting "a nabob in triumph, throwing rough diamonds to the young fifers to play at marbles." He is, he asserts, a conscientious man "and never runs the same recruit through more than three regiments, and that only when we have been hard pressed for a review." Moll Flagon one may take as the typical soldier's wife of the day, an adept at marauding on a campaign, and always ready to marry the first soldier handy as soon as widowed. Her costume is "a Soldier's coat over her petticoat, she carries a Gin-bottle by her Side and a Short Pipe in her Mouth." Her sentiments are free and easy, not to say gay and fancy; she has a song:

Sing and quaff,
Dance and laugh,
A fig for care or sorrow;
Kiss and drink,
But never think.
'Tis all the same to-morrow.

One has no objection whatever to soldiers of all ranks kissing and drinking, but the advice "never think" should be carefully eschewed by all young officers who hope to rise in their profession. Think, but for heaven's sake, never *say* what you think.

It is interesting to note that in this play Burgoyne anticipates our old friend Mr. Jorrocks in a couplet in a hunting song:—

> The Chase of Old Britons was ever their care
> Their sinews it brac'd, 'twas the image of war.

It will be remembered that Mr. Jorrocks said " 'Untin' is the sport of Kings, the image of war without its guilt, and only five and twenty per cent of its danger."

But Gentleman Johnny's chief claim to renown as a dramatist rests upon *The Heiress* which had an extraordinary success. Mrs. Inchbald says it "attracted vast sums of money from the East as well as the West part of the metropolis." By which she means that the citizens living East of Temple Bar as well as the fashionable world of St. James flocked to see it. That amazing man, Mr. Genest, who, although a parson, appears to have spent his whole time at the theater, writes in his *Some* (one ought to underline the *Some) Account of the English Stage:* "Drury Lane, 14th Jan. 1786 *The Heiress* by Gen. Burgoyne: the best new comedy since *The School for Scandal.** . . . It was acted thirty times in the course of the season." This, for those days, was a long run. *The Heiress* which was written at Lord Derby's seat, Knowsley, was dedicated to Lord Derby, and the celebrated Miss Farren (an honored and ancient

*Arthur Murphy, the translator of *Tacitus* and biographer of Garrick, used exactly the same words of it.

name in the annals of the English stage) who played the leading female part, later on, on the death of the first Lady Derby, in whose honor *The Maid of the Oaks* had been written, married Lord Derby. So it was quite a family affair. Even "Horry" approved of it, saying it was "the genteelest comedy in the English language." He read it twice in one day and liked it better than anything he had ever seen since *The Provoked Husband.** The plot consists of the usual complications and misunderstandings. In the last act somebody asks, "Why did you keep the secret from me?" Well, the real answer is, if he hadn't there would have been no play. Which reminds me of a story, very castaneous, of a band of Barnstormers. An actor, promoted to an important part, totally forgot his cue and rushed on several acts too soon. Dropping on one knee—probably the wrong one—he exclaimed "Please, Your Graice, we 'ave cut off the Dook of Buckingham's 'ead."

"Oh, you 'ave, 'ave you?" came the indignant reply; "then you've been and spoilt the 'ole of the bloomin' play."

*The Heiress* has a major and a minor hero, Lord Gayville and Mr. Clifford, and a major and a minor heroine, Lady Emily (the part Miss Farren played) and Miss Alton who turns out to be the heiress and sister to Clifford. The most entertaining character is Mr. Alscrip, a rascally old attorney. He is really a dreadful old man. The plot necessitates Miss Alton taking the post of lady companion to Miss Alscrip and the aged libertine tries to make love to her.

---

*This appears to have been Walpole's criterion. Writing of Sheridan's *School for Scandal* he said, "I have seen Sheridan's new comedy and like it much better than any I have seen since *The Provoked Husband*." This, by the way, was by Colley Cibber.

"But how to begin?" says he, "my usual way of attacking my daughter's maids will never do." So he tries a fresh gambit, addresses her as "Beauteous Stranger" and in less than three minutes "Kisses her fingers with rapture" exclaiming the while "Oh! the sweet little twiddle-diddles." No wonder Miss Alton considers him "a very strange old man."

The dialogue, here and there, is entertaining. Two minor characters, Mr. Blandish and his sister (not Serena), hangers-on of society, keep a lying-in list and send kind inquiries "to be delivered at the doors before the first load of straw"* and, in the case of spinsters, inquiries as to the "Angora kittens and the last batch of Java sparrows." There is a description by Lord Gayville of the Sim Tappertit of the day, "one of those beings peculiar to this town who assume the name of gentleman, upon the sole credentials of a boot, a switch, and round hat—the *things* that escape from counters and writing-desks to disturb public places, insult foreigners and put modest women out of countenance." Mr. Brown in *Evelina* is very like this. Old Alscrip has one excellent speech: "What a change have I made to please my unpleasable daughter! Instead of my regular meal at Furnivall's Inn, here I am transported to Berkley Square, to fast at Alscrip House, till my fine company come from their morning ride two hours after dark. Nay, it's worse if I am carried among my great neighbours in Miss Alscrip's suite as she calls it. My Lady looks over me, my Lord walks over me, and sets me in a little tottering cane chair, at the cold corner of the table—though I have

*This may puzzle a modern generation. It is years since I have seen straw laid down in the West End streets. And yet babies continue to be born.

NEVER PERFORMED.

At the Theatre-Royal in Drury Lane,

This preſent SATURDAY, Jan. 14, 1786,

Will be preſented a NEW COMEDY, called

# The HEIRESS.

THE PRINCIPAL CHARACTERS BY

Mr. KING,
Mr. PALMER,
Mr. PARSONS,
Mr. BADDELEY,
Mr. WILSON, Mr. CHAPLIN,
Mr. BANNISTER jun.
Mr. AICKIN,
Mr. R. PALMER,
And Mr. SMITH.
Miſs POPE,
Mrs. CROUCH,
Mrs. WILSON,
Mrs. LOVE, Miſs TIDSWELL,
Mrs. BOOTH, Miſs BARNES,
And Miſs FARREN.

The Prologue to be ſpoken by Mr. KING,
And the Epilogue by Miſs FARREN.

With Variety of New Scenes, Dreſſes, and Decorations.

In Act II. a Song in Character, by Mrs. CROUCH.

To which will be added

# The QUAKER.

Steady by Mr. BANNISTER,
Solomon by Mr. PARSONS,
Eaſy by Mr. WRIGHTEN,
And Lubin by Mr. SUETT,
Gillian by Mrs. FORSTER,
Cicely by Mrs. LOVE,
And Floretta by Mrs. WILSON.

Places for the Boxes to be taken of Mr. FOSBROOK at the Theatr

Bill for Burgoyne's play *The Heiress*

a mortgage upon the house and furniture, and arrears due of the whole interest. It's pleasant though to be well dressed. Lord! the tightness of my wig and stiffness of my cape give me the sense of the pillory—plaguey scanty about the hips, too, and the breast something of a merry-thought reversed." In one scene there is a curious parallel to Dickens. Lady Emily is instructing Miss Alscrip in demeanor, elocution and deportment.

> "My dear Miss Alscrip, what are you doing? I must correct you as I love you. Sure you must have observed the drop of the underlip is exploded since Lady Simpermode broke a tooth. *(Sets her mouth affectedly.)* I am preparing the cast of the lips for the ensuing winter—thus—it is to be called the Paphian mimp.
>
> "*Miss Alscrip.* *(Imitating)* I swear I think it pretty—I must try to get it.
>
> "*Lady Emily.* Nothing so easy. It is done by one cabalistical word, like a metamorphosis in the fairy tales. You have only, when before your glass, to keep pronouncing to yourself Nimini-primini—the lips can not fail of taking their plie.
>
> "*Miss Alscrip.* Nimini-primini, imini, mimini, oh! it's delightfully infantine! and so innocent, to be kissing one's own lips.
>
> "*Lady Emily.* You have it to a charm."

I do not know if Charles Dickens had ever seen, or read, *The Heiress,* but this passage is very like that in *Little Dorrit,* "Papa, potatoes, poultry, prunes and prisms—all very good words for the lips."

In any case "nimini-primini" became a catch-word

which lasted on well into the nineteenth century. I myself have recollections of it as being used, rather in derision, by aunts of mine who probably had seen revivals of *The Heiress* when they were young, and whom the word had struck as something quaint.

Although I love old plays, for I think you get from them a far more vivid notion of the life of the period than you do from the novels, I doubt if *The Heiress* would bear reviving. Just as it is doubtful if in one hundred years' time anybody will revive *The Second Mrs. Tanqueray,* or *The Importance of Being Earnest. The Heiress* was translated into many languages and ran through many editions. That with which I am acquainted is embellished by two plates, which are really very delightful. One represents Lord Gayville, with a very elegant leg, kneeling before Miss Alton (Clifford) whose waist is very high up, with Miss Alscrip, with towering ostrich-plumes upon her head, in the indignant background. The other shows a duel in Hyde Park, which appears to be a kind of Forest of Arden.

Burgoyne also translated from the French Sedaine's *Richard Cœur de Lion* which is remembered for the song "O Richard! O mon Roi!" The part of Florestan was played by Mr. Caulfield, a name very familiar and dear to Handsome Jack. The librettos of operas, with the exception of those by the immortal "poet Bunn," are but dreary reading, so we will leave Lion Heart alone.

Burgoyne had, like most eighteenth-century dramatists, a great fondness for what one might (pedantically) call onomatopœic names, that is to say names which suggest a person's nature and character. You will find, for example, in his comedies such names as Lady Cypher, Mrs. Squabble, Lord Flimzey, Lady Squander, Dolly

Dump, Lord Dangle,* Billy Vapid, Quicksilver Jack (a professional deserter, "he was hanged at last in Berlin after having served six different princes in the same pair of shoes"), Lady Spite, Mrs. Scanty, Billy Skim, Secret Tom, Lady Newchapel (a Methodist) and so on. Sheridan and most eighteenth-century dramatists also invented names like these but the great master of this curious art of expressive nomenclature was a far more serious writer, John Bunyan. Witness his Pliable, Wordly Wiseman, Talkative of Prating Row, Pickthank, Lords Letchery, Love-Lust and Carnal Delight, Feeble-Mind, No-Good, Turn-about, By-ends of Fair-speech and Lady Feigning. The habit still continues in Christmas Pantomimes where you may still meet such characters as Baron Blowhard and the Earl of Bodega.

As *The Heiress* was the best of Burgoyne's excursions into the drama, so was his plan for tinkering with *As You Like It* his worst. He tries to translate *As You,* as actors call it, into eighteenth-century phraseology. Thus, Rosalind is given a song of which one stanza is:

> "To be honest and fair is too much for our share
> Impartially nature replies,
> Ere that Phœnix I make, let me see for his sake
> A man that's deserving the prize!"

There is a lilt about this which reminds one of the lyric written in honor of Mr. Pecksniff at Todger's:

> "All hail to the vessel of Pecksniff the sire
> With favouring breezes to fan
> While Tritons flock round him and proudly admire
> The architect, artist and man."

*There is also a Dangle in Sheridan's *The Critic.*

And oddly enough the hunting-song which in Burgoyne's version becomes:

> "Ah! the dappled fool is stricken,
> See him tremble—see him sicken,
> All his worldly comrades flying,
> See him bleeding, panting, dying.
> From his eyelids wan and hollow
> How the big tears follow—follow,
> Down his face in piteous chace,
> How they follow, follow, follow
> Without stop, drop by drop,
> How they follow drop by drop!"

bears, I think, a remarkable likeness to:

> "Can I view thee, panting, lying
> On thy stomach, without sighing,
> Can I unmoved see thee dying
> On a log
> Expiring frog!"

"The next verse is still more touching," said Mr. Leo Hunter, but I will not quote it, hoping that if you have forgotten it, you will refresh your memory by looking up the text.

Horace Walpole said, "Burgoyne's battles and speeches will be forgotten, but his delightful comedy of *The Heiress* still continues the delight of the stage and one of the most pleasing domestic compositions." I think he is wrong. No one, certainly, reads Burgoyne's speeches now, but who in the world ever does, in cold blood, read speeches? Nobody, except perhaps the orators who make them. And sometimes they read them when they deliver them, if they can't learn them by heart, as old Sam Rogers said of Lord Dudley, whom he did not like:

"Ward has no heart, they say, but I deny it,
He *has* a heart—and gets his speeches by it."

But Saratoga will never be forgotten, for it was the beginning of the end of the War of Independence.

But one should not blame Gentleman Johnny because his plays lie undisturbed on the top shelf. It is not the business of a general to write plays, any more than it is the business of a dramatist to fight battles. Mr. Shaw and Mr. Henry Arthur Jones, to mention only two names, have fought many battles ("My dear Wells") on paper, but I am sure that both would admit that they would cut but a poor figure at a General Headquarters. Generals have certainly on occasion, like Burgoyne, written verse. A famous living general published many years ago a little volume of poetry. I rescued it from what was then called The Tuppenny Box where it was lying cheek by jowl with old sermons, old pamphlets on The Sewage Question, out of date school-books, and all the kind of cagmag which people so generously gave away during the war when they were asked to send books to our Tommies in the field. I took it home and read it. And when, the next day, with a vague idea that I had been cheated, I took it back to the second-hand bookseller and offered it to him for one penny, his face became distorted with a horrible sneer, and he laughed sardonically.

So I will not give the author's name.

## II

### AUTHORITIES

RESEARCH has been, rather unkindly, defined as "taking something out of a book which nobody has ever read and putting it into a book which nobody ever will read." This is a hard saying, calculated to annoy bibliographers. There is certainly a tendency nowadays for very detailed and minute bibliography which often results in one's not being able to see the wood for the trees. In compiling a bibliography of this kind, where it concerns the life of an individual, you begin by referring to the entry in the books of the physician who saw your hero into the world, you indicate where his Glaxo bill is to be found and the sum paid for his first rocking-horse, and so you continue till you end with the undertaker's account. This form of enthusiastic, detailed, Scotland Yardish research reminds me of a saying of Sir Owen Seaman, who, dealing with the activities of a Bronte enthusiast, remarked that he collected every possible item connected in any way whatsoever with that amazing family, including "Photographs of Patrick Bronte's boots."

I do not profess, life, like Sam Weller's "wision," being limited, to have read all the books and documents in which John Burgoyne's name appears. The manuscripts which deal with his military career are to be found in the Public Record Office, and copies of many of his slightly verbose letters are in the Manuscripts Department of the British Museum. He made such a stir in his day that all the more important of his writings got into print, many of them being (rather as if they were eggs) "laid" before Parliament.

The United States is as rich in Burgoyniana as England, and I should like to repeat here my great indebtedness to Mr. D. C. Mearns who has sent me much and most valuable material which does not exist in this country, in the shape of extracts from many publications and from the Manuscripts in the Library of Congress. Without his help this book would have been but "a bald and unconvincing narrative."

All the books which appear in the following list I have read, some of them under that Great Dome in Bloomsbury where the presiding genius, my old friend Mr. F. D. Sladen, will tell you where to find everything about anything. I believe that if you were to ask him what song the Sirens sang, he would, with no great delay, whistle it to you. Many of these books, of course, are in the War Office Library and, as librarian there, I have never hesitated to give myself permission, as a student of military history, to borrow and pore over at home anything I wanted. An "eminent" (to annex the epithet usually attached to "divines") librarian, overwhelmed with the number of books which came under his care, once observed in despair, "The librarian who reads is lost." I don't agree. I think it would have been more true had he said, "The librarian who does not read will be found out." In any case, I have read all I could discover about John Burgoyne, but I am painfully aware that I yet may be found out. And I say in all sincerity that I hope those who find me out will either come and see me and find me in, or else write and tell me of my shortcomings.

ADAMS (C. F.) *Studies, Military and Diplomatic.* 8vo. 1911.

ALMON (J.) *The Debates and Proceedings of the British House of Commons from 1743 to 1774.* 8vo. 1766-75.

ALMON (J.) *The Parliamentary Register; or, History of the Proceedings and Debates of both Houses of Parliament from 1774.* 8vo. 1775, etc.

ANBUREY (T.) *Travels through the Interior Parts of America; in a series of letters,* 2 vols. 8vo. 1789.

ANDREWS (J.) *History of the War with America, France, Spain and Holland, 1775-83.* 4 vols. 8vo. 1785-86.

BATCHELDER (S. F.) *Burgoyne and his Officers in Cambridge, 1777-78.* 8vo. 1926.

BAXTER (J. P.) *The British Invasion from the North. The Campaigns of Generals Carleton and Burgoyne from Canada, 1776-77, with the Journal of Lieut. W. Digby of the 53rd, or Shropshire Regiment of Foot.* 8vo. 1887.

BELCHER (Rev. H.) *The First American Civil War. First period, 1775-78. With chapters on the Continental or Revolutionary Army and on the Forces of the Crown.* 2 vols. 8vo. 1911.

BOYNTON (Capt. E. C.) *History of West Point and Its Military Importance during the American Revolution.* 8vo. 1864.

BRIEF *Examination of the Plan etc. of the Northern Expedition in America and of the surrender of the Army under the command of Lieutenant-General Burgoyne.* 8vo. 1789.

BURGOYNE (Lieut.-Gen. J.) *A Letter from Lieut.-Gen. B. to his Constituents, upon his late resignation; with the correspondence between the Secretaries of War and him, relative to his return to America.* 12mo. 1779.

BURGOYNE (Lieut.-Gen. J.) *A State of the Expedition from Canada, as laid before the House of Commons by Lieut.-Gen. B. and verified by evidence, with a collection of authentic documents, etc.* 4to. 1780.

BURGOYNE (Lieut.-Gen. J.) *Orderly Book of Lieut.-Gen. J. B., from his Entry into the State of New York until his surrender at Saratoga.* Edited by E. B. O'Callaghan. 4to. 1860.

BURGOYNE (Lieut.-Gen. J.) *The Dramatic and Poetical Works of J. B.,* 2 vols. 8vo. 1808.

CANADA, *General Staff, Historical Section. A History of the Organisation, Development and Services of the Military and Naval Forces of Canada from the Peace of Paris in 1763 to the present time. With illustrative documents.* Vol. 2.—*The War of the American Revolution. The Province of Quebec under the Administration of Governor Sir Guy Carleton, 1775-78.* 8vo. 1920.

CARRINGTON (Col. H. B.) *Battles of the American Revolution, 1775-81. Historical and military criticism, with topographical illustration.* 8vo. 1877.

COBURN (F. W.) *A History of the Battle of Bennington, 1777.* 1912.

COFFIN (C.) *History of the Battle of Breed's Hill,* by Major Generals W. Heath, H. Lee, J. Wilkinson and H. Dearborn. Compiled by C. C. 8vo. 1835.

COOLIDGE (G. A.) *Brochure of Bunker Hill, with heliotype views.* Revised edition, with account of the centennial. 12mo.

CREASY (Sir E. S.) *Fifteen Decisive Battles of the World.* 8vo. 1864.

CRESSWELL (N.) *Journal of, 1774-77.* 8vo. 1924.

CURTIS (E. E.) *The Organisation of the British Army in the American Revolution.* 8vo. 1926.

DEANE (C.) *Lieutenant-General J. Burgoyne and the Convention of Saratoga.* 8vo. 1877.

DE FONBLANQUE (E. B.) *Political and Military Episodes in the latter half of the eighteenth century. Derived from the life and correspondence of the Right Hon. John Burgoyne, General, Statesman, Dramatist.* 8vo. 1876.

DE PEYSTER (Brev. Maj.-Gen. J. W.) *Major-General Philip Schuyler and the Burgoyne Campaign in the summer of 1777.* 8vo. 1877.

DONKIN (R.) *Military Collections and Remarks.* 8vo. 1777.

DRAKE (S. A.) *Burgoyne's Invasion of 1777.* 12mo. 1889.

EGLESTON (T.) *The Life of John Paterson, Major-General in the Revolutionary Army. 2nd edition.* 8vo. 1898.

ESSAY *on Modern Martyrs.* 8vo. 1780.

EELKING (M. V.) *Die deutschen Hülfstruppen im nord-amerikanischen Befreiungskriege.* 2 pts. 8vo. 1863.

EELKING (M. V.) *German Allied Troops in the North*

*American War of Independence, 1776-83.* 4to. 1893.

EELKING (M. V.) *Memoirs and Letters and Journals of Major-General Riedesel. Translated from the original German of M. von E. by W. L. Stone.* 2 vols. 8vo. 1868.

FISHER (S. G.) *True History of the American Revolution.* 8vo. 1902.

FISKE (John) *The American Revolution.* 2 vols. 8vo. 1891.

FITZMAURICE (E., Baron) *Life of William, Earl of Shelburne, afterwards first Marquess of Lansdowne.* 8vo. 1875-76.

FORTESCUE (Hon. Sir J. W.) *A History of the British Army.* 8vo. 1899, etc.

GENTLEMAN'S MAGAZINE. *Passim.*

GRAHAM (Col. H.) *History of the Sixteenth, the Queen's Light Dragoons (Lancers), 1759 to 1912.* 4to. 1912.

GREENE (Maj.-Gen. F. V.) *The Revolutionary War and the Military Policy of the United States.* 8vo. 1911.

HADDEN (J. M.) *Journal in Canada and on Burgoyne's Campaign, 1776-77.* 4to. 1884.

HATCH (L. C.) *The Administration of the American Revolutionary Army.* 8vo. 1904.

HEADLEY (J. T.) *Washington and his Generals.* 2 vols. 8vo. 1847.

HEATH (Maj.-Gen. W.) *Heath's Memoirs of the American War (Reprinted).* 8vo. 1904.

HENLEY (Col. D.) *Proceedings of a Court Martial held for the trial of Colonel D. Henley, accused of ill-treatment of the British Soldiers.* 8vo. 1778.

HISTORICAL MANUSCRIPTS COMMISSION. *Abergavenny, Carlisle, Dartmouth, Dropmore, Kenyon, Knox, Lothian, Round, Stopford Sackville MSS.*

HOWE (Lieut.-Gen. Sir W.) *The Narrative of Lieut.-Gen. Sir W. Howe, in a Committee of the House of Commons, on the 29th April, 1779, relative to his conduct during his late command of the King's Troops in North America; to which are added, Some Observations upon a pamphlet entitled "Letters to a Nobleman."* 4to. 1780.

HUDLESTON (F. J.) *The Misfortune at St. Cas. (In the United Service Magazine).* 8vo. 1907.

JACKSON (R.) *A View of the Formation, Discipline and Economy of Armies. 3rd edition.* 8vo. 1845.

JUNIUS: *including letters by the same writer. New edition.* 8vo. 1875.

KINGSFORD (W.) *The History of Canada.* Vol 6. 8vo. 1893.

LAMB (R.) *An Original and Authentic Journal of Occurrences during the late American War, to 1783.* 8vo. 1809.

LAMB (R.) *Memoirs of his own Life.* 8vo. 1811.

LANGWORTHY (E.) *Memoirs of the Life of the late Charles Lee.* 8vo. 1792.

LEE (Charles) *The Lee Papers. (New York Historical Society.)* 8vo. 1872-76.

LEES (Maj. A. W. H.) *The True Account of Saratoga. (In Journal of the Royal United Service Institution.)* 8vo. 1913.

LOSSING (B. J.) *The Pictorial Field-Book of the Revolution: or, Illustrations, by pen and pencil, of the history, biography, etc., of the War for Independence.* 2 vols. 4to. 1851-52.

LOSSING (B. J.) *The Life and Times of Philip Schuyler.* 12mo. 1860.

LOWELL (E. J.) *The Hessians in the Revolutionary War.* 8vo. 1884.

LUCAS (Sir C. P.) *A History of Canada.* 8vo. 1909.

MARTIAL BIOGRAPHY, *or Memoirs of the Most Eminent British Military Characters.* 12mo. 1804.

MOORE (F.) *Diary of the American Revolution from newspapers and original documents.* 2 vols. 8vo. 1859-60.

MUMBY (F. A.) *George III and the American Revolution: the Beginnings. (History in Contemporary Letters.)* 8vo. 1924.

NEILSON (C.) *An Original, Compiled and Collected Account of Burgoyne's Campaign and the memorable battles of Bemis's Heights.* 12mo. 1849.

PAUSCH (G.) *Journal of Captain Pausch, of the Hanau Artillery during the Burgoyne Campaign.* 4to. 1886.

PULSIFER (D.) *An Account of the Battle of Bunker Hill, compiled from authentic sources. With General Burgoyne's account of the battle.* 12mo. 1875.

REMEMBRANCER, *The, 1777.* 8vo. 1777.

RIEDESEL (Gen. F. A., Baron von) *Briefe und Berichte des Generals und der Generalin von Riedesel während des nord-amerikanischen Kriegs, 1776, bis 1783.* 8vo. 1851.

RIEDESEL (F. C. L., Baroness von) *Die Berufs-Reise nach Amerika. Briefe der Generalin von Riedesel.* 8vo. 1800.

RIEDESEL (F. C. L., Baroness von) *Letters and Memoirs Relating to the War of American Independence.* 12mo. 1827.

RIEDESEL (F. C. L., Baroness von) *Letters and Journals relating to the American War of the Revolution. Translated by W. L. Stone.* 8vo. 1867.

ROYAL INSTITUTION OF GREAT BRITAIN. *Report on American Manuscripts in the Royal Institution of Great Britain.* 2 vols. 8vo. 1904-06.

ST. CLAIR (A.) *Proceedings of a General Court Martial for the Trial of Major-General St. Clair. (Reprint.)* 8vo. 1881.

SACKVILLE (G., Lord) *The Trial of the Rt. Hon. Lord George Sackville.* 8vo. 1760.

SCHUYLER (P.) *Proceedings of a General Court Martial for the Trial of Major-General Schuyler. (Reprint.)* 8vo. 1880.

SCOTS MAGAZINE. 8vo. 1777.

SCULL (G. D.) *The Evelyns in America, 1608-1805. Edited by G. D. S.* 4to. 1881.

SMITH (W. H.) *The St. Clair Papers.* 2 vols. 8vo. 1882.

STEDMAN (C.) *History of the Origin, Progress and Termination of the American War.* 2 vols. 4to. 1794.

STONE (W. L.) *Ballads and Poems relating to the Burgoyne Campaign.* 4to. 1893.

STONE (W. L.) *The Campaign of Lieutenant-General J. Burgoyne and the Expedition of Lieutenant-Colonel B. St. Leger.* 12mo. 1877.

STONE (W. L.) *Centenary Celebration of Burgoyne's Surrender.* 8vo. 1877.

STONE (W. L.) *Letters of Brunswick and Hessian Officers during the American Revolution. Translated (from Schlozers Briefwechsel) by W. L. S.* 4to. 1891.

STONE (W. L.) *Visits to the Saratoga Battlegrounds.* 8vo. 1895.

TREVELYAN (Sir G. O.) *The American Revolution.* 8vo. 1899-1907.

TYLER (M. C.) *Literary History of the American Revolution, 1763-83.* 8vo. 1897.

TUCKERMAN (B.) *Life of General P. Schuyler, 1733-1804.* 8vo. 1904.

VAN TYNE (C. H.) *The American Revolution, 1776-83.* 8vo. 1905.

WADDINGTON (R.) *La Guerre de Sept Ans. Histoire diplomatique et militaire.* 8vo.

WALPOLE (H.) *Letters on the American War of Independence.* 8vo. 1908.

WALWORTH (E. H.) *Saratoga: the Battle, Battle Ground, Visitors' Guide.* 8vo. 1877.

WALWORTH (E. H.) *Battles of Saratoga, 1777.* 8vo. 1891.

WASHINGTON (Gen. G.) *Official Letters to the Honorable American Congress, written, during the War between the United Colonies and Great Britain, by his Excellency, G. W., Commander-in-Chief of the Continental Forces, now President of the United States. (American State Papers.)* 2 vols. 8vo. 1795.

WERTHERN (V.) *Die hessischen Hülfstruppen in nord-amerikanischen Unabhängigsheitkriege, 1776-83.* 8vo. 1895.

WILKINSON (James) *Memoirs of my own Times.* 3 vols. 8vo. 1816.

WORTLEY (Hon. Mrs. E. S.) *A Prime Minister and his Son. From the correspondence of the 3rd Earl of Bute and of Lt.-General the Hon. Sir Charles Stuart, K. B., etc. (Letters to Lord Bute from America.)* 8vo. 1925.

WRAXALL (Sir N. W.) *Historical Memoirs of my own Times. New edition.* 8vo. 1904.

## III

### JOHN BURGOYNE'S APPOINTMENTS AND PROMOTIONS.

A certain John Burgoyne was appointed Sub-Brigadier in the 3rd Troops of Horse Guards, 9. 8. 1737. Retired c. 13. 11. 41. Possibly the same, it being quite customary to appoint boys to such posts, especially if well connected, as Burgoyne was.

| | | | | |
|---|---|---|---|---|
| Cornet | 1st Dragoons | 23. | 4. | 1744. |
| Lieut. | do. | 23. | 2. | 45. |
| Captain | do. | 1. | 7. | 45. |
| | Retired October 1751. | | | |
| Captain | 11th Dragoons | 14. | 6. | 56. |
| Capt.-Lieut. & Lt.-Col. | Coldstream Guards | 10. | 5. | 58. |
| Lt.-Col. Comdt. | 16th Light Dragoons | 4. | 8. | 59. |
| Brevet Col. | | 8. | 10. | 62. |
| Col. | 16th Light Dragoons | 18. | 3. | 63-1779 |
| Major-Gen. | | 25. | 5. | 72. |
| Lieut.-Gen. | | 29. | 8. | 77. |
| Col. | 4th Foot | 7. | 6. | 82. until death. |

Governor of Fort William 1769 until 1779 (£300 p. a.)

# INDEX

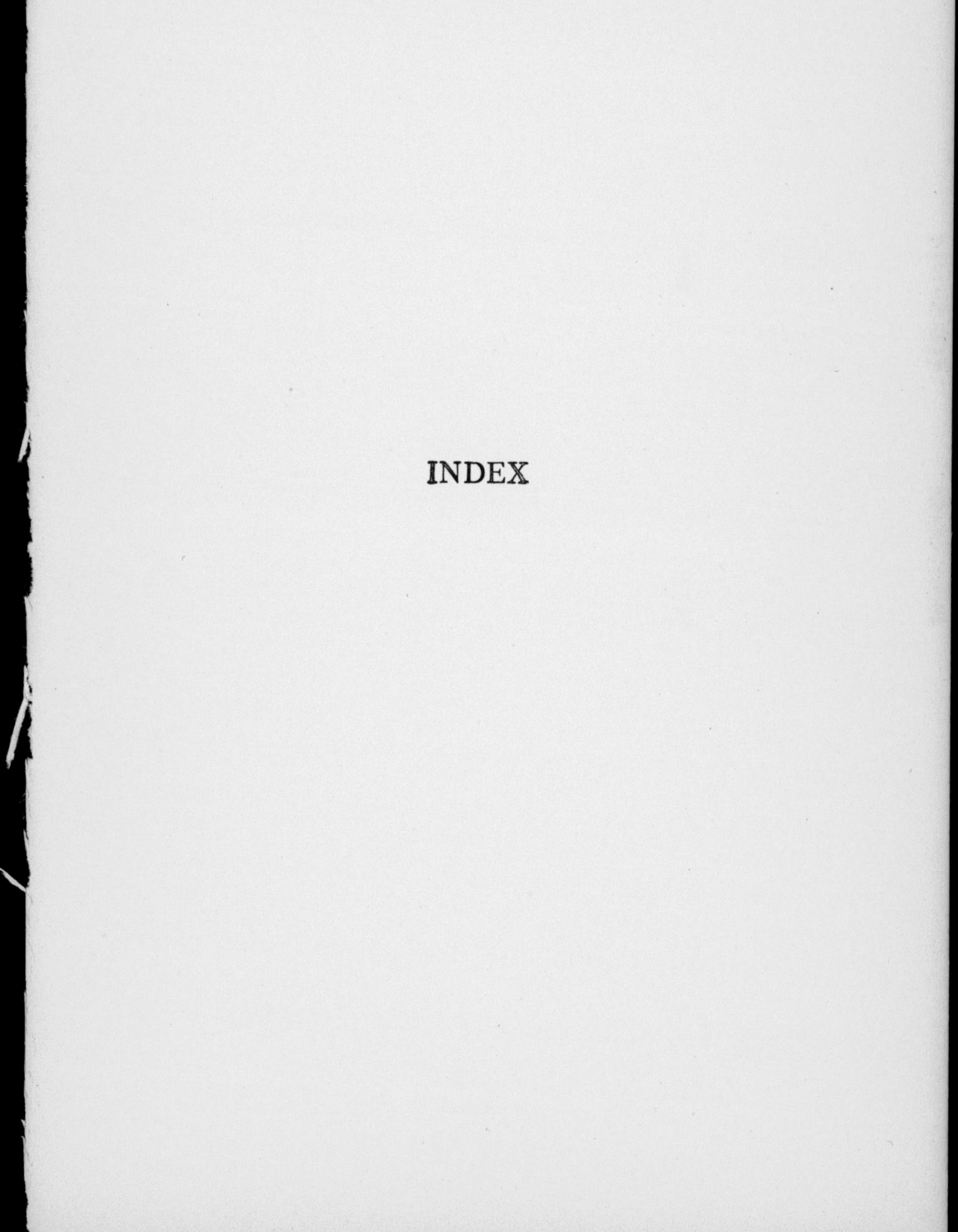

# INDEX

# INDEX

INDEX

# INDEX

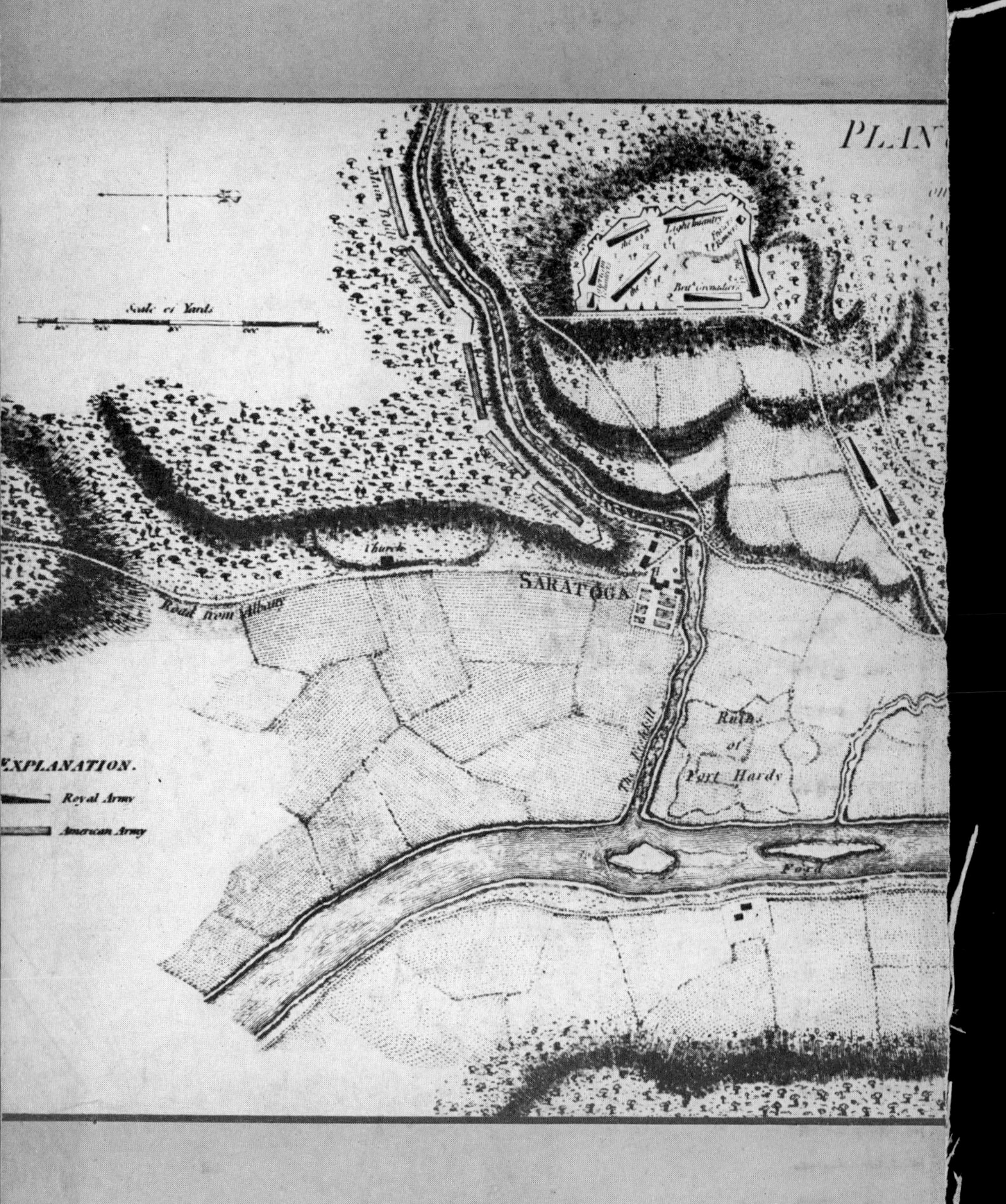

PLAN
Scale of Yards
Light Infantry
Brit. Grenadiers
Church
SARATOGA
Road from Albany
Ruins
of
Fort Hards
Ford
EXPLANATION.
Royal Army
American Army